Representing Auschwitz

The Holocaust and Its Contexts

Series Editors: **Olaf Jensen**, University of Leicester, UK and **Claus-Christian W.Szejnmann**, Loughborough University, UK
Series Editorial Board: Wolfgang Benz, Robert G. Moeller and Mirjam Wenzel

More than 60 years on, the Holocaust remains a subject of intense debate with ever-widening ramifications. This series aims to demonstrate the continuing relevance of the Holocaust and related issues in contemporary society, politics and culture; studying the Holocaust and its history broadens our understanding not only of the events themselves but also of their present-day significance. The series acknowledges and responds to the continuing gaps in our knowledge about the events that constituted the Holocaust, the various forms in which the Holocaust has been remembered, interpreted and discussed, and the increasing importance of the Holocaust today to many individuals and communities.

Titles include:

Nicholas Chare and Dominic Williams (*editors*)
REPRESENTING AUSCHWITZ
At the Margins of Testimony

Olaf Jensen and Claus-Christian W. Szejnmann (*editors*)
ORDINARY PEOPLE AS MASS MURDERERS
Perpetrators in Comparative Perspectives

Karolin Machtans and Martin A. Ruehl (*editors*)
HITLER – FILMS FROM GERMANY
History, Cinema and Politics since 1945

Simo Muir and Hana Worthen (*editors*)
FINLAND'S HOLOCAUST
Silences of History

Tanja Schult
A HERO'S MANY FACES
Raoul Wallenberg in Contemporary Monuments

Forthcoming titles:

Olaf Jensen (*editor*)
HISTORY AND MEMORY AFTER THE HOLOCAUST IN GERMANY, POLAND, RUSSIA AND BRITAIN

The Holocaust and Its Contexts Series
Series Standing Order ISBN 978–0–230–22386–8 Hardback
978–0–230–22387–5 **Paperback**
(*outside North America only*)

You can receive future titles in this series as they are published by placing a standing order. Please contact your bookseller or, in case of difficulty, write to us at the address below with your name and address, the title of the series and the ISBN quoted above.

Customer Services Department, Macmillan Distribution Ltd, Houndmills, Basingstoke, Hampshire RG21 6XS, England

Representing Auschwitz
At the Margins of Testimony

Edited by

Nicholas Chare
Lecturer in Gender Studies, University of Melbourne

and

Dominic Williams
Montague Burton Fellow in Jewish Studies, University of Leeds

palgrave
macmillan

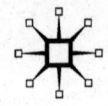

Editorial matter, selection and introduction © Nicholas Chare and
Dominic Williams 2013
Individual chapters © Respective authors 2013
Foreword © Eva Hoffman 2013
Softcover reprint of the hardcover 1st edition 2013 978-1-137-29768-6

All rights reserved. No reproduction, copy or transmission of this
publication may be made without written permission.

No portion of this publication may be reproduced, copied or transmitted
save with written permission or in accordance with the provisions of the
Copyright, Designs and Patents Act 1988, or under the terms of any licence
permitting limited copying issued by the Copyright Licensing Agency,
Saffron House, 6–10 Kirby Street, London EC1N 8TS.

Any person who does any unauthorized act in relation to this publication
may be liable to criminal prosecution and civil claims for damages.

The authors have asserted their rights to be identified as the authors of this
work in accordance with the Copyright, Designs and Patents Act 1988.

First published 2013 by
PALGRAVE MACMILLAN

Palgrave Macmillan in the UK is an imprint of Macmillan Publishers Limited,
registered in England, company number 785998, of Houndmills, Basingstoke,
Hampshire RG21 6XS.

Palgrave Macmillan in the US is a division of St Martin's Press LLC,
175 Fifth Avenue, New York, NY 10010.

Palgrave Macmillan is the global academic imprint of the above companies
and has companies and representatives throughout the world.

Palgrave® and Macmillan® are registered trademarks in the United States,
the United Kingdom, Europe and other countries.

ISBN 978-1-349-45217-0   ISBN 978-1-137-29769-3 (eBook)
DOI 10.1057/9781137297693

This book is printed on paper suitable for recycling and made from fully
managed and sustained forest sources. Logging, pulping and manufacturing
processes are expected to conform to the environmental regulations of the
country of origin.

A catalogue record for this book is available from the British Library.

A catalog record for this book is available from the Library of Congress.

Contents

List of Illustrations   vii

Foreword   viii
Eva Hoffman

Acknowledgements   xi

Notes on Contributors   xii

Introduction: Representing Auschwitz – At the Margins of Testimony   1
Nicholas Chare and Dominic Williams

1 The Harmony of Barbarism: Locating the Scrolls of Auschwitz in Holocaust Historiography   11
Dan Stone

2 On the Problem of Empathy: Attending to Gaps in the Scrolls of Auschwitz   33
Nicholas Chare

3 'The Dead Are My Teachers': The Scrolls of Auschwitz in Jerome Rothenberg's *Khurbn*   58
Dominic Williams

4 Chain of Testimony: The Holocaust Researcher as Surrogate Witness   85
Anne Karpf

5 What Remains – Genocide and Things   104
Ulrike Kistner

6 Representing the Einsatzgruppen: The Outtakes of Claude Lanzmann's *Shoah*   130
Sue Vice

7 Reconciling History in Alain Resnais's *L'Année dernière à Marienbad* (1961)   151
Hannah Mowat with Emma Wilson

8 Gender and Sexuality in Women Survivors' Personal
   Narratives   174
   Cathy S. Gelbin

9 Art as Transport-Station of Trauma? Haunting Objects in
   the Works of Bracha Ettinger, Sarah Kofman and Chantal
   Akerman   194
   Griselda Pollock

10 Coda: Reading Witness Discourse   222
   Hayden White

Index   227

Illustrations

5.1–5.17 Photographs of material remains at
Auschwitz-Birkenau taken by Ulrike Kistner 105–113
7.1 Stills from *L'Année dernière à Marienbad/Last Year in Marienbad*, Dir. A. Resnais (Optimum Home Entertainment, 2005 [1961]) [on DVD] 161
7.2 Still from *L'Année dernière à Marienbad/Last Year in Marienbad*, Dir. A. Resnais (Optimum Home Entertainment, 2005 [1961]) [on DVD] 165
7.3 Stills from *L'Année dernière à Marienbad/Last Year in Marienbad*, Dir. A. Resnais (Optimum Home Entertainment, 2005 [1961]) [on DVD] 168
8.1 Still from interview with Irmgard K. for the *Archive of Memory*, Moses Mendelssohn Zentrum für europäisch-jüdische Studien (Universität Potsdam). Courtesy of the interviewee's family 190
9.1 Freud's desk with the diary of Uziel Lichtenberg and the notebooks of Bracha (Lichtenberg) Ettinger. Bracha L. Ettinger, *Father you see?* (series n° 2), installation view at *Resonance/Overlay/Interweave*, Sigmund Freud study room, Freud Museum, London, 2 June–29 July 2009, curated by Griselda Pollock. Photograph © Bracha L Ettinger 2009. Courtesy of the artist 195
9.2 Freud's table with mother's spoon. Bracha L. Ettinger, *Father you see?* (series n° 2), installation view at *Resonance/Overlay/Interweave*, Sigmund Freud study room, Freud Museum, London, 2 June–29 July 2009, curated by Griselda Pollock. Photograph © Bracha L Ettinger 2009. Courtesy of the artist 197

Foreword

Eva Hoffman

Nearly 70 years after the Holocaust, and as we contemplate the enormous amounts of study and response dedicated to that event since its occurrence, we can see that catastrophes of these dimensions and complexity demand, and generate, not one but many kinds of investigation and genres of testimony. There was, immediately after the event, the legal documentation of the Nuremberg Trials; there were, in the years following the war (and before the coming down of the Iron Curtain), systematic attempts undertaken by relevant institutions in Eastern Europe – for example, the Jewish Historical Institute in Warsaw – to collect survivors' and witnesses' oral narratives and written accounts. There were early memoirs, many of them still pulsating with the horror and moral uncertainties of the event, and great numbers of later chronicles, written from a more remote distance and sometimes marked by certain formulaic notions of how the Holocaust should be remembered. There have been visual documentaries and massive later projects of documentation, such as the Spielberg Archives. Perhaps one should also count among genres of response the many works of the imagination, some of them deeply illuminating, with their transformations of personal and collective experience into forms of literature and art.

And there has been, throughout, the invaluable work of historical research and interpretation. This important and affecting collection of scholarly essays reaches back, from our temporal perspective, to the dark root of the event, and examines documents which have emerged from the very centre of the inferno. The fragments of text under scrutiny, produced by the Sonderkommando who worked in the gas chambers of Auschwitz, seem to represent, especially in their half-destroyed form, not so much acts of written recollection, as enactments of direct, almost physical witnessing; emanations from the underworld, driven by a compelling need to reach the world above, to record and tell. Primo Levi has famously said that the true witnesses of the annihilation did not speak. The Scrolls of Auschwitz are as close as we can come to hearing voices from the site of death.

What is the historical status of such documents? As some of the essays included here suggest, there has been a long-standing controversy in

Holocaust studies (indeed, in historiographical debates altogether) about the veridical value of personal testimony. At the same time, it is clear that our knowledge of the Holocaust – and of other historical atrocities – would be immeasurably impoverished without the evidence of personal memory and witness. Various genres of documentation and testimony provide different kinds of insight and call for different kinds of recognition. It is perhaps only from the multiple strata of knowledge and interpretation that a fuller comprehension of the overwhelming events can emerge. Factual and statistical information, and the understanding of chronology, topography and overall structure of events are clearly crucial to our grasp of the Holocaust; but insight into the victims' experiences, as these were lived within particular situations, and from within particular perceptions and subjectivities, is also essential to comprehend the human meanings of atrocity.

It is the merit and interest of this thought-provoking collection that it addresses various kinds of sources and registers of response. Included here are analyses of historical methodology, but also reflections on film and poetry, and the pressures on artistic form exerted by traumatic knowledge. There are considerations, among others, of post-Holocaust memory and its passage across the generations, the impact of fragmentary objects retrieved from catastrophe – as well as the kinds of empathy or detached understanding which such memories and artefacts demand and evoke.

What kind of response is called for – or possible – to the evidence inscribed, or implicit, in the Auschwitz Scrolls? It is hard, when confronted with these shards of darkness, to avoid moral ambivalence or confusion. The Sonderkommando, whose written traces we have here, functioned in the blackest part of what Primo Levi called 'the grey zone', and they performed terrifying tasks. The extreme ambiguities of the circumstances in which the Scrolls were written may account for the long delay in scholarly response to them; but those ambiguities are part of the difficult knowledge brought to us by the Shoah's extremity.

But perhaps the most powerful aspect of the Scrolls' significance is the very fact of their existence. In the closest proximity to the horrifying processes of annihilation, and facing their own almost certain death, the scribes of Auschwitz were determined that what happened there should not be deleted from human memory or knowledge; against all odds, they maintained their 'ability to think', necessary for the act of writing, and the desire to understand their surely nearly incomprehensible situation. Perhaps the only comparable documents to emerge from the Holocaust are the Ringelblum Archives, discovered on the grounds of the Warsaw Ghetto and containing meticulously gathered information about daily life within its confines before the extinction. In both cases, the documents testify, over and above the specific facts recorded in them, that the need to register the evidence of suffering and terrible injustice – to give expression to one's own existence, so that it is not entirely lost – is a fundamental and profound part of being human. In turn, the desire to respond to those voices – to preserve that evidence and to restore justice even in memory – is what makes history a reparative as well as an analytical enterprise. 'If none of us survives, at least let that remain,' Emmanuel Ringelblum wrote as he confronted his own certain death. The essays in this collection augment our knowledge and capacity to understand part of that which has remained.

Acknowledgements

We wish to thank the British Academy and the Elisabeth Barker bequest for their help in making the research behind much of this volume possible. We are also obliged to the Auschwitz-Birkenau State Museum and, in particular, to Wojciech Płosa for help during our visits to archives there.

For their intellectual and, often, practical support, we are grateful to Suzannah Biernoff, Bryan Cheyette, Maria-Luisa Coelho, Vanessa Corby, D. Ferrett, Benjamin Hannavy-Cousen, Peter Kilroy, Milena Marinkova, Maria Mileeva, Angela Mortimer and Roy Wolfe. A specific debt is also owed to Jacqueline Rose for encouraging further research into the Scrolls of Auschwitz.

We are also thankful to the commissioning and production teams at Palgrave, particularly Clare Mence and Devasena Vedamurthi, who were a pleasure to work with throughout, and to our series editors, Olaf Jensen and Claus-Christian Szejnmann.

Contributors

Nicholas Chare is Lecturer in Gender Studies at the School of Culture and Communication, University of Melbourne. His publications include the books *Auschwitz and Afterimages* (2011) and *After Francis Bacon* (2012). He is working on a book (with Dominic Williams) on the Scrolls of Auschwitz, to be called *Matters of Testimony*.

Cathy S. Gelbin is Senior Lecturer in German at the University of Manchester. She specializes in German-Jewish culture, Holocaust studies, gender and film studies. From 1995 to 1998, she was coordinator of the Archiv der Erinnerung (Archive of Memory). Her publications include *An Indelible Seal: Race, Hybridity and Identity in Elisabeth Langgässer's Writings* (2001) and *The Golem Returns: From German Romantic Literature to Global Jewish Culture 1808–2008* (2011).

Eva Hoffman is an internationally renowned writer and Senior Researcher in Creative Writing at Kingston University. Her most important publications include *Lost in Translation: Life in a New Language* (1989), *Exit into History: A Journey Through the New Eastern Europe* (1993), *Shtetl: The Life and Death of a Small Town and the World of Polish Jews* (1997), *The Secret* (2002), *After Such Knowledge: Memory, History and the Legacy of the Holocaust* (2004) and *Time* (2009).

Anne Karpf is a writer and sociologist, contributing regularly to *The Guardian* and other publications, and broadcasting on BBC Radios 3 and 4. Her books include a family memoir, *The War After: Living with the Holocaust* (1997). A recipient of the British Academy Thank-Offering to Britain Fellowship, she is Reader in Professional Writing and Cultural Inquiry at London Metropolitan University.

Ulrike Kistner teaches in the Department of Philosophy at the University of Pretoria, South Africa. Her interests lie at the interface between aesthetic theory and political philosophy. Her recent publications include articles on theorizations of totalitarianism, on conceptualizations of the political and on the sense of the common.

Hannah Mowat is a PhD candidate in the Department of French at the University of Cambridge. Her thesis focuses on the role of gesture in the works of contemporary Francophone visual artists.

Griselda Pollock is Professor of Social and Critical Histories of Art and Director of the transdisciplinary Centre for Cultural Analysis, Theory and History at the University of Leeds. She is co-editor with Max Silverman of *Concentrationary Cinema: Aesthetics and Political Resistance in Night and Fog by Alain Resnais (1955)* (2012). She has just completed *After-Images/After-Effects: Trauma and Aesthetic Transformation in the Virtual Feminist Museum* (2013) and is completing a monograph on Charlotte Salomon, *The Nameless Artist*.

Dan Stone is Professor of Modern History at Royal Holloway, University of London. He is the author or editor of 14 books, including *Histories of the Holocaust* (2010), *The Oxford Handbook of Postwar European History* (ed., 2012), *The Holocaust, Fascism and Memory: Essays in the History of Ideas* (2013) and *Saving Europe: The Rise and Fall of the Postwar Consensus* (2014).

Sue Vice is Professor of English Literature at the University of Sheffield. Her most recent books are *Shoah* (2011) and *Representing Perpetrators in Holocaust Literature and Film* (2013), co-edited with Jenni Adams. She is working on a study of literary hoaxes and false memoirs, to be called *Textual Deceptions*.

Hayden White is Professor Emeritus in the History of Consciousness Department at the University of California, Santa Cruz. His most recent books include *Figural Realism: Studies in the Mimesis Effect* (2000) and *The Fiction of Narrative* (2010).

Dominic Williams is Montague Burton Fellow in Jewish Studies, University of Leeds. He is co-editor of *Modernist Group Dynamics: The Politics and Poetics of Friendship* (2008). He is working on a book (with Nicholas Chare) on the Scrolls of Auschwitz, to be called *Matters of Testimony*.

Emma Wilson is Professor of French Literature and the Visual Arts at the University of Cambridge, Course Director of the MPhil in Screen Media and Cultures and a Fellow of Corpus Christi College. Her recent publications include *Alain Resnais* (2006) and *Love, Mortality and the Moving Image* (2012).

Introduction: Representing Auschwitz – At the Margins of Testimony

Nicholas Chare and Dominic Williams

The Holocaust is frequently described in bounded terms. It is defined as an event possessing distinct existential, geographical and temporal borders. This explains why the barbed wire fences erected around concentration and extermination camps, fences that formed their physical boundary, have become a powerful trope for expressing boundaries of knowledge and understanding. The fence stands as a metaphor for limits to comprehension. Griselda Pollock adroitly illustrates the unbridgeable divide the fence has come to represent through her analysis of Margaret Bourke White's photograph of 'Survivors at Buchenwald, April 1945'. Pollock writes: 'while they look at us, the spectators, the concentrationees are divided from us by a barbed wire fence that cuts horizontally across their vertically striped garb as a barely visible barrier that is, none the less, an absolute division. What these men have seen and what they will never cease to carry as images burned into hunger and pain-dulled minds, our sight of them from this side of that frontier cannot imagine' (2007, p. 276). In this reading, the wire marks a limit point beyond which the minds of those not interned in the camps cannot journey in the sense that they cannot adequately conceive of the experiences endured by the inmates. This failure to ideate is contrasted by Georges Didi-Huberman who, also drawing on photographs to make his point, contends that Auschwitz 'is only imaginable' (2003, p. 62).

The positions of Didi-Huberman and Pollock are, however, not as distant as this initial contrast implies. Both share a profound commitment to thinking through the potential communicability of aspects of the experience of the Shoah. Pollock's work on the artistic practice of the psychoanalyst Bracha Ettinger, for example, demonstrates a belief in the communicability of trauma. For Pollock, painting invokes 'its spectators to become partners in a testimonial exploration of the sharing of trauma transported into the present' (2007, p. 181). In an earlier discussion of the Bourke-White photograph, Pollock argues that 'not to look back, not to consider again and again this horizon of our present that is cut into history at that razored wire, is to obliterate all that which these men look for in meeting whoever is there, on the other side' (2007, p. 192). The fence simultaneously marks a seeming limit and signals an obligation to try and see beyond it.

Like all boundaries, that around the Holocaust shifts and is subject to dispute. At what point did it start: 1933, 1935, 1939, 1941? Where did it take place? In the ghettos, the transports, the concentration camps, the sites of extermination? There is also debate in relation to the physical boundaries of Auschwitz. The disputes over the Carmelite convent established outside (or inside?) the grounds of Auschwitz I in the 1980s show that this is contested (Rittner & Roth, 1991). As equally does the fact, noted by Debórah Dwork and Robert Jan van Pelt, that the 'Arbeit Macht Frei' sign was an internal barrier within Auschwitz I (1996, pp. 360–361).

Although our cover image, of a pond close to crematoria IV and V into which ashes were dumped, is in fact situated 'inside' Auschwitz-Birkenau, the trees represented here also served as an internal barrier between the crematoria and the rest of the camp. What went on in the crematoria, for example, was subject to speculation and uncertainty even within Auschwitz. The Sonderkommando especially, those tasked with the running of the crematoria, walled up in their blocks in the men's camp or finally confined to the crematoria themselves, became mythologized figures with whom many other prisoners found it impossible to empathize (Levi, 1988, p. 35). The trees, and the fences that supplemented them, were barriers against imagination, which not so much kept outsiders in complete ignorance of what happened beyond them, but offered them the possibility of not imagining. Barriers of this kind, obstacles to insight, persist in the present. Hermann Langbein, for instance, writes that 'the boundary lines that were crossed by forced labor of this kind cannot be crossed in thought after the fact' (2004, p. 194). And yet Primo Levi suggests that imagining is what we need to do: we should 'meditate on the story of "the crematorium ravens": with pity and rigour' while suspending judgement on them (1988, pp. 42–43).

Levi's reflections on the Sonderkommando form part of his famed essay on the 'Grey Zone', a profound meditation on moral ambiguity motivated by events during the Holocaust. The essay draws on witness accounts produced after the event for aspects of its understanding of the actions of the Sonderkommando and the behaviour of Chaim Rumkowski. Levi mentions depositions given by survivors and legal testimony (pp. 34–35). The influence of forms of witnessing produced retrospectively can therefore be felt. For some, testimony to the Shoah only becomes possible retroactively. In his key essay 'An Event without a Witness', for example, Dori Laub argues that only from outside the boundary of the Shoah was it possible for true witnessing of the event to take place. Even though he does acknowledge that attempts were made to record what happened and inform the outside world, they were, he believes, 'doomed to fail'. The 'degree to which bearing witness was required, entailed such a measure of awareness and of comprehension of the event [...] that it was beyond the limits of human ability (or willingness) to grasp, to transmit, or to imagine [...]. The event could thus unimpededly proceed as *though* there were no witnessing whatsoever, *no witnessing that could decisively impact on it*' (Laub, 1992, p. 84).

Laub's model of testimony seems to demand that the witness himself or herself be able to put boundaries upon the event, to have some sense of its dimensions, to have an outside to which he or she can speak. Indeed, equating 'witnessing' with 'witnessing that could decisively impact on it' suggests that a true witness should help to limit the event. Such demands on a witness are of course impossible, but they reveal the way in which the traumatic model of testimony relies on a 'within' from which it is impossible to tell what is within and what is without. The boundary necessary for comprehension, or claiming, of the Holocaust experience, the scission between within and without, can only be instituted belatedly. It is necessary to establish a gap between within and without in the psyche of the individual survivor in order to mend the 'historical gap which the event created in the collective witnessing' (p. 84).

Such a tendency to concentrate on testimony produced retrospectively has offered many positive insights into the Holocaust experience. As numerous survivors attested, the concentration camp, or the ghetto, or the extermination site, was a world which ran by entirely different rules. Many had difficulty articulating what had happened and difficulty finding people who would listen. The awareness that silence could be meaningful, and needed to be attended to, was an important one. But the danger has become that we listen to nothing other than silence and that we refuse to accept any other way of representing the Shoah. We risk presenting the event as an ungraspable enormity that was barely experienced, let alone understood by its victims. *Representing Auschwitz* seeks to demonstrate that this way of approaching the Holocaust itself places a boundary on testimony, one which needs to be questioned (cp. Cesarani & Sundquist, 2012). As part of this process of questioning, it offers a number of in-depth considerations of one key example of testimony from inside the event, the manuscripts, known as the Scrolls of Auschwitz, buried by members of the Sonderkommando in the grounds of the crematoria at Birkenau.

The Scrolls are only one instance – perhaps the most extraordinary – of testimony produced from within some of the sites where the Shoah was implemented. As Eva Hoffman points out in her foreword, a large archive was generated in the Warsaw Ghetto by the Oyneg Shabes group. Writing from ghettoes is now relatively well known: not only diaries such as those by Chaim Kaplan and Mary Berg, but also poetry such as that of Yitskhok Katznelson and Avrom Sutzkever. Despite all the difficulties of writing in the ghetto, however, it was far easier than writing from within concentration camps. In her major study of testimony, Zoë Waxman (2006) makes a clear and important distinction between the literature of the ghettoes and that produced in camps. She mentions only two examples of the latter: the Sonderkommando manuscripts and the report recorded by Oyneg Shabes under the name of 'Jakob Grojanowski' (whom Patrick Montague (2012) has identified as Szlama Winer), the most extensive written testimony from Chełmno (qtd. in full in Gilbert, 1987, pp. 252–279). In fact, concentration and extermination camps produced more writing than this. In concentration camps in Germany and Holland, diaries were occasionally kept by prisoners who were usually in positions of privilege (Herzberg, 2008; see Laqueur, 1991). And if 'Grojanowski's' account should be counted as testimony from an extermination site, then so should Rachel Auerbach's interview with Abraham Krzepicki, who had escaped to the Warsaw Ghetto from Treblinka (Kassow, 2007, pp. 287–293 & 309–310; Krzepicki, 1979). Such accounts, produced within one part of a system while documenting another part, raise questions about where the boundaries of the event lie. The borders between different geographical locations and experiential situations were, even if only rarely, permeable.

The members of the Sonderkommando in Birkenau also made some attempt to record what had happened in other parts of the system of the 'Final Solution', with one of them, Leib Langfuss, relating accounts of Bełżec, and another, Zalman Loewenthal, preserving a document and artefact from the Łódź Ghetto (Mark, 1985). The document, a diary, had presumably been found by him amongst clothing and other personal effects left in the undressing room by those about to be gassed. He had recognized its testimonial value and therefore adopted the role of archivist. The addendum he wrote to accompany the diary looks ahead to a time when historians and psychologists will be striving to understand the 'diabolical cruelty' of the Nazis (Loewenthal, 1985, p. 236). The fact Loewenthal believes in such a future demonstrates how knowledge of German military setbacks was common in the camps. He also refers to the uprising in the Warsaw Ghetto and seeks to make a qualitative distinction between conditions in Łódź and Warsaw. Loewenthal is therefore carefully signalling what specific insights the diary potentially holds for its coming readership. The addendum and diary show how artefacts and information traversed boundaries.

A detailed consideration of testimony from within, such as that of Langfuss and Loewenthal, shows that there is not a straightforward way of delineating a boundary between it and testimony produced from outside. Even the Sonderkommando were producing their documents with a future, and therefore an outside, in mind and undertook a variety of strategies to help it reach there. The careful concealment and packaging up of manuscripts, just like the thought put into the way in which the documents were written, were all part of a strategy to get the writings to a reader, to bring the events home to him or her. Their writings are material traces crossing a boundary, transformed in that crossing, unable to be confined to one side or the other, and carrying something of the other side with them. They are designed to cross to an outside, but also, once on that outside, to enable readers to cross back in their imaginations. An element of retrospectivity is built into the documents.

The aim of this volume is not, therefore, to offer another realm of testimony, which operates by entirely different laws, but rather to open a dialogue between these texts and other forms of testimony and cultural memory. While they have been used by historians, we note perhaps a tendency in the writings on diaries produced in ghettos and concentration camps to mine them for information rather than *read* them. The work done by scholars of testimony and cultural memory is precisely what needs to be followed, showing how these texts work their material. Of course, some of these documents are straightforward cries for help, or ways of saying goodbye, or calls for revenge, attempts to record the basic facts under the most restrictive and overwhelming circumstances. Letters written in Yiddish and Polish by prisoners forced to work in Chełmno are examples of these (Dafni & Kleiman, 1991, pp. 119–122). Only a few can be considered fully formed literature, such as the last poems of Miklós Radnóti, written on a death march and dug up from the mass grave in which his body had lain for two years (see Babus et al., 2009). But they need to be seen as part of a continuum, in which the writers call upon the resources that they have available. The ways in which the documents have been written are significant. 'Grojanowski's' report from Chełmno (as told to the Wassers) is emotional and full of pathos, revealing a troubled but continuing religious sensibility. Abraham Krzepicki's account of Treblinka, with its sardonic sub-headings ('A Ukrainian Tries to Cheer Us Up' and 'How to Attract the Attention of a German') which may have been supplied by Rachel Auerbach (they feature in her account of Treblinka too), has a mordant sense of irony and the absurd. Already, between them, these witnesses and their interviewers are making some kind of meaning from what they have only just escaped.

It is not only written testimony that requires this kind of analysis. There were also acoustic attestations to the camp experience, songs composed in the Lagers (Rosen, 2010, pp. 110–119). And more attention has probably been paid to art from the camps (including Auschwitz) than to other forms of representation from within (as Bohm-Duchen (1994, p. 42) points out; see e.g. Kaumkötter et al., 2005; Mickenberg, Granoff & Hayes, 2003). Nonetheless, there are images which have failed to receive the reading they deserve, not least (until recently) the Sonderkommando photographs. A member of the Sonderkommando surreptitiously took four photographs of aspects of the process of the mass killings at Birkenau (Didi-Huberman, 2003; Stone, 2001). The negatives were then smuggled to the main camp where they were concealed in a tube of toothpaste by Helena Dantón and spirited out to members of the Polish Resistance. Further documentation of the extermination process is provided by the unknown artist with the initials 'MM', whose *Sketchbook from Auschwitz*, discovered in the men's camp at Birkenau, has recently been published (Sieradzka, 2011). 'MM' uses his pictures to weave together histories of concentration camp inmates and deportees taken straight to the gas chambers. He also demonstrates some interest in the psychology of the SS, who pose nonchalantly alongside wraith-like figures drained of humanity. The variety of forms which we see in retrospective testimony, therefore, can also be observed in those produced from within the event.

The collection does not seek to privilege this witnessing from within but, rather, by way of judicious comparisons with retrospective testaments, strives to examine the possibilities and problems it presents for the theorization of Holocaust testimony. These readings do not simply say that testimony from within works by an entirely different set of rules from retrospective testimony. Rather they show how there cannot be a point from which testimony is excluded. What the readings of the

Scrolls propose is a dialectic between two poles. The way in which we read them must be different from our approach to other documents and yet we find concerns which scholars of other forms of testimony have raised also present in these texts.

In the chapters that focus on the Scrolls, Dan Stone shows that Zalman Gradowski provides ways of understanding the perpetrators which speak to the explanations of Adorno and Arendt, and that Loewenthal anticipates the questions historians would ask. He carefully locates the Scrolls in a wider context of holocaust historiography as a whole and in particular within the questions that testimony has posed for historians. Nicholas Chare examines ethical questions around empathy and bearing witness in relation to testimonies produced within the event, focussing on the Sonderkommando photographs, the Scrolls and film footage from Liepāja of a mass execution. Dominic Williams shows the ways in which the Scrolls can be read with the resources of the post-war avant-garde and can be seen to offer models of writing for it. He analyses how cultural responses to the Scrolls also have a profound significance that requires investigating. Ulrike Kistner considers materials preserved at Auschwitz and addresses the system of exchange and absolute fungibility of all matter in the camp. Anne Karpf provides a powerful meditation on the significance of personal investment in Holocaust scholarship that takes the Scrolls as its starting point. She draws on ideas from psychoanalysis to perceptively address the reception of testimony.

The volume then turns to forms of witnessing produced retrospectively yet which seek to foster connections with the event, to cross boundaries of time and place. Similarly to the Scrolls and the Sonderkommando photographs, many of them have had difficulty fitting into accepted models of testimony. In addition, they address some of the same issues that have figured in the discussions of the Scrolls. The different positions of power and ability to witness, the role of gender and sexuality, questions of empathy and imagination, and the function of material objects as means of attestation, as well, of course, as the limits that have been placed on testimony, are themes that carry over from the first to the second half of the collection.

In her reading of *Shoah* (Dir. Claude Lanzmann, 1985), Shoshana Felman sees Lanzmann's film as fostering a connection between the inside and outside of the Holocaust (Felman & Laub, 1992, pp. 204–283; p. 232). Sue Vice has also interpreted *Shoah* as linking past and present, focussing 'on the past only as it makes itself felt in the present' (2011, p. 39). In 'Images of Death: Claude Lanzmann's Einsatzgruppen

Interviews', Vice discusses why Claude Lanzmann decided to leave out his interviews with the Einsatzgruppen members from *Shoah*. Her nuanced analysis exposes the heterogeneity of Holocaust experiences. The experiences of the Einsatzgruppen victims differed considerably from those interned in concentration camps or sent to extermination camps and fall outside efforts to frame the Shoah as exemplary of modernity gone awry.

In 'A Matter of Memory or a Remembrance of Matter? Tracing the Gesture in Alain Resnais's *L'Année dernière à Marienbad*', Hannah Mowat and Emma Wilson think through the difficulty of placing boundaries on the texts that function as testimony. Through an inspiring close analysis of sub-narrative elements in *L'Année dernière à Marienbad* (Dir. Alain Resnais, 1961), particularly at the level of the film's gestural economy, including its cinematography, Mowat and Wilson track how the film presents visual echoes, after-images, of the Holocaust experience. Cathy S. Gelbin's chapter, 'Are Holocaust Narratives Gendered?', forms a significant addition to recent efforts to acknowledge previously ignored women's Holocaust testimonies (Hedgepeth & Saidel, 2010; Loew, 2011; Waxman, 2006). Gelbin concentrates on the ways in which women survivors articulate or suppress issues related to their sexuality in video testimony.

Griselda Pollock's 'Art as Transport-station of Trauma? Haunting Objects in the Works of Sarah Kofman, Chantal Akerman and Bracha Ettinger' uses three case studies to examine aesthetic dimensions to witnessing. Pollock draws on Bracha Ettinger's idea of 'wit(h)nessing' to examine how art and literature open vital spaces for provisionally containing and communicating traumatic experiences. Judith Butler (2011, p. 150) has suggested that 'both in her psychoanalytic theory and in her visual art, there is for Ettinger always a question of an exilic tradition, a problem of borders, a question of what passes from one domain to another, and in what form and through which medium that passage is made.' She reads Ettinger's work as developing a new vocabulary for understanding the transgenerational transmission of trauma. Pollock deftly tracks how such a transmission, a 'traumatic wit(h)nessing' comes into being in the art of Ettinger, Akerman's film-making and Kofman's writing.

As a coda to the collection, Hayden White uses Saul Friedländer's *Nazi Germany and the Jews, 1933–1945: The Years of Extermination, 1939–1945* as a starting point to reflect on the distinct character of 'crafted' or artistic testimony. This addendum builds on White's ground-breaking work on the way language intervenes between facts and their interpretation, and is never matter of fact, always carrying a metaphoric potential (White, 2004). Without explicitly discussing the Scrolls, the remarks about informational versus expressive testimony provide crucial insight into how the documents buried by the Sonderkommando might be understood. They are produced out of a desire to attest to both emotional and factual aspects of the camp experience. Theirs was carefully crafted evidence designed to carry beyond the limits of Auschwitz and represent their experiences to an audience living in less desperate times. It is hoped that this volume can contribute in some small way to bringing the existence of these vital documents, and a sense of their richness and complexity as forms of testimony, to a broader audience.

Works cited

Babus, A., et al. (2009) 'O Poet Live in Purity Now', Exhibition of the Library of the Hungarian Academy of Sciences, 5 May–5 June 2009 [online version] Available at: <http://radnoti.mtak.hu/index-en.htm> [Accessed 3 December 2012].
Bohm-Duchen, M. (1994) 'Ways of Seeing the Unseeable', *Jewish Quarterly* (Spring), 41–45.
Butler, J. (2011) 'Disturbance and Dispersal in the Visual Field', in C. de Zegher & G. Pollock (eds.) *Art as Compassion* (Brussels: ASA Publishers), pp. 149–165.
Cesarani, D. & Sundquist, E. (eds.) (2012) *After the Holocaust: Challenging the Myth of Silence* (London: Routledge).
Dafni, R. & Kleiman, Y. (eds.) (1991) *Final Letters: From the Yad Vashem Archive* (London: Weidenfeld and Nicholson).
Didi-Huberman, G. (2003) *Images malgré tout* (Paris: Les Éditions de Minuit).
Dwork, D. & van Pelt, R. (1996) *Auschwitz: 1270 to the Present* (New York and London: Norton).
Felman, S. & Laub, D. (1992) *Testimony: Crises of Witnessing in Literature, Psychoanalysis, and History* (London: Routledge).
Gilbert, M. (1987) *The Holocaust: The Jewish Tragedy* (London: Fontana).
Hedgepeth, S. & Saidel, R. (2010) *Sexual Violence against Jewish Women during the Holocaust* (Waltham: Brandeis University Press).
Kassow, S. (2007) *Who Will Write Our History?: Rediscovering a Hidden Archive from the Warsaw Ghetto* (London: Penguin).
Kaumkötter, J., et al. (eds.) (2005) *Kunst in Auschwitz/Sztuka w Auschwitz* (Bramsche: Rasch Verlag).
Krzepicki, A. (1979) 'Eighteen Days in Treblinka', in A. Donat (ed.) *The Death Camp Treblinka: A Documentary* (New York: Holocaust Library).
Langbein, H. (2004) *People in Auschwitz* (Chapel Hill: University of North Carolina Press).
Levi, P. (1988) *The Drowned and the Saved* (London: Michael Joseph).
Loew, C. (2011) *The Memory of Pain: Women's Testimonies of the Holocaust* (Amsterdam: Rodopi).

Loewenthal, Z. (1985) 'Addendum to the Łódź Manuscript', in B. Mark, *The Scrolls of Auschwitz*, S. Neemani (trans.) (Tel Aviv: Am Oved), pp. 236–240.

Mark, B. (1985) *The Scrolls of Auschwitz*, S. Neemani (trans.) (Tel Aviv: Am Oved).

Mickenberg, D., Granoff, C. & Hayes, P. (eds.) (2003) *The Last Expression: Art and Auschwitz* (Evanston, IL: Mary and Leigh Block Museum of Art, Northwestern University).

Montague, P. (2012) *Chełmno and the Holocaust: The History of Hitler's First Death Camp* (London: I. B. Tauris).

Pollock, G. (2011) 'Death in the Image: The Responsibility of Aesthetics in *Night and Fog* (1955) and *Kapò* (1959)', in G. Pollock & M. Silverman (eds.) *Concentrationary Cinema: Aesthetics as Political Resistance in Alain Resnais's Night and Fog* (Oxford: Berghahn).

Rosen, A. (2010) *The Wonder of their Voices* (Oxford: Oxford University Press).

Sieradzka, A. (ed.) (2011) *Szkicownik z Auschwitz/The Sketchbook from Auschwitz* (Oświęcim: Państwowe Muzeum Auschwitz-Birkenau)

Stone, D. (2001) 'The Sonderkommando Photographs', *Jewish Social Studies* 7:3, 132–148.

Vice, S. (2011) *Shoah* (Basingstoke and New York: Palgrave Macmillan).

Waxman, Z. (2006) *Writing the Holocaust: Identity, Testimony, Representation* (Oxford: Oxford University Press).

White, H. (2004) 'Figural Realism in Witness Literature', *Parallax* 10:1, 113–124.

1
The Harmony of Barbarism: Locating the Scrolls of Auschwitz in Holocaust Historiography

Dan Stone

Holocaust historiography

The writing of history tends towards order, towards the elimination of contingency and towards claims that become common knowledge. One such widely held view is that the victims of the Holocaust could not understand what was happening to them or were unable to make sense of their experiences as they were unfolding. In some cases, this claim is accurate: the Jews of Hungary, for example, felt, with understandable complacency, that their position as Magyar citizens was untouchable and that the disaster that had befallen their co-religionists elsewhere in Europe would pass them by (Miron, 2004; Szalai, 2004).

In Holocaust historiography, which is a massive, sophisticated field of historical scholarship, one finds numerous such examples (see Stone, 2010b, 2013). Perhaps the most famous, and most hotly contested, is the role played by the *Judenräte* (Jewish Councils) in the Polish ghettos in 'collaborating' with the deportation process (Arendt, 1977, pp. 117–119; Diner, 1992; Michman, 2004; Trunk, 1996). Taken as a whole, however, the field remains methodologically rather restricted and restrained, even though it is no longer confined to political history but also encompasses social history and approaches that focus on gender, religion and memory. This is most notably the case with respect to the use of testimony, as we will see. The debate about the Nazis' decision-making process for the 'Final Solution' is still rightly central to historians' concerns, as illustrated in the major empirical studies that have appeared in recent years, especially those by Christopher Browning (2004) and Peter Longerich

(2010). But there is also a slowly growing tendency to bring together the perpetrator narrative with the experiences of the victims in what Saul Friedländer calls an 'integrated history'.

Furthermore, the range of subjects with which Holocaust historians concern themselves has broadened immensely since the opening up of new archives after the end of the Cold War. There are now detailed local and regional studies of the Holocaust in most parts of Europe, although some key books remain to be written, such as a monograph on the Holocaust in Poland to place alongside Yitzhak Arad's study of the Soviet Union and Jean Ancel's on Romania, or on Slovakia, where the literature is as yet relatively undeveloped. But we now know in great detail about the unfolding of the Holocaust in Western Europe, in Ukraine, Romania, Hungary, Serbia and the western USSR, and the literature on Greece, Scandinavia and other outlying areas is growing all the time.

When it comes to the camps, the relationship of the murder of the Jews to the concentration camp system in general is now much better understood, thanks to the work of historians such as Karin Orth, Nikolaus Wachsmann and Dieter Pohl, the general lesson being that most Holocaust victims were not murdered in camps at all and that the death camps need to be understood as separate from the camps run by the SS's IKL (*Inspektion der Konzentrationslager*, Concentration Camps Inspectorate), a point that raises problematic questions for attempts to reintroduce the figure of the 'concentration camp' into contemporary discussion as the telos or most revealing synecdoche of modernity.[1] Quite large groups of Jews even survived the war thanks to being kept in forced labour camps that were outside of the SS-run system, in camps run by local councils and businesses across occupied Europe (Dreyfus & Gensburger, 2011; Gruner, 2006). However, despite the massive literature, there is a still a need for a standard monograph on Auschwitz, and for more work on Operation Reinhard, which constituted the heart of the killing process and on which there are very few monographs and not many more scholarly articles.

The mention of the Operation Reinhard camps should also remind us that most of the Holocaust's victims came from Poland and further east, in Ukraine, Belarus and the Baltic States (see Brandon & Lower, 2008; Snyder, 2010). The nature of the killing process, especially in the western USSR, is hard to recreate for lack of sources, but finally research is underway into the short-lived ghettos that existed in this massive region and the nature of the face-to-face killing process as it transpired on the ground. Because Auschwitz became, for understandable reasons, the symbol and synecdoche of the murder of the Jews, and because the Operation Reinhard camps and the Einsatzgruppen killings were for many years overlooked (because of lack of sources, communist instrumentalization in the 'antifascist' narrative or Cold War totalitarianism theory), the vast number of religious Jews, who made up the majority of Holocaust victims, who mostly lived and were murdered in Poland and eastern Europe, have, until recently, received little attention. Historians, too, have finally started working seriously on the so-called 'death marches' and on the massive operation to plunder and dispossess Jews (Blatman, 2011; Dean, 2008; Dean, Goschler & Ther, 2007).

The topic of plunder is especially important, thanks to its resonance with the explosion of interest in compensation payments for slave labour and restitution of looted assets and bank accounts that took up so much time and effort in the 1990s. Michael Marrus (2009) reasonably wonders whether the claim that it was not all about money is entirely true, but his and others' recent work helps us to understand the profound sense of the need to win at least 'some measure of justice' by illustrating not just the scale of plunder across Europe – from whole national economies fleeced by the Nazi occupation, to institutions set up to coordinate the theft of objects (especially the *Einsatzstab Reichsleiter Rosenberg* (Grimsted, 2006)), to individual, poor, eastern European looters enriching themselves at the expense of their equally poor Jewish neighbours – but providing us with the anthropological insight that human identity is to a large extent bound up with the things we own, the loss of which contributes to a loss of identity. The rediscovery of this subject, now more or less shorn of the Marxist assumptions about Nazism's relationship with big business which drove research in the 1960s, has given rise to a massive literature, from company studies, such as Daimler Benz, Deutsche Bank or Volkswagen, to studies of the banking, insurance and clearing systems and international trade with the Third Reich. What they show is the vast extent of everyday complicity in the regime and the willingness of big business to serve the Third Reich and to profit from the opportunities that it offered to them (for an introduction, see Kobrak and Schneider, 2004).

All of these different aspects of the Holocaust – and many more besides – mean that the historiography is varied and rich. All of them, to a greater or lesser extent, deal with victims as well as perpetrators, for historians are no longer content merely to rely on Nazi documents with their illusion of officialdom and hence 'reliability'. Methodologically speaking, perhaps the most exciting and productive development is the impact of cultural history (Stone, 2009). Here one needs to make the distinction between histories of cultural institutions (theatre or music in the ghettos and camps, for example) or of 'high art' and a cultural history that seeks, anthropology style, to recover meaning and meaning-production by people in the past. This is something that can be done for the victims of the Holocaust, where the challenge is to explain how meaning-production broke down or was sustained in the face of events that exceeded previous experience, and for perpetrators. In the latter case, investigating the Nazis' (or, more broadly, the German population's) own processes of meaning-production might seem a risky and less than tasteful enterprise. The argument would be that it is necessary to enter into a Nazi mindset in which the dynamic that gave rise to genocide can be analysed in relation to the narratives that Germans employed to make sense of the world at the time. A number of German historians are currently engaged in such a task and the initial results are fruitful indeed (e.g. Confino, forthcoming; Gross, 2010; Kühne, 2010; Neumann, 2010), as long as one does not succumb to the temptation of granting the Nazis' own concepts and ambitions – such as the creation of a *Volksgemeinschaft*, or racial community – more credibility than they deserve (see Kershaw, 2011). This historical sensibility has gradually awakened historians' interest in the potential uses of testimony, primarily survivor testimony, but also, if we can use the word 'testimony' with all its resonances of listener compassion and arduous telling, for perpetrators and fellow travellers.

That said, it is striking that some key texts from the Holocaust period have been neglected, much to the detriment of historical understanding. Historians are, for example, starting to discover the recorded testimonies made by David Boder in Displaced Persons (DP) camps in the immediate post-war period and texts originally in Yiddish are finding their way into the consciousnesses of historians beyond the small circle of people who could always read them and were aware of their significance (Cesarani & Sundquist, 2012; Rosen, 2010). Among the most noteworthy of all such documents is the collection of writings now known as the Scrolls of Auschwitz, texts written by members of the Sonderkommando (the Special Squad) in Auschwitz-Birkenau, who then buried them in the ground next to the gas chambers and crematoria. This collection of documents, the first of which was dug up immediately after the camp's liberation in 1945 and the last of which was discovered in 1980, constitutes a unique view into the very heart of darkness.[2] The manner of the texts' production and discovery is itself remarkable, but they are made even more precious by virtue of being some of the very few documents to have been produced by Holocaust victims from within the death camps themselves. Furthermore, for the most part, these are highly literate and thoughtful texts and not, as one might assume, hastily-scribbled lists of factual information. And yet they have rarely featured in historical scholarship on the Holocaust.

Although the first of the Scrolls was discovered straight after the war, the authors of the earliest synthetic histories of the murder of the Jews had not yet registered them. Léon Poliakov's in many ways remarkable book *Harvest of Hate* (1956, original French 1951) discusses the Sonderkommando's tasks in Birkenau, as well as the uprising of October 1944, but does not mention the men's hidden writings. The same is true of Gerald Reitlinger's important study, *The Final Solution* (1953) and of Lord Russell of Liverpool's popular work, *The Scourge of the Swastika* (1956). Despite its far greater detail than the above-mentioned books, Raul Hilberg's masterpiece, *The Destruction of the European Jews*, also says nothing about the Scrolls. The same applies to Nora Levin's 1968 book, *The Holocaust*. And despite her focus on the Jewish victims of the Holocaust, Lucy Dawidowicz mentioned neither the Sonderkommando men nor their writings in her standard work, *The War against the Jews 1933–45* (1975), perhaps precisely because to do so might, at a time when the Sonderkommando were still regarded with some suspicion, have distracted from that focus.

These early historians are not to be blamed for not sharing our concerns. But what their works suggest is how quickly the documents acquired at the Nuremberg Trials became the standard reference point for understanding the genocide of the Jews, and how anything else – especially documents made by the victims – tended to be overlooked. And despite the changes in sensibility amongst historians, the Scrolls are still for the most part passed over. For example, recent research on the post-war institutes and historians who set about the process of fact-finding and writing the first studies of the murder of the Jews – in itself, a very important addition to our narrative of Holocaust historiography's development – does not mention the Scrolls, even in the Polish context (e.g. Cesarani & Sundquist, 2012; Jockusch, 2008; Tych, 2008).

Later historical syntheses continued in this vein of not mentioning the Scrolls, even when the Sonderkommando men themselves were discussed. Leni Yahil (1990, p. 521) quotes the 'anonymous author' of one of the manuscripts (Leib Langfuss), but does not discuss the nature of the source, referring to it only to provide evidence of the deportation of the Jews of Shavli. Tellingly, the one notable exception to this trend is Martin Gilbert's *The Holocaust* (1986), a book written almost exclusively on the basis of victims' testimonies in a deliberate attempt to counter the deadening effect of concentrating on Nazi documentation.

Gilbert gives a brief account of the texts' discovery and, throughout the book, cites extensively from Loewenthal and, briefly, from Gradowski (pp. 820; pp. 515–516, 649–653, 744–746, 749–750; p. 730).[3] More recently, some historians have mentioned the texts – Dwork and Van Pelt (2002, pp. 358–360) or Friedländer (2007, pp. 580–582), for example – though without much reflection on the nature of the sources themselves.[4] Others, whose research is resolutely perpetrator centred, do not mention them at all. All in all, then, it is fair to say that these texts, whilst their existence is acknowledged, have not been incorporated into the major synthetic accounts of the Holocaust and are thus not part of most people's consciousness when they think of that event's major documents. This is a situation that is crying out to be remedied, as has also been the case for the four photographs taken by the Sonderkommando men (Didi-Huberman, 2003; Stone, 2001).

What are the reasons why these extraordinary documents have been neglected? That is a question that requires some understanding of the main trends of Holocaust historiography, especially the tendency amongst historians to prefer 'official' Nazi documents to those produced by the Jewish victims, as if the latter are somehow less objective than the former. Although many historians, especially Israeli ones, have long looked to diaries and other material produced by Jews in the Third Reich, in Nazi-occupied Europe, in the ghettos and camps, somehow, the Scrolls have been left out, perhaps because the Sonderkommando men themselves were regarded in the first post-war decades with some suspicion – almost as collaborators in some quarters (Levi, 1989, pp. 22–51) – and perhaps because their writings contradicted the widespread view that there could not be Jewish documents from the death camps, first, because of a lack of available writing materials, second, because the Jews were in no fit condition to think of writing and, third, because (as was widely believed) the victims could not comprehend what was happening to them and certainly were unable to represent the events. This suspicious attitude, whether held unconsciously or not, is replicated in the general reluctance amongst historians to make use of post-war Jewish testimonies. That reluctance has been steadily eroded over the last decade or two and it is to these changing attitudes towards testimony on the part of Holocaust historians that I now turn.

Historians and the use of testimony

Holocaust historians have traditionally disregarded testimony as a source, just as historians in general are wary of post-hoc accounts and prefer 'non-intentional sources' (Pendas, 2009). Robert Wolfe, US national archivist of captured German records, says that 'Memoirs, oral history, courtroom testimony, and sworn affidavits are indirect and unavoidably subjective. None of these is immediate, contemporaneous, objective, or unaffected by hindsight.' By contrast, he claims, 'the most reliable sources are *primary textual* sources, contemporaneous in fact and purpose, provided they are authentic' (Wolfe, 1995, pp. 5, 6). Lucy Dawidowicz and Raul Hilberg, who otherwise took very different stances on whether sources produced by perpetrators or victims were the most valuable for historical understanding of the Holocaust, concurred on the question of the *type* of sources historians should use, with Hilberg arguing that Holocaust testimonies are all basically the same, following a generic pattern, and that only rarely does one find anything in them that helps one to understand 'the "before" and "after" enclosing the Holocaust years' (Hilberg, 1988, p. 19; see also: Dawidowicz, 1981, pp. 129–130; Hilberg, 2001). Historians continue to make such claims, with telling comments along these lines by Peter Novick and others being easy to find.

In response to this sort of blanket dismissal, historians sought to affirm the usefulness of testimony, sometimes going so far as to employ testimony more or less indiscriminately and/or as the major source for their studies. The best example here is Gilbert's *The Holocaust*, already referred to above. Finally, we see historians such as Saul Friedländer incorporating testimonies from the Holocaust period into an 'integrated' history as 'voices of the victims' along with more familiar Nazi and Jewish sources, although he too makes little use of survivors' accounts. This approach has given rise to some thoughtful criticisms. Amos Goldberg (2009), in particular, whilst admiring Friedländer's achievement in his two-volume study, argues that to employ testimonies and diaries as 'voices' is hardly daring in an age that has become familiar with oral history and which is suffused with 'ego-documents' such as misery memoirs, and that Friedländer even inadvertently replicates the subject position of the Jewish victim by treating these sources not as glimpses into fully-rounded human beings but as disembodied 'voices' which serve the purpose of putting the Nazis' actions into fuller perspective. Tony Kushner (2010) and Zoë Waxman (2010a) also both criticize Friedländer for not engaging with diaries and testimonies as closely as he could have done, in Waxman's case adding that such an engagement would more clearly illuminate the gendered aspects of the Holocaust. Nevertheless, as Dominick LaCapra notes, Friedländer's approach 'may itself be a manner of staying close to, if not keeping faith with, the "voices" of victims rather than giving greater conceptual or theoretical perspective on them', a statement which can be read as both criticism and approval (2011, p. 87). Indeed, there is now a highly sophisticated historiography of testimony, especially in relation to diaries (e.g. Garbarini, 2006). One might be tempted to cite victims' texts without theoretical accompaniment, as a way of refusing to stifle the past with historical commentary or determinism, but one might equally well seek to problematize the very notion of a source by granting testimony some special epistemological significance. This latter approach, in fact, has become quite a common and productive way of proceeding in literary-historical analysis, as we will see below.

Amongst historians, however, we see most recently renewed attempts to treat testimony as a source like any other, responding quite explicitly against those historians who intuitively dismiss its validity. Christopher Browning is the prime mover here, both for perpetrators (*Ordinary Men*) and victims (*Remembering Survival*). These are both adventurous books, methodologically speaking, and they depend on a well-defended claim that the use of a substantial number of testimonies which agree in many respects is defensible from a historian's perspective. It is especially interesting to note that Browning, who was, let us recall, Raul Hilberg's doctoral student, has stressed the reliability of testimonies as sources and displayed great sensitivity as well as historical skill in handling them. In contrast to the often-untested, run-of-the-mill claim of historians that long-term memory is unreliable, Browning (2010, p. 9) asserts that, having spent time working with the testimonies of survivors of the Starachowice labour camp, he 'now share[s] the counterintuitive conclusion of psychologist Henry Greenspan that the lack of differences between early and late survivor testimonies is "most noteworthy and remarkable"'. In contrast to Friedländer, as Goldberg (2012, p. 83) notes, 'It is notable that Browning does not perceive Jews as a national or cultural community, but rather as a group of victims struggling jointly and separately for their survival and for the survival of each of the group's members'. These Jews are not 'voices' but the main focus of Browning's research, a group of victims struggling to survive. Browning was fortunate to have a critical mass of testimonies from Starachowice available to him, thus allowing him to create a kind of 'control' for testing the testimonies against each other and against other records. He notes that for the historian, testimonies present special problems as source material, not least because it is tempting, out of respect for the survivor, to treat testimonies less critically than other sources and because in the popular imagination, survivors and certain testimonies have acquired iconic status. But he correctly notes that all sources are problematic, none are transparent and thus argues, convincingly in my opinion, for the critical use of survivor testimonies in the writing of Holocaust history. Nevertheless, for Browning, it remains the case that testimonies should be used by historians just as any other sort of evidence and be subject to source critique.

The 'crisis of testimony'

At the same time as these trends and counter-trends have developed in the historiography of the Holocaust, there has also grown up a large and probably more influential analysis of testimony which, first, regards the twentieth century as the 'age of testimony' and, second, simultaneously talks about a 'crisis of testimony' brought about by the events of the twentieth century. This crisis consists of the fact that trauma exceeds cognition, implying that the articulation of testimony is infinitely deferred and infinitely uncognizable. At its most extreme – in the works of Shoshana Felman and Cathy Caruth – trauma is made into a master trope for understanding the present *tout court*. Where all are traumatized, testimony is itself thrown into disarray and we find ourselves immersed in what critics have called a 'traumaculture' or 'wound culture' in a 'pathological public sphere' (Luckhurst, 2003; Seltzer, 1997; see also: Alexander et al., 2004; Edkins, 2003; Leys, 2000; Luckhurst, 2008; Tal, 1996).

How can historians respond to this notion of a 'crisis of testimony'? It seems on first glance barely possible, for as Richard Crownshaw (2010, p. 27) argues, 'In the universalisation of trauma and confusion of text and event, witness and secondary witness, the identities of those remembered and those remembering and the contexts in which acts of recollection take place are eclipsed if not altogether dehistoricised'. The criticisms raised against trauma theory of late in the humanities by scholars such as Wulf Kansteiner (2002, 2004; see also: Klein, 2000)[5] have been met in turn by what we might call a 'defence literature' which argues that one should not throw the baby out with the bath water, that is to say, that whilst aspects of the critique are well taken, it might be going too far to abandon the concept altogether. Didier Fassin and Richard Rechtman (2009), for example, readily acknowledge that the term 'trauma' is over-used and that the idea of being traumatized can be applied to almost any scenario one wishes. As practitioners and therapists, they nevertheless argue that the mockery of the language of 'victimization' is a 'sophisticated but classic way of denying injustice, inequality, and violence'. Trauma theory is, in this reading, more than just a predictable barometer of culture: 'Thus, while trauma emerges in the context of an ethos of compassion that is characteristic of our era, it is also a tool used in a demand for justice' (pp. 278, 279).

In terms of writing a history that is responsive to trauma, I suggest that, for the time being, we follow Judith Butler and Hayden White. Butler, in an article on White, writes that 'There is a task at work in testimony that is different from the transmission and preservation of a sequence of events.' There is a need for figuration, not just bare facts in writing history; or rather, 'need' does not quite do justice to the point: one cannot write historical analysis without figuration. Otherwise one writes mere annals or chronicles (and as we know from White, these forms also contain within them incipient tropes, such as metaphor, allegory or emplotment) (Butler, 2009, p. 285). Talking specifically about the Holocaust, White (2004, p. 118; see also: White, 2005) writes that 'even the most rigorously objective and determinedly "clear" and literal language cannot do justice to the Holocaust without recourse to myth, poetry, and "literary" writing'. This is a statement that is of course applicable to all historical writing. The Holocaust does not raise unique issues for historians, but it does bring out with particular clarity the inherent epistemological difficulties of writing history, perhaps because of the powerful moral pressures historians operate under when writing about it.[6]

What does this mean for the historian's use of testimony? It means that, on the one hand, there can be greater openness and receptivity towards it; since it is clear that history is a form of poetics, there is no reason to exclude testimony on the basis that it is 'unscientific'. But testimony also challenges some of the basic epistemological foundations of historiography. This is not an argument for sentimentality or special pleading; historians are rightly wary of the sanctification of survivors and the attendant risk of turning testimonies into sacred texts (Waxman, 2010b). But a testimony is more than just a 'source'. As Karyn Ball (2008, pp. 43–44) passionately writes, responding to Daniel Goldhagen's use of survivor testimony as a counterpoint to Nazi documents, 'Traumatic events challenge historians to open these gates [separating a 'betrayed minority' from a 'self-entitled majority'] by divesting themselves of a scientific equanimity that is barbaric in the face of genocide' (2008).

Going even further than Ball's criticisms of scientism, in his 'Afterword' to Marc Nichanian's *The Historiographic Perversion* (2009), Gil

Anidjar contests the notion that testimony is something that should be upheld as evidence, a 'discourse of proof' or 'a document for the archive'. Testimonies, he argues, following the Armenian literary scholar Nichanian, should be read as monuments – 'Finally rid of the fact and of the historians' history! Finally rid of the reality principle!' (pp. 145, 152). For a historian, this is of course problematic. But it is important to acknowledge what Anidjar (and Nichanian) are trying to say here, which is that testimony, especially perhaps traumatic testimony, is too important to be incorporated into the archive, to become simply one more piece of evidence that historians can employ. Rather, testimony is the archive breaker, it has the potential to shatter the homogenizing platitudes (i.e. the problem of speaking 'flatly') that historical discourse and historical epistemology can become, most notably when dealing with traumatic events. Historiography is a discourse that is not amenable to trauma, because the 'historicization operation' does not take kindly to events or moments that cannot be placed into a chronological continuum. That is, by the way, an explanation for both the radicalism and the conservatism of western history: radical because nothing is fixed, everything – even human nature – is time bound and subject to change; conservative because it presents permanent change via a theory of time that is unidirectional and in which the past cannot invade the present as presence, even when the past is most contested in the present, as in the 'memory wars' of recent years (Stone, 2012a). Faced with a situation where testimony stages its own impossibility – in Levi's terms, the real witnesses did not survive – testimony requires the ability of 'saying the inside from the outside' (Felman, 1992, p. 249; see also: Sumic-Riha, 2004). All history in a sense says the inside from the outside – the subjects of the historian's text are normally no longer present. But this fact is rarely allowed to trouble the historiographical operation; indeed it is the basic condition of its functioning. As Browning (2010, p. 8) quite reasonably says, 'Claiming that survivor testimony must be accorded a privileged position not subject to the same critical analysis and rules of evidence as other sources will merely discredit and undermine the reputation and integrity of Holocaust scholarship itself'. Perhaps the best we can do is to conclude that historians such as Browning and theorists of history such as Anidjar or White are talking in two different registers. Whilst it is entirely fair for historians to insist on trying to assess the empirical accuracy of any given statement they wish to analyse in a survivor testimony, it is also productive to insist that testimonies serve purposes other than establishing single factual truth claims. Let us allow both possibilities to co-exist, albeit uneasily.

Testimony and the Scrolls of Auschwitz

Finally, how can we think about the Scrolls of Auschwitz in the context of this discussion? Whilst acknowledging the simultaneous existence of different registers of thought or of different regimes of truth, the Scrolls of Auschwitz do have some important ramifications for the kind of theorizing of testimony and trauma that has become so familiar in cultural and literary studies. Unearthed with the help of former Sonderkommando colleague Shlomo Dragon under the auspices of the Soviet investigation commission on 5 March 1945, Zalman Gradowski's text, written apparently in late 1943, and reburied by, presumably, mid-September 1944 (a covering note is dated 6 September), is, along with another manuscript by Gradowski and later texts by Leib Langfuss and Zalman Loewenthal,[7] among the most remarkable documents to have emerged from Auschwitz-Birkenau, indeed to have emerged from the Holocaust per se. Seen and read together with the four photographs taken secretly by the Sonderkommando in August 1944, they are perhaps the most significant victim-produced documents that we have from Auschwitz.[8]

First, they are not testimonies in the sense I have mostly been discussing so far, that is, they are not survivor accounts but are part of the history of the Holocaust, coterminous with it, not written afterwards. Indeed, their calling to us from the place of the dead is what is so remarkable about them. They exemplify the fact that, as Alexandra Garbarini memorably puts it, Holocaust diarists set about 'writing themselves into the future' (2006, p. 5) or, as Nicholas Chare similarly writes, explicitly of Loewenthal, 'He is writing back from death toward life' (2006, p. 65). But they are also, of course, not 'diaries' in the traditional sense; even the dated section of Langfuss's writings appears to have been written retrospectively. Nevertheless, they are also not 'unintentional documents', for they explicitly address the outside world, the audience that the texts' authors hoped they would one day find. They are testimonies from within the event.

More important, the extraordinary self-awareness that the Sonderkommando men's texts display seems to problematize Dori Laub's assertions that contemporaneous witness sources were unable to comprehend the context in which they were produced and that only survivor testimonies could, with the benefit of hindsight, bring some kind of retrospective rehumanization of the victims. Laub, led by his definition of trauma, writes that

> The historical imperative to bear witness could essentially *not be met during the actual occurrence*. The degree to which bearing witness was

required, entailed such an outstanding measure of awareness and of comprehension of the event – of its dimensions, consequences, and above all, of its radical *otherness* to all known frames of reference – that it was beyond the limits of human ability (and willingness) to grasp, to transmit, or to imagine. There was therefore no concurrent 'knowing' or assimilation of the history of the occurrence. The event could thus unimpededly proceed *as though* there were no witnessing whatsoever, *no witnessing that could decisively impact on it.*

(1992, p. 84; see also: Chare, 2006, p. 41)

Whilst Laub's claim might hold true in general, this sort of theoretical statement loses its powerful impact in the face of the writings of the Sonderkommando men. They are neither written from the inside nor from the outside, but, as Chare (2006, p. 65) writes, they 'move from death world to life world and back'.

Let us stop for a moment and actually recall some of the texts, which are often referred to but rarely examined in detail as texts. Zalman Gradowski's text, hidden in a wax-sealed bottle, is clearly the work of an educated man, with a strong sense of literary style. His narrative invites the reader in, addressing itself directly to him or her, and creating a gradually heightening sense of tension as the promise of retelling terrible deeds gets more and more intense. This is not a text written in quiet contemplation, but it is also not a text hastily scrawled in the hope of making known a few basic facts. The facts, which are soberly and shockingly recounted, are contained within a narrative, or better a declamatory journey, that forces the reader into long, unremittingly bleak encounters with the process of mass murder on the one hand and provides a framework for analysing them on the other. Its combination is Dante's *Inferno* and 'an undercutting Jewish anguish', as David Suchoff (1999, p. 61) describes another lesser-known Yiddish text from Auschwitz.[9] It is a remarkably prescient text in terms of the scholarly concerns it adumbrates, for example, with its play on the dialectic of civilization and barbarism – 'The more highly developed a culture, the more cruel its murderers, the more civilized a society, the greater its barbarians' – and the emphasis on the willing submission of individuals to Nazi ideology – 'This violent pirate and his gang have begun their tortures by crushing their egos, sacrificing their souls to their Aryan God' (Gradowski, 1985, pp. 175, 177). When one considers that at the same time that Gradowski was writing these words in Birkenau, Horkheimer and Adorno were writing their not dissimilar *Dialectic of Enlightenment* in exile in California, the true importance of his writings becomes clear, that is, not just as a text that met its purpose of being found and testifying to the conditions of its production, but in terms of its remarkable content.[10] Gradowski's text also provides a rare insight into the way in which the Sonderkommando men were inducted into their role and how they were forced to come to terms with the murder of their families and then with what the Nazi authorities were expecting them to do for the short time they were supposed to remain alive. This combination of a lachrymose conception of Jewish history – under the circumstances, hardly objectionable – with a penetrating critical intelligence makes Gradowski's the most fascinating of the Sonderkommando writings, formally speaking.

Leib Langfuss's texts, buried at the end of November 1944, are more thematic, recounting remarkable moments in the history of the killings, such as when the naked Rabbi Moshe Friedman addressed the Oberscharführer, threatening him with the destruction of the German people in return for attempting to destroy the Jews, and describing moments of sadistic violence, from sexual abuse to the starvation of Russian POWs. Importantly, Langfuss also provides a list of the transports of inmates cremated in Birkenau between 9 and 24 October 1944 (Langfuss, 1985, 206–215). Langfuss's identity as the author of these texts was established by Esther Mark, Ber Mark's wife, in her research to prepare the Scrolls of Auschwitz for publication (Mark, 1985, pp. 166–170).

Thanks to the ravages of being buried for far longer – they were not unearthed until 1961 and 1962 – Zalman Loewenthal's texts are hardest to read, with many gaps. They also recount details of sexual torture at the start of the German occupation of Poland and in the ghettos, as well as the deportation and murder process. Significantly, though, Loewenthal provides more detail of the resistance movement amongst the Sonderkommando men than do Gradowski or Langfuss, as well as an account of the uprising. One can also reasonably make the assumption that Loewenthal was the historian or archivist of the group, for his writings were buried along with those of others: the Łódź diary in the 1961 find and the two longer texts by Langfuss. His own writings also make repeated references to historians and he even appears to suggest how historians should go about dealing with the manuscripts, especially the Łódź diary, to which he attached a short addendum which remains partly legible. Turning from the Łódź diarists and chroniclers to the author of the diary buried along with his own text, Loewenthal tantalizingly suggests that 'you will have here, in the accumulated material – – – a [cl]ear picture of everything, that is, the whole situation, economic, spiritual, and sanitary'. And he goes on, revealing clearly his admiration for the historical approach: 'As you see, a [certain] man interested in history took the trouble to collect pictures, facts, reports, and just information, which will certainly interest the future historian who will come here and be of advantage to him. As for them the historian will have [to] labour no less than on the horrors [which] his[tory] can – – – every fact on human dignity – and on those who ask why?' (Loewenthal, 1985b, p. 238). These words first of all produce in the historian today a chilling realization that he or she is being addressed by a colleague from the heart of Auschwitz – in itself startling enough – but they soon bring one back to reality with their sober (and sombre) discussion of the hard facts. Particularly with respect to Chaim Rumkowski's 'rule' over the Łódź Ghetto, Lowenthal foreshadows many later debates:

> But I cannot imprison in my heart [these things without adding] a few words on the great mistake we all ma[de] thinking that they needed people for labour. They really need them[.] But [the] matter of destroying the Jews is his – – – first priority. Above all – – – this will be depicted by the rese[ar]chers, in the future the historians and afterward the psychologists a clear and definite picture of the histo[ry] of the events and the suffering... (p. 239)

Indeed, historians and other scholars, not to mention law courts and popular representations of the ghetto, have struggled since the end of the war to assess Rumkowski's role and to try to understand how a man so universally disliked managed to keep the Łódź Ghetto in existence until the late summer of 1944. The reality is that, despite the appearance he liked to project, that decision on the usefulness and the continued existence of the ghetto was out of Rumkowski's hands and was taken by local authorities in Litzmannstadt (Łódź) and the broader region of the Warthegau in the face of SS opposition (Horwitz, 2008; Stone, 2010b, pp. 86–88). Loewenthal explains already in 1944 the understandable mistake that *Judenrat* leaders such as Rumkowski (but also others, such as Ephraim Barasz in Białystok, Jacob Gens in Vilna or Moshe Merin in Sosnowiec) made: believing that by fulfilling what the German authorities demanded of them, they might stand a chance of surviving. In fact, with the temporary exception of Łódź, war production came second in priority to the 'Final Solution'. For the historian, then, it is terrible to think of what we have lost, as well as gratifying to consider what we have. Loewenthal ends his addendum to the Łódź manuscript, demanding: 'Keep looking! You will [still] – – – find more.' Loewenthal the historian wanted as complete an archive as possible.

All three of these authors were aware of the impossibility of telling everything, but that is hardly different from a historian's account. As testimony, these texts clearly show that it was possible for the Nazis' victims to take some cognizance of what was happening to them, even in the last circle of Hell and even without the benefit of having an overview of the 'Final Solution' as a whole. Loewenthal (1985a, p. 235) was adamant, as he ended his account, that his and his colleagues' writings would aid the process of explaining to the world that what had happened at Auschwitz had opened up a 'deep pit' in 'the very heart of civilised Europe'.

Thus, whatever the reasons for these texts' neglect at the hands of historians, it is surely time to acknowledge that sometimes the victims – perhaps, paradoxically, especially those at the very heart of the killing process – did have the resources not only to understand, however partially, what was happening to them and to the Jews of Europe, but also to provide representations of the events in different forms and styles. These representations contradict the assumption that there can be no representation of the Holocaust from within the event itself or the assertion that it is immoral or impossible to provide one afterwards. As another unknown diarist from the Łódź ghetto wrote: 'To say that it is unimaginable, undescribable [sic], unspeakable, un...un...un...etc. and etc., is to have said nothing!'[11] Indeed, Gradowski's description of music in the camps might just as well be a summary of his own text, which is a powerful and – hard to say though it is – *beautiful* (in the sense of being formally poised) meditation which recalls the life of the mind of Gradowski's world before Auschwitz. When Gradowski recounts his surprise at hearing music in Auschwitz, he manages to sum up the outrage with scholarly precision: 'What can this mean? Music in the death camp, sounds of life on the island of death? In this battlefield of labour, to excite our souls with the magic sound of life from the past, here in this great cemetery, where everything breathes death and destruction; can it be that the life of yesteryear can be imagined – – – but here anything is possible. This is the harmony of barbarism; this is the reason of sadism' (1985, p. 202).

Notes

I am very grateful to Nicholas Chare and Dominic Williams for their helpful comments on the first draft of this chapter.

1. I am thinking here of the work of Giorgio Agamben. For an analysis that persuasively argues that Agamben is returning contemporary discussion to

the notion of the *'univers concentrationnaire'* introduced after World War II by David Rousset, see Moyn (2010). On Agamben, see also Giaccaria & Minca (2011) and Takayoshi (2011).
2. The name 'Scrolls of Auschwitz' comes from Ber Mark's volume (1985); that book, though important, does not however contain all the known writings of the Sonderkommando men. Another text by Zalman Gradowski (1988), 'The Czech Transport: A Chronicle of the Auschwitz *Sonderkommando'*, which contains a detailed description of the killing process, has been translated into English. The complete document from which this part is taken is available in French (Gradowski, 2001). Another text, as yet translated only into German (from Yiddish) by Langfuss ('Aussiedlung' ['Resettlement']) can be found in Bezwińska et al. (1996, pp. 73–129). Sadly, several of the originals have been lost and exist now only in transcript, although most of them survive, held in various institutions. See the discussion in Chare (2011, pp. 77–78).
3. It should be noted that the long passage cited by Gilbert on pp. 649–653 is attributed by Mark not to Loewenthal but to Langfuss (see Mark, 1985, pp. 212–214).
4. Revealingly, Friedländer also mentions Gradowski in the last, moving paragraphs of his book (p. 663) as one of the significant Jewish 'voices' that appear throughout the text.
5. I have discussed these texts in more detail in 'Beyond the Mnemosyne Institute' (Stone, 2010a).
6. I have discussed this in more detail in *Constructing the Holocaust* (Stone, 2003). See also my introduction to Stone (2012b), and also Confino (2012).
7. In addition to these texts, a letter written in French by Chaim Herman was found in 1945; a diary by an unknown author written in the Łódź Ghetto and buried along with one of Loewenthal's was unearthed in 1961, and a letter in Greek by Marcel Nadjary was found in 1980.
8. See brief comments by Friedler, Siebert and Kilian (2005, pp. 107–108) and Cohen (1994, pp. 522–534). For the unknown author's text on the Łódź Ghetto uncovered in July 1961 along with an addendum by Loewenthal, see Gumkowski, Rutkowski & Astel, 1967. Loewenthal's addendum is also available in English in Mark, *The Scrolls of Auschwitz*, as I discuss below.
9. This is a reference to Avraham Levite's introduction to a projected anthology of writings by Jews in Auschwitz, an anthology which has never been found.
10. A useful essay amongst the massive literature on Horkheimer and Adorno is Jacobs, 2005. For the recollections of another former Sonderkommando man, Eliezer Eisenschmidt, and of Gradowski, see the interview in Greif (1995, pp. 207–208).
11. In English in original, including misspelling of 'indescribable'. The diarist wrote in Polish, English, Hebrew and Yiddish. See Loewy & Bodek (1997, p. 72) for the German translation and the reproduction section after page 100 for the original.

Works cited

Alexander, J., et al. (eds.) (2004) *Cultural Trauma and Collective Identity* (Berkeley: University of California Press).

Anidjar, G. (2009) 'Against History', afterword to M. Nichanian, *The Historiographic Perversion* (New York: Columbia University Press, 2009), pp. 125–159.
Arendt, H. (1977) *Eichmann in Jerusalem: A Report on the Banality of Evil* (New York: Penguin).
Ball, K. (2008) *Disciplining the Holocaust* (Albany: State University of New York Press).
Bezwińska, J., et al. (eds.) (1996) *Inmitten des grauenvollen Verbrechens: Handschriften von Mitgliedern des Sonderkommandos* (Oświęcim: Staatliches Museum Auschwitz-Birkenau).
Blatman, D. (2011) *The Death Marches: The Final Phase of Nazi Genocide* (Cambridge, MA: Harvard University Press).
Brandon, R. & Lower, W. (eds.) (2008) *The Shoah in Ukraine: History, Testimony, Memorialization* (Bloomington: Indiana University Press).
Browning, C. (2004) *The Origins of the Final Solution: The Evolution of Nazi Jewish Policy, September 1939–March 1942* (London: William Heinemann).
Browning, C. (2010) *Remembering Survival: Inside a Nazi Slave-Labor Camp* (New York: W.W. Norton).
Butler, J. (2009) 'Primo Levi for the Present', in F. Ankersmit, E. Domańska & H. Kellner (eds.) *Re-figuring Hayden White* (Stanford: Stanford University Press).
Cesarani, D. & Sundquist, E. (eds.) (2012) *After the Holocaust: Challenging the Myth of Silence* (London: Routledge).
Chare, N. (2006) 'The Gap in Context: Giorgio Agamben's *Remnants of Auschwitz*', *Cultural Critique*, 64, 40–68.
Chare, N. (2011) *Auschwitz and Afterimages: Abjection, Witnessing and Representation* (London: I.B. Tauris).
Cohen, N. (1994) 'Diaries of the *Sonderkommando*', in Y. Gutman & M. Berenbaum (eds.) *Anatomy of the Auschwitz Death Camp* (Bloomington: Indiana University Press/Washington, DC: United States Holocaust Memorial Museum), pp. 522–534.
Confino, A. (2012) *Foundational Pasts: The Holocaust as Historical Understanding* (New York: Cambridge University Press).
Confino, A. (forthcoming) *A World without Jews* (New Haven: Yale University Press).
Crownshaw, R. (2010) *The Afterlife of Holocaust Memory in Contemporary Literature and Culture* (Houndmills: Palgrave Macmillan).
Dawidowicz, L. (1977) *The War against the Jews 1933–45* (Harmondsworth: Penguin).
Dawidowicz, L. (1981) *The Holocaust and the Historians* (Cambridge, MA: Harvard University Press).
Dean, M. (2008) *Robbing the Jews: The Confiscation of Jewish Property in the Holocaust, 1933–1945* (New York: Cambridge University Press).
Dean, M., Goschler, C. & Ther, P. (eds.) (2007) *Robbery and Restitution: The Conflict over Jewish Property in Europe* (New York: Berghahn Books).
Didi-Huberman, G. (2003) *Images malgré tout* (Paris: Éditions de Minuit).
Diner, D. (1992) 'Historical Understanding and Counterrationality: The Judenrat as Epistemological Vantage', in S. Friedländer (ed.) *Probing the Limits of Representation: Nazism and the "Final Solution"* (Cambridge, MA: Harvard University Press), pp. 128–142.

Dreyfus, J.-M. & Gensburger, S. (2011) *Nazi Labour Camps in Paris: Austerlitz, Levitan, Bassano, July 1943–August 1944* (Oxford: Berghahn Books).
Dwork, D. & van Pelt, R. (2002) *Holocaust: A History* (London: John Murray).
Edkins, J. (2003) *Trauma and the Memory of Politics* (Cambridge: Cambridge University Press).
Fassin, D. & Rechtman, R. (2009) *The Empire of Trauma: An Inquiry into the Condition of Victimhood*, R. Gomme (trans.) (Princeton: Princeton University Press).
Felman, S. (1992) 'The Return of the Voice: Claude Lanzmann's *Shoah*', in S. Felman & D. Laub (eds.), *Testimony: Crises of Witnessing in Literature, Psychoanalysis, and the History* (New York: Routledge), pp. 204–283.
Friedländer, S. (2007) *The Years of Extermination: Nazi Germany and the Jews 1939–1945* (London: HarperCollins).
Friedler, E., Siebert, B. & Kilian, A. (2005) *Zeugen aus der Todeszone: Das jüdische Sonderkommando in Auschwitz* (Munich: Deutscher Taschenbuch Verlag)
Garbarini, A. (2006) *Numbered Days: Diaries and the Holocaust* (New Haven: Yale University Press).
Giaccaria, P. & Minca, C. (2011) 'Nazi Bio-Geopolitics and the Dark Geographies of the *Selva*', *Journal of Genocide Research*, 13:1&2, 67–84.
Gilbert, M. (1987) *The Holocaust: The Jewish Tragedy* (London: Fontana).
Goldberg, A. (2009) 'The Victim's Voice and Melodramatic Aesthetics in History', *History and Theory*, 48, 220–237.
Goldberg, A. (2012) 'The History of the Jews in the Ghettos: A Cultural Perspective', in D. Stone (ed.) *The Holocaust and Historical Methodology* (New York: Berghahn Books).
Gradowski, Z. (1985) 'Writings', in B. Mark, *The Scrolls of Auschwitz*, S. Neemani (trans.) (Tel Aviv: Am Oved), pp. 173–205.
Gradowski, Z. (1988) 'The Czech Transport: A Chronicle of the Auschwitz *Sonderkommando*', in D. Roskies (ed.) *The Literature of Destruction* (Philadelphia: Jewish Publication Society), pp. 548–564.
Gradowski, Z. (2001) *Au coeur de l'enfer*, B. Baum (trans.) (Paris: Éditions Kimé).
Greif, G. (1995) *Wir weinten tränenlos: Augenzeugenberichte der jüdischen "Sonderkommandos" in Auschwitz* (Cologne: Böhlau Verlag).
Grimsted, P. (2006) 'The Postwar Fate of Einsatzstab Reichsleiter Rosenberg Archival and Library Plunder, and the Dispersal of ERR Records', *Holocaust and Genocide Studies*, 20:2, 278–308.
Gross, R. (2010) *Anständig geblieben: nationalsozialistische Moral* (Frankfurt/M: S. Fischer).
Gruner, W. (2006) *Jewish Forced Labor under the Nazis: Economic Needs and Racial Aims, 1938–1944* (New York: Cambridge University Press).
Gumkowski, J., Rutkowski, A. & Astel, A. (eds.) (1967) *Briefe aus Litzmannstadt*, P. Lachmann & A. Astel (trans.) (Cologne: Friedrich Middelhauve Verlag).
Hilberg, R. (1988) 'I Was Not There', in B. Lang (ed.) *Writing and the Holocaust* (New York: Holmes and Meier, 1988), pp. 17–25.
Hilberg, R. (2001) *Sources of Holocaust Research: An Analysis* (Chicago: Ivan R. Dee).
Horwitz, G. (2008) *Ghettostadt: Łódź and the Making of a Nazi City* (Cambridge, MA: Harvard University Press).

Jacobs, J. (2005) 'Horkheimer, Adorno, and the Significance of Anti-Semitism: The Exile Years', in D. Kettler & G. Lauer (eds.) *Exile, Science, and Bildung: The Contested Legacies of German Émigré Intellectuals* (New York: Palgrave Macmillan, 2005), pp. 157–168.

Jockusch, L. (2008) 'Chroniclers of Catastrophe: History Writing as a Jewish Response to Persecution before and after the Holocaust', in D. Bankier & D. Michman (eds.) *Holocaust Historiography in Context: Emergence, Challenges, Polemics and Achievements* (Jerusalem: Yad Vashem 2008), pp. 135–166.

Kansteiner, W. (2002) 'Finding Meaning in Memory: A Methodological Critique of Collective Memory Studies', *History and Theory*, 41, 176–197.

Kansteiner, W. (2004) 'Genealogy of a Category Mistake: A Critical Intellectual History of the Cultural Trauma Metaphor', *Rethinking History*, 8:2, 193–221.

Kershaw, I. (2011) '"Volksgemeinschaft": Potenzial und Grenzen eines neuen Forschungskonzepts', *Vierteljahrshefte für Zeitgeschichte*, 59:1, 1–17.

Klein, K. (2000) 'On the Emergence of *Memory* in Historical Discourse', *Representations*, 69, 127–150.

Kobrak, C. & Schneider, A. (2004) 'Big Business and the Third Reich: An Appraisal of the Historical Arguments', in D. Stone (ed.) *The Historiography of the Holocaust* (Houndmills: Palgrave Macmillan), pp. 141–172.

Kühne, T. (2010) *Belonging and Genocide: Hitler's Community, 1918–1945* (New Haven: Yale University Press).

Kushner, T. (2010) 'Saul Friedländer, Holocaust Historiography and the Use of Testimony', in C. Wiese & P. Betts (eds.) *Years of Persecution, Years of Extermination: Saul Friedländer and the Future of Holocaust Studies* (London: Continuum, 2010), pp. 67–79.

LaCapra, D. (2011) 'Historical and Literary Approaches to the "Final Solution": Saul Friedländer and Jonathan Littell', *History and Theory*, 50, 71–97.

Langfuss, L. 'The Horrors of Murder', in B. Mark, *The Scrolls of Auschwitz*, S. Neemani (trans.) (Tel Aviv: Am Oved), pp. 206–215.

Laub, D. (1992) 'An Event without a Witness: Truth, Testimony and Survival', in S. Felman & D. Laub (eds.), *Testimony: Crises of Witnessing in Literature, Psychoanalysis, and the History* (New York: Routledge), pp. 75–92.

Levi, P. (1989) *The Drowned and the Saved* (London: Abacus).

Levin, N. (1968) *The Holocaust: The Destruction of European Jewry 1933–1945* (New York: Thomas Y. Crowell Company).

Leys, R. (2000) *Trauma: A Genealogy* (Chicago: University of Chicago Press).

Loewenthal, Z. (1985a) 'Writings', in B. Mark, *The Scrolls of Auschwitz*, S. Neemani (trans.) (Tel Aviv: Am Oved), pp. 216–235.

Loewenthal, Z. (1985b) 'Addendum to the Łódź Manuscript', in B. Mark, *The Scrolls of Auschwitz*, S. Neemani (trans.) (Tel Aviv: Am Oved), pp. 236–240.

Longerich, P. (2010) *Holocaust: The Nazi Persecution and Murder of the Jews* (Oxford: Oxford University Press).

Luckhurst, R. (2003) 'Traumaculture', *New Formations*, 50, 28–47.

Luckhurst, R. (2008) *The Trauma Question* (London: Routledge).

Mark, B. (1985) *The Scrolls of Auschwitz*, S. Neemani (trans.) (Tel Aviv: Am Oved).

Mark, E. (1985) 'Notes on the Identity of the "Anonymous" Author and on His Manuscript', in B. Mark, *The Scrolls of Auschwitz*, S. Neemani (trans.) (Tel Aviv: Am Oved), pp. 166–170.

Marrus, M. (2009) *Some Measure of Justice: The Holocaust Era Restitution Campaign of the 1990s* (Madison: University of Wisconsin Press).

Michman, D. (2004) 'Jewish Leadership in Extremis', in D. Stone (ed.) *The Historiography of the Holocaust* (Houndmills: Palgrave Macmillan), pp. 319–340.

Miron, G. (2004) 'History, Remembrance, and a "Useful Past" in the Public Thought of Hungarian Jewry, 1938–1939', *Yad Vashem Studies*, 32, 131–170.

Moyn, S. (2010) 'In the Aftermath of Camps', in F. Biess & R. Moeller (eds.) *Histories of the Aftermath: The Legacies of the Second World War in Europe* (New York: Berghahn Books), pp. 49–64.

Neumann, B. (2010) *Die Weltanschauung des Nazismus: Raum, Körper, Sprache* (Göttingen: Wallstein).

Pendas, D. 'Testimony', in M. Dobson & B. Ziemann (eds.) *Reading Primary Sources: The Interpretation of Texts from Nineteenth- and Twentieth-Century History* (London: Routledge, 2009), pp. 226–242.

Rosen, A. (2010) *The Wonder of Their Voices: The 1946 Holocaust Interviews of David Boder* (New York: Oxford University Press).

Seltzer, M. (1997) 'Wound Culture: Trauma in the Pathological Public Sphere', *October*, 80, 3–26.

Snyder, T. (2010) *Bloodlands: Europe between Hitler and Stalin* (London: The Bodley Head).

Stone, D. (2001) 'The Sonderkommando Photographs', *Jewish Social Studies*, n.s., 7:3, 131–148.

Stone, D. (2003) *Constructing the Holocaust* (London: Vallentine Mitchell).

Stone, D. (2009) 'Holocaust Historiography and Cultural History', followed by forum discussion, *Dapim: Studies on the Shoah*, 23, 52–93.

Stone, D. (2010a) 'Beyond the Mnemosyne Institute: The Future of Memory after the Age of Commemoration', in R. Crownshaw, J. Kilby & A. Rowland (eds.) *The Future of Memory* (New York: Berghahn Books), pp. 17–34.

Stone, D. (2010b) *Histories of the Holocaust* (Oxford: Oxford University Press).

Stone, D. (2012a) 'Memory Wars in the "New Europe"', in D. Stone (ed.) *The Oxford Handbook of Postwar European History* (Oxford: Oxford University Press) pp. 714–731.

Stone, D (ed.) (2012b) *The Holocaust and Historical Methodology* (New York: Berghahn Books).

Stone, D. (2013) *The Holocaust, Fascism and Memory: Essays in the History of Ideas* (Houndmills: Palgrave Macmillan).

Suchoff, D. (1999) 'A Yiddish Text from Auschwitz: Critical History and the Anthological Imagination', *Prooftexts*, 19, 59–69.

Sumic-Riha, J. (2004) 'Testimony and the Real: Testimony between the Impossibility and Obligation', *Parallax*, 10:1, 17–29.

Szalai, A. (2004) 'Will the Past Protect Hungarian Jewry? The Response of Jewish Intellectuals to Anti-Jewish Legislation', *Yad Vashem Studies*, 32, 171–208.

Takayoshi, I. (2011) 'Can Philosophy Explain Nazi Violence? Giorgio Agamben and the Problem of the "Historico-Philosophical" Method', *Journal of Genocide Research*, 13:1&2, 47–66.

Tal, K. (1996) *Worlds of Hurt: Reading the Literatures of Trauma* (New York: Cambridge University Press).

Trunk, I. (1996) *Judenrat: The Jewish Councils in Eastern Europe under Nazi Occupation* (Lincoln: University of Nebraska Press).

Tych, F. (2008) 'The Emergence of Holocaust Research in Poland: The Jewish Historical Commission and the Jewish Historical Institute (ŻIH), 1944–1989', in D. Bankier & D. Michman (eds.) *Holocaust Historiography in Context: Emergence, Challenges, Polemics and Achievements* (Jerusalem: Yad Vashem), pp. 227–244.

Waxman, Z. (2010a) 'Towards an Integrated History of the Holocaust: Masculinity, Femininity, and Genocide', in C. Wiese & P. Betts (eds.) *Years of Persecution, Years of Extermination: Saul Friedländer and the Future of Holocaust Studies* (London: Continuum, 2010), pp. 311–321.

Waxman, Z. (2010b) 'Testimonies as Sacred Texts: The Sanctification of Holocaust Writing', *Past and Present*, Supplement 5, 321–341.

White, H. (2004) 'Figural Realism in Witness Literature', *Parallax*, 10:1, 113–124.

White, H. (2005) 'Introduction: Historical Fiction, Fictional History, and Historical Reality', *Rethinking History*, 9:2–3, 149.

Wolfe, R. (1995) 'Nazi Paperwork for the Final Solution', in J. Pacy & A. Wertheimer (eds.) *Perspectives on the Holocaust: Essays in Honor of Raul Hilberg* (Boulder: Westview Press), pp. 5–19.

Yahil, L. (1990) *The Holocaust: The Fate of European Jewry* (New York: Oxford University Press).

2
On the Problem of Empathy: Attending to Gaps in the Scrolls of Auschwitz

Nicholas Chare

> There is no document of civilization which is not at the same time a document of barbarism. And just as such a document is not free of barbarism, barbarism taints also the manner in which it was transmitted from one owner to another.
>
> (Benjamin, 1999, p. 248)

Making things clear

In the last months of the operation of the 'death factory' at Auschwitz-Birkenau a number of manuscripts were buried in the grounds of the crematoria at Birkenau by members of the Sonderkommando, or Special Squads. Some of these remarkable documents were recovered after the liberation of the camp and are now collectively known as the Scrolls of Auschwitz. In addition to the manuscripts, the men also interred quantities of teeth. These had been extracted from the mouths of those murdered in the gas chambers and were, like the writings, intended to form a kind of testimony. Teeth, which comprise of four kinds of tissue of differing densities, are more durable than bone. They are more likely to persist, to survive the passage of time. The teeth provided physical evidence of the murders referenced by the documents. The Sonderkommando, therefore, engaged in a combination of activities in an effort to convey something of the crimes that surrounded them. They bore witness through words and bodily matter. The words can be understood to put the teeth in context and the teeth to lend substance to the words. The burying of writings and bodily remains had a singular aim: to leave a trace. Zalman Gradowski writes that the documents were buried so that 'traces can be found of millions of slaughtered people' before going on to state that 'a lot of teeth have been buried here, we've done this, [...] sowed as many as possible over the entire area, in order that the world should be able to find material [thingly] traces of millions of murdered people' (Gradowski, 1985, p. 205).[1]

Traces provide evidence of the former presence or existence of something. The trace is not the thing in its entirety. It is a vestige of it, a left-over or survival. Gradowski and other members of the Sonderkommando were seeking to leave these traces, these remnants and residues to act as signs, pointers for what had happened. Words and things were concealed in order to index the murders committed there. These traces were left in the belief that there would be a concerted effort by the Nazis to destroy all indications of the genocide they had perpetrated. They were conceived of as forms of evidence, intended to act as spurs to remembrance, and also as incitements to revenge. In the aftermath of the liberation of Auschwitz-Birkenau, over a period of time, some of the buried writings were found, their worth was recognized and they were, albeit sometimes by circuitous routes, usually archived and preserved. The teeth, by contrast, went unremarked. They were lost amidst the mass of ash and bone fragments that fill and form the soil at Birkenau. The survival of words, of written communications composed in the midst of the machinery of mass murder, was what was taken to be extraordinary. These documents endured against the odds. They were frequently damaged by the effects of their concealment, rendered partially illegible, yet much writing persisted.

It is possible to interpret the decay and dirt that interrupts the extant originals of the Sonderkommando manuscripts as constituting a further layer of testimony in addition to the account provided by the written words. The pages of the notebook Langfuss used for his composition *Der Geyresh*, for example, have become pockmarked, scarred by accumulated grime and the effects of moisture. This smutting and staining, which supplements the written narrative, provides a complementary account of the circumstances in which the document was produced and then hidden. *Der Geyresh* and the other ravaged Scrolls of Auschwitz can therefore be understood as palimpsests. Elsewhere I have already explored the crucial importance this subsequent 'text', one written by acid, earth and water, forms as a mode of bearing witness to Auschwitz (Chare, 2011, pp. 77–91). In my earlier account, however, I only briefly touched on the way this secondary story generated by contingency is perceived, in the case of the Auschwitz Museum, to be one that mars rather than intensifies the first.

The restoration work carried out on the paper of the final manuscript to be discovered, the letter written by Marcel Nadjary that was found in 1980, is informative in this context. When it was unearthed the pages of the manuscript, which were photographed in black and white, were discoloured and tattered. The letter has, however, now been restored by the Auschwitz Museum. The pages have been treated and are therefore cleaner. The tears have also been repaired. The aim of this exercise appears to be to magnify the clarity of the written account, the primary text. The secondary narrative has, to a large extent, been excised, treated as a taint that requires cleansing. This has led the foxing on the pages of the letter to be blanched, the tears knitted, and any holes to be filled with paper of a similar colour and weight. The aim has been to remove all indications of decay and render the manuscript as close as possible to the condition when it was written, in other words, to restore it. Salvador Muñoz Viñas (2005, p. 17) defines the objective of restoration to be 'to return [an] object to a better, less damaged state'. The conservators are seeking to undo the effects of oxidation and simultaneously improve the legibility of the letter. The consequence of this perceived damage to the paper, its evidentiary value in relation to how the letter was transmitted from a writer facing almost certain death in Auschwitz to a contemporary reader at ease in the camp archive, is therefore perceived as unimportant. Ideally all traces of this passage from within the event to its aftermath would be removed.

The celebrated paper restorer Max Schweidler (2006) regarded paper as akin to skin and described his activities as comparable to those of a physician. Schweidler refers to paper under his care as 'the patient' (pp. 49, p. 52). He calls foxed or decayed paper 'diseased' (p. 46). In Schweidler's eyes, the actions of restorers were therefore curative. The way the conservation team at Auschwitz have treated Nadjary's letter suggests they view their actions as similarly remedial. The rents and stains are injuries rather than another form of testimony that should be preserved. The aim is to achieve spotlessness. It is to minimize gaps in comprehension and to maximize intelligibility. Other manuscripts from the archive are now also undergoing restoration and may be receiving a similar treatment. Their 'health' is being assessed based upon their legibility and lack of tarnish and corrective measures are being contemplated.

The interventions made to the Nadjary letter (techniques which may in future also be applied to manuscripts by Langfuss and Loewenthal) are comparable to the alterations made to reproductions of photographs taken by Alex, a member of the Sonderkommando, in August 1944.

For Georges Didi-Huberman, these images have been manipulated for two reasons. One motivation is the desire to transform the pictures into *icons* of horror (2003, p. 50). This has led the image which shows naked women in the foreground walking past the photographer to be reframed, cropped and retouched, this last action including the crafting of a countenance and breasts being lifted and affirmed. For Didi-Huberman, 'this aberrant doctoring [...] reveals a crazed wish to *give a face* to what is no more than movement, blurring, incident, in the image itself' (p. 50). In this context, it seems that the aim is to provide horror with a singular identity, an individual likeness. Through the addition of detail the picture comes closer to achieving the status of the boy held at gunpoint in the Warsaw Ghetto, a sharp portrait for whom a number of possible identities have been offered, who is burdened with standing for the millions of other children murdered in the Holocaust. The second impetus to alter this and the other images is 'with the aim of making them more *informative* than they were in their original state' (p. 50). Adjustments are carried out to enhance the documentary force of the pictures. It is this second impulse which informs the efforts to purify the Scrolls of seemingly non-documentary matter. The difference between the restoration processes that are being undertaken in relation to the manuscripts and the interventions carried out on the photographs in their reproduction is that the original photographs are not being doctored whereas the writings by the Sonderkommando, the actual texts rather than reproductions, are being physically modified. The motivation to do this in the interests of intelligibility is understandable, yet, as will become clear, ultimately misplaced. What follows is a series of reflections on the implications of this drive for clarity of expression in testimony for bearing witnessing to the Holocaust more broadly.

On the problem of empathy...

Didi-Huberman suggests that the changes made to the photographs taken covertly by Alex pare them of their phenomenological import. The various alterations deprive the pictures of the condition of urgency that accompanied their taking. This sense of haste and pressure, of anxiety and furtiveness, is embodied in the lack of clarity and poor centring of the images. Didi-Huberman reconstructs the actions, the feelings of Alex from close attention to what other viewers of the images, those who have altered them in reproduction, have perceived to be their failings. The mass of shadow in the first two photographs caused by the physical structure of the crematorium, which is often cropped in reproduction, becomes a means by which Didi-Huberman accesses Alex's cunning and his fear. In the blurred image of the women walking (its haziness caused both by their and the photographer's motion) urgency is detected, a fearful vigour (Didi-Huberman, p. 63). The photographs are therefore, as becomes markedly clear in the description of the picture just discussed, passageways to empathy.

Didi-Huberman writes that despite the image being assailed by a lack of visibility, when we are confronted by it we are made to feel the 'shattering [*bouleversante*] *obligation* of an *empathic* gesture' on our part (p. 63). The photographs demand that we imagine our way into them. For Didi-Huberman, 'Auschwitz *is only imaginable*' and the photographs provide a vital spur to such an envisioning (p. 62).[2] This imagining requires the viewer to stand as Alex did, withstand what he experienced. In the images of the incineration pits that Alex steals, for example, Didi-Huberman joins him in sensing 'the cracklings of grease, the smells, the shrivelling of human flesh' (p. 22). These sounds, odours, contractions emerge from out of a disturbance in the field of vision, out of the fog of smut, bone ash and grease that obscures the bodies of those murdered, out of seemingly superfluous visual matter. Didi-Huberman, however, sees through these cinders or rather sees into them. His description embodies the empathetic gesture he suggests is a stipulation of seeing the images.

Didi-Huberman does not provide a gloss on this complex concept, which has had a varied history.[3] It is obvious from his descriptions of the four images taken by Alex, however, that he feels that, through an imaginative recreation of the photographer's physical endeavours, his psychic state can be restored. This is evident, for example, in Didi-Huberman's discussion of the second photograph taken outwards from within the gas chamber. This closer and more frontal picture shows that Alex has become 'emboldened' (Didi-Huberman, p. 22). The composition reveals the movements that led up to it. These in turn reveal the photographer's state of mind. There is a belief in *Images malgré tout* that the feeling of another's motion can cause the feeling of their emotion to be shared as well. There is a connection between reproducing another's kinaesthetic sensations and participating in their feelings. This echoes Edith Stein's (1989, p. 68) phenomenological conception of empathy. She contends that spontaneous movement is necessary for empathy to occur. Her general theorization of empathy is informative in that it appears, in many ways, to resonate with Didi-Huberman's implicit understanding of the term. Stein states that empathy is 'the experience of a foreign consciousness' (p. 14). This experience is a non-primordial one, at a remove from feeling rather than first hand and immediate, although it announces a primordial one (the primordial here being understood as 'raw' feeling or perception). It is also one 'in which foreign primordiality', another's direct experience of phenomena, 'becomes apparent' (Stein, p. 17). Empathy is being in feeling with another, rather than understanding another's feelings, in the sense that it is the inhabiting of another's emotional state not its simulation.

For Stein, empathy is something beyond representation. It is given directly rather than achieved via association and inference (Stein, p. 24). Didi-Huberman's reference to the shattering obligation to empathize when confronted by the photographs, with its emphasis on the violent upset the images cause, implies a shock to thought. The drive to empathize manifests itself, first and foremost, physically. It is, as Stein suggested, not a deliberative process. It is a gesture and it is also an act, an action, of resemblance (Didi-Huberman, p. 63). It is a travelling with the image. In the photograph of the naked women, for Didi-Huberman, the viewer moves with the women and the photographer, whilst simultaneously being moved by that accompanying motion (p. 63). By going along with these figures, getting in step with them, he shares in their feelings, anxieties. Empathy is a way of moving beyond words, and by extension images, as a means by which to understand foreign phenomena, feelings and sensations, even if its catalyst is a word or image. Stein writes:

> if there were no possibility of empathy, of transferring the self into another's orientation, their statements about their phenomenal world would always have to remain unintelligible, at least in the sense of a complete fulfilling understanding in contrast with the mere empty understanding of words. Statements can fill the breach and supplement where empathy fails. Possibly they may even serve as points of departure for further empathy. But in principle they cannot substitute for empathy. (p. 65)

For Didi-Huberman, Alex's photographs, or more specifically the reveries they engender, provide a point of departure, a springboard, for such empathy. The images therefore constitute a means of bridging the gap between the present and the past, of traversing the break between the inside and the outside of Auschwitz. This conception of empathy as a means of crossing borders echoes Stein's. She also describes acts of empathy in terms of boundary crossings (p. 64). For her, empathy is a being here and there rather than a moving from here to there (p. 64).

It is a combining of positions rather than a shift from one position to another. Susan Leigh Foster's (2011, p. 164) summary of the philosopher's conception of empathy is informative here: 'for Stein empathy was the bodily experience of feeling connected to the other, while at the same time knowing that one was not experiencing directly the other's movements or feelings'. Empathy is the bringing into being of a knowing distance. Dominick LaCapra's (2001, pp. 41–42) idea of 'empathic unsettlement', a non-appropriative response to another's traumatic experience that provides insight into their feelings, involves a familiar detachment that can be compared to this intimate discretion. The Sonderkommando photographs, which Dan Stone (2001, p. 133) describes as offering a sort of closeness to events as well as emphasizing distance, generate an empathic response of the kind Stein conceives of. The film from which these photographs were developed was, of course, also physically carried, smuggled, from inside Birkenau to outside. Their empathic capability likewise permits a journeying in the other direction via the physical responses they hold the potential to engender.

The kind of empathy Didi-Huberman believes can be felt in relation to the Sonderkommando photographs, however, is potentially not restricted to those images. It becomes highly disquieting to consider this kind of felt witnessing in the context of other testimony produced from within the Holocaust. The film footage shot by Reinhard Wiener in 1941 in Latvia of members of a Jewish forced labour detachment being executed whilst standing in a pit, for example, can, in some ways, be said to hold a comparable phenomenological import to the photographs. Joshua Hirsch (2004, pp. 1–3) briefly discusses this footage in *Afterimage*, using it as a way to begin his investigation into the capacity for cinema to transmit historical trauma. He recounts how Wiener's film was placed in a trunk and buried in a pigsty by his mother in 1945 when the family farm became close to the front line of advancing allied troops. Wiener retrieved it from there after the war and eventually sent it to Yad Vashem.

The film is under two minutes long and consists of 18 shots in total. The projection speed employed when screening the footage may make the events it depicts appear to unfold faster than they did in real time. Excessive rapidity, for instance, is particularly apparent when figures are shown shovelling earth. The footage involves several jumps caused by Wiener shifting position slightly, seemingly to get a clearer view. In common with the Sonderkommando photographs, two of the lines of movement the viewer can accompany are the cameraman and the soon-to-be-murder victims, who are made to run to the pit where they will be executed. These distinct kinetic possibilities, markedly different forms of motions and emotions, will be discussed shortly. There are, however, at least four positions available here, two other possible sets of bodies to inhabit, which merit attention.

The pit Wiener films is not in a remote location. It is situated on the outskirts of the town of Liepāja and buildings, perhaps houses, are visible in the background. A crowd, forming the third standpoint the viewer can associate with, has gathered in the foreground and to the left and right of the site of the murders. There are more people visible on an embankment or escarpment in the background. The killings are plainly a local spectacle. In this short footage, Dori Laub's contention that the Holocaust was an event without a witness is lent corroboration by the chilling indifference of these bystanders. Their 'lack of responsiveness' to the massacre unfolding in front of their eyes is communicated by the dearth of motion they display (Felman & Laub, 1992, p. 81). The feelings held in this standing by, this relative inaction of looking on, the sentiment accompanying it, are either apathy or fascination. When people do demonstrate significant movement, as happens in the ninth shot of the sequence, in which a head pops into frame at the left, or in the tenth shot, when a number of people can be seen jostling, it is to get a better view. The viewer therefore baulks despite Didi-Huberman's imperative, which is not restricted to the Sonderkommando photographs, to 'imagine'. The footage potentially provides insights into the failure of onlookers to assume the position of witness by signalling their complicity. It also reveals a disturbing aspect to empathy. It can carry us to feelings of others that we do not, or should not, wish to know.

This links with the fourth available position in the footage, that of the perpetrators. The many soldiers in the clip also provide possible points of transference, possible foreign bodies the viewer can enter into and empathically understand. Their movements are mainly directed towards forcing the Jewish men towards the pit as quickly as possible, to policing the space around it and to shooting the men in the pit dead. The motions of the soldiers are not ones a well-balanced viewer would wish to merge with, be moved by. The only possible exception to this judgment might be the actions of a soldier who appears in the eleventh shot of the sequence. This individual, who is standing at the right edge of the frame, turns away from the pit as soil is being shovelled onto the bodies of those murdered. He walks away from this scene of atrocity, turning his back on it, hands to his face, perhaps his nose, a gesture that does not suggest indifference, rather unease, anxiety. This may, perhaps, be a sign of the psychological strain that made the Nazi's turn to the 'Brack method' to accomplish their genocidal aims (Stone, 2010, p. 190). His gestures could signal the trace of a conscience. This man may demonstrate a comparable revulsion at what is occurring to that of the soldier who ran up to Wiener as he was approaching Liepāja and told him not to walk any further because something terrible was happening up ahead (Hirsch, p. 1). The actions of the soldier in the footage are, however, isolated. They contrast starkly with those of the soldier immediately in front of him, for example, who continues to watch, hand on hip, as the bodies are buried.

Tellingly, Wiener did not heed the warning of the other soldier and continued into the town until he located the site of the massacre. The cuts and jump cuts in the footage signal his motions. They can be easily tracked, followed, entered into. It seems Wiener arrived or began filming during a lull in the killing before a vehicle turned up with more victims. The first shot of the footage shows the pit where the murders take place in the middle distance. This is shortly replaced by one in which the back of a truck can be seen in the foreground. Local Jewish men who were evidently its passengers are filmed running from it towards the pit which they jump down into. The back of the lorry is closed. Shortly afterwards it has disappeared, evidently sent to pick up more victims. Wiener then shifts position, moves forwards, and a shot shows the truck after it has arrived again or the arrival of a different vehicle. The pit must now be behind Wiener and to his left. He moves again, turning to his left for the next shot which shows the men from the truck being led past him. He then moves further left and forwards so that the next shot shows the pit in closer proximity than before. The men can be seen lining up in the pit. They are then killed by the firing squad. A dog skitters in the foreground, scared by the sound of the rifles.

Wiener has now witnessed multiple murders first hand more than once and has filmed them for the first time. He continues filming, recording earth being shovelled over the corpses and, by coincidence, captures the seemingly perturbed soldier. He then returns to his former location between the pit and the truck to shoot footage of more men arriving. His camera follows the men, tracks them as they run from right to left towards the pit, the edge of which comes into view. Wiener then shifts position again in an effort to centre on the pit. He catches the end of another set of executions, bodies crumpling to the ground. This is followed by a shot of five or six further victims running to the pit, a soldier following close behind them. Wiener then moves in close proximity to the pit. He must be filming from near to its edge. The footage is grainy but it appears the victims are forced to turn their backs on their executioners. They are murdered. Wiener records soil being shovelled over the dead shortly afterwards.

This footage, like the Sonderkommando photographs, has phenomenological significance. Wiener's spontaneous movements, repeated actions, express a story. They also provide a space for motional imagining, for empathic understanding. It is, however, a form of witnessing to atrocity that is perversely confident rather than furtive. There is no anxiety betrayed here, Wiener goes about his ghastly business unimpeded and exhibits a curious self-assurance. He later claimed that whilst shooting the footage he was agitated and 'shivering all over' (Hirsch, p. 3). The calm documentation of process, the calculated choice of shots, belies this. His gradual forward motion towards the pit in the sequence is unnerving. The imagination does not wish to engage with his brutal tenacity, his willingness to approach, his capacity to record from at the edge of the pit, this last act betraying far more than a mere wish to document. The time devoted to this endeavour, less than two minutes, is also obscenely long. There is a moment after which the rationale of bearing witness can no longer justify the act of filming. Wiener's tarrying is therefore aberrant. His ability to get close to the 'action', his capacity to shift, turn, advance, also kinetically signals his alliance with those perpetrating the murders. He has the power to move freely. He is damned by the ease and excess of his actions.

The fourth position, the final obvious set of motions the viewer can enter into, is those of the victims. The men are obviously bewildered and fearful. They are bullied towards the pit, forced to run there, climb down into it. The viewer is, fortunately, separated from the expressions of these individuals in their final moments. There is a distance that renders this horror unknowable, an experiential gap that cannot be traversed. What these men are going through should, in any case, remain unimaginable. The anxiety in the photographs discussed by Didi-Huberman forms a general atmosphere. The photographs show the aftermath of murder and its antecedents. They do not, however, show the moment of death. Both the film and the photographs present possible points of identification with bodies in their final frantic moments. Several of the accounts in the Scrolls also present potential instances of empathic connection with victims of Nazi atrocity.

Ways of seeing

The footage shot by Wiener is also comparable to the four photographs taken by Alex and the Scrolls of Auschwitz in that it is testimony produced from within the Holocaust. It is, however, also markedly different as an example of interior witnessing. From an historian's perspective, it attests to murders carried out by the Einsatzgruppe rather than to those committed in the death camps. It is also made by a German soldier, a perpetrator, rather than an internee. The photographs and manuscripts produced by the Sonderkommando were acts of resistance. Wiener's film, on the other hand, by way of its openness, reveals his collusion in the events that are unfolding in front of him. There are, however, still ways in which a consideration of the Wiener film alongside these other testaments to the Holocaust can be instructive in relation to ethical questions around testimony. The Wiener footage, for example, is particularly graphic. It is noteworthy that although it can still be understood as summoning projection, it leaves little to the imagination. Crucially, as will be discussed in due course, this contrasts with the photographs by Alex and with the accounts of mass murder present in the Scrolls.

The testimonies of the Sonderkommando, like Wiener's film, have a suspect status as witness accounts. The photographs have generated considerable controversy, with Claude Lanzmann claiming 'they are images without imagination' (Didi-Huberman, p. 118). The Scrolls of Auschwitz, on the other hand, have been remarkably neglected given their astonishing depth and complexity. The wariness exhibited towards the photographs and writings, is, however, understandable given that some may view the actions of the Sonderkommando as morally questionable. Didi-Huberman, for instance, glosses over the significance of the relative freedom of Alex's movements. The inmate is similar to Wiener in that he walks with a degree of autonomy that contrasts with those he photographs (although he is dissimilar in that his camera is concealed). The fact Alex must be furtive also translates into a lack of clearness in his images which contrasts starkly with the comparatively crisp footage shot by the German. Like Alex, the writers of the Scrolls also betray the concessions they enjoyed as prisoners in that they produced the manuscripts. They had the materials and time to compose written accounts, the energy and opportunity to do so. Nevertheless, their accounts still had to be written surreptitiously and then concealed.

The members of the Sonderkommando can therefore be understood to unwillingly occupy the position of hinge between perpetrator and victim. This status is pivotal, making their witnessing possible. Their ambiguous, undecided status carries them outside the trapping roles of executioner and victim that are identified by Laub as rendering testimony from within the event impossible (Felman & Laub,

p. 81). For Laub, no historical insider could fail to be contaminated by the event, either by their complicity or their abject victimhood. The Sonderkommando are – it is inescapable – unwilling facilitators of mass murder yet their acts of resistance demonstrate that they are not straightforward collaborators. They are also obviously victims, although they are not victims to the extent that their identity ceased to exist (as Laub claims happened to all victims) (p. 82). They were not reduced to animal status and therefore what Edith Wyschogrod describes as the symbolic truths of human existence were not annulled in them (1985, p. 114). In the 'death-world' of Birkenau, to borrow Wyschogrod's descriptor for all the camps, they retained the capacity to give an account of their present, to interpret events and look to a future beyond them. The acts of photographing and writing gesture to a life world, these linguistic expressions address another, elsewhere. The Special Squad members were able to retain their sense of identity and their ability to attest to the circumstances they found themselves in because the Nazis continued to recognize their humanity. This is evident in Miklós Nyiszli's (1973, p. 60) disturbing account of the easy merriment that surrounded a football match organized between the number one crematorium's SS guards and the Sonderkommando within view (and, presumably, smell) of the smoking chimneys of the crematoria. The Sonderkommando had an exceptional status that positioned them outside of Laub's generalized Holocaust experience.

The uncertain standing of the Sonderkommando was recognized by the members themselves and several worried they would be perceived as collaborators. Chaim Herman's (1973, p. 184) letter to his wife, for example, which was found buried in a heap of human ashes in February 1945, urges her not to have a bad opinion of him despite what will be written about the actions of the Special Squads. Primo Levi (1989, pp. 36–43) also famously frames the Sonderkommando as the epitome of the Grey Zone. The testimonies produced in 1943 and 1944 by these men who worked, and for a time lived, in the crematoria tellingly possess none of the savage clarity of Wiener's film. Alex's photographs are indistinct and present a fragmentary narrative of murder. The Scrolls foster hazy picturing of the events they describe. This distinction is crucial when it comes to considering the moral implications of following Didi-Huberman's dictum to 'only imagine'.

Gradowski employs film as a metaphor at several points in his writings. He writes, for example, of prisoners on the train journey to Auschwitz: 'It seems as if they are imprisoned in a mobile fortress, watching a film of this world in all its colours, from which its prisoners must now forever take their leave' (Gradowski, 1985, p. 183). He also refers to memory in cinematic terms writing of inmates reminiscing about their former freedom: 'They review the film of their years gone by, forever vanished, and the horror of the cruel reality in which they find themselves is projected before their eyes' (Gradowski, 2001, p. 60). These references to motion pictures, however, are used to signal detachment from the world outside, with its rich sensory experiences, and also from the past. Film is figured as an elsewhere. It exists at a frustrating distance and is used as a trope by which to communicate the agonizing estrangement from past experiences that constituted camp life. Additionally, of course, the filmic references in Gradowski's writings form a memory trace of the author's past cultural life.

A film such as Wiener's could never have been made by the Sonderkommando at Birkenau. The technology required would be too unwieldy to use surreptitiously and also difficult, if not impossible, to procure. For the Sonderkommando, film existed only as memory and metaphor. The photographs are, however, close to film in the sense of the immediacy they offer. The written testimonies also possess a strong visual component. They can also be interpreted as graphic. The vivid use of visual imagery is evident, for example, in Gradowski's lengthy account of the fate of a Czech transport of women and men. He writes of the arrival of the women: 'We are all stunned. There are alluring bodies, full of attraction and charm, draped in these threadbare, long tattered, timeworn clothes' (Gradowski, 2001, p. 83). Gradowski goes on to provide a poetic description of the visible appeal of these women:

> So many heads with black, brunette, blonde curls, and the odd grey head, looked at us with their deep, enchanting, generous dark eyes. We saw before our eyes young lives, bubbly, quivering, effervescent, burgeoning, brim with vigour, like roses still blossoming in a garden, in full bloom. Fresh, bathed in rain, wet with morning dew. (pp. 83–84)

This passage of description comprises one of the most disturbing aspects of any of the manuscripts due to the palpable desire it communicates by way of an unnerving floridity. The flowery prose is undoubtedly, in part, judicious with the liveliness of the women emphasized via the detailed description as a means to make their imminent deaths all the more horrific. There is, however, also plainly a pleasure in looking betrayed by the elaborate, even orchidaceous, depiction. This joy in female appearance recurs slightly later, when Gradowski refers to the women as having skin as white as alabaster. The analogy conjures images of stone sculptures and suggests the women possess an aesthetic appeal. In his retrospective testimony, the Sonderkommando member Shlomo Venezia also frames an encounter with the corpse of a striking woman in these terms: 'one day, among the corpses brought out of the gas chamber, the men found the body of an incredibly beautiful woman. She had the perfect body of ancient statues' (2009, p. 97).

Gradowski's (2001, p. 86) sculptural metaphor enables him to look ahead to the time when he foresees that the white alabastrine bodies will be 'spattered with human waste'. This sullying does indeed occur as he writes later, as part of a description of the aftermath of the gassing of the women, that 'you pull the corpse across the chill dirty cement floor, and its lovely smooth alabaster body sweeps up all the muck, the filth in its path'. The reader is therefore presented with a studied composition. In the space of a few pages a prediction is seen to become reality. The stylistic strategy, foreseeing and then confirming events, operates to reinforce the fact that Gradowski knows what he is talking about. He has seen it all before. It also functions to emphasize that the murders are an open-ended process rather than a singular event. The set of contrasts between the now and the future is additionally powerful because it communicates the way the members of the Sonderkommando, with their insider knowledge, already looked upon the living as dead: 'From this pearly mouth, teeth will be torn along with flesh, blood will gush. From this finely chiselled nose two red, yellow, or white streams will flow. And the gas will cause this white and rosy face to become red, blue or black' (p. 86).

Furthermore, in some passages, there may be a desire to hold onto aspects of these women by way of the enduring present of the prose. Gradowski knows the women will shortly be reduced to ashes. He later specifies the time it takes to completely burn a body as twenty minutes (p. 114). This understanding comes from past experience and, of course, because he is writing about the group of women retrospectively. It is obvious, however, that during the murders he was already mentally noting details. The text becomes a way of leaving traces of these lost lives, albeit faint, fragmentary ones. Individual identities, what Gradowski refers to as 'worlds,' have disappeared yet the text functions as their remnant (p. 114). The murdered women are nameless yet some are individualized by way of their recounted actions. Through a cataloguing of distinct attitudes and behaviours, Gradowski provides a sense of the heterogeneous personalities crammed into the undressing room. As Gideon Greif suggests, he seeks to 'bestow on them a small touch of humanness' (2005, p. 30). Some of the women cry, others are silent, several, calm, talk of their situation with members of the Sonderkommando (Gradowski, 2001, p. 85).

Despite the laudable aspects informing Gradowski's endeavour just outlined, however, parts of the narrative remain deeply unnerving. It is obvious from the elaborate account of the appearance and vitality of the female prisoners, from what we might describe as Gradowski's taking of his descriptive pleasures, that they are largely viewed as sexual objects by him and, presumably, by the other members of the Sonderkommando.[4] Venezia seeks to deny this in his *ex post facto* account which frames the fascination with the beautiful woman in solely aesthetic terms: she is 'pure image' rather than a source of impure thoughts (p. 98). It is noteworthy, however, that in the same paragraph as he mentions this event he states of the undressing room: 'you didn't pay any attention; you had no right to feel moved' (p. 98). Gradowski's account shows that this suggested indifference, this lack of anguish or desire for those about to die, was not the reality.

The fact that members of the Sonderkommando had the energy, the libido, to look in this way, to appreciate, desire, in these circumstances, is itself insightful. It reaffirms the uncommon physical vigour that came with the unique privileges (such as access to significant quantities of food) that they benefited from. Herman boasts of his health in the letter to his wife (p. 185). This energy is embodied in the capacity to write and is also manifest in what is written about. It becomes a kind of evidence available to the historian who is attentive to traces of forces and motions. Gradowski's aberrant vitality enables him to possess a sex drive and also to craft his writing, to figure and construct similes. The energy that sustains these activities is made possible by his willingness to work in the crematoria, to facilitate the workings of the death factory. He has strength that is absent from most of those in the camp. Such vivacity is denied to them. His physical well-being renders him closer to the perpetrators than to their victims.

Gradowski's way of seeing also positions him alongside the Nazi officials he tells of, who have come to take visual pleasure in the sight of the women (2001, p. 89). He describes a young woman as railing at these officials for their lasciviousness and drawing attention to their sadistic gaze yet his vivid account of the undressing room leaves him open to similar condemnation. The officials, however, do not share his exhilaration at the songs of resistance the women perform from within the gas chamber as they await their fate (pp. 93–95). The account reinforces Gradowski's ambiguous status in relation to both victims and executioners. It is nonetheless possible to align his way of looking at the women with a scopic mastery bordering on the sadistic comparable to that discussed by Griselda Pollock in her reading of Gillo Pontecorvo's *Kapò* (2011, p. 267). This prospect arises because he looks upon the women as alive yet dead. His narrative therefore raises comparable concerns to those identified by Pollock about feminized, aestheticized death. The figures of beautiful women are often employed to cover 'insupportable signs of lack, deficiency, transiency and promise their spectators the impossible – an obliteration of death's ubiquitous "castrative" threat to the subject' (Bronfen, 1992, p. 64). The perfection of the image of Woman in Gradowski is not, however, maintained. Woman's castrative potential surfaces, for instance, in the prophetic visions of her leaking corpse. What Elisabeth Bronfen refers to as 'insupportable signs of lack' is plain to see (p. 64).

It is nevertheless still noteworthy that even within the event Woman is chosen to represent the process of industrial murder. This also frequently occurs retrospectively including in Alain Resnais's *Night and Fog* (Pollock, p. 285). Gradowski's account prefigures later masculine, heterosexual viewing dynamics in which naked women and clothed men represent the genocidal aims of the death-world (Pollock, p. 286). The repaired femininity of Alex's photographs after they have been retouched similarly contributes to this way of seeing, endeavours to engineer such a perspective. Gradowski's potential reduction of Woman to a general symbol for genocide is, however, offset by the individuality he grants to two women. One is a mother who berates the Nazi officials and warns them of their own impending fate given their losses on the Russian front. The other is the woman discussed earlier who castigates the officials for their lechery. In both these instances, the Nazis are reminded that a similar fate soon awaits them. The mother implicitly affirms that victims and executioners share in vulnerability when she suggests the officials will have their living bodies 'torn to pieces' (Gradowski, 2001, p. 90). The executioner will soon exchange places with the victim. By drawing attention to this, the women invite the executioners to empathize with their fate, to feel what they feel, to experience what will also befall them soon enough. If the murderers accept this summons then they will discover a chilling common humanity, the 'cauterization of conscience' caused by the labelling of the Jews as sub-human will briefly be undone (Cohen, 1993, p. 7).

Gradowski's account also demonstrates awareness of an individual's ability for empathy and of the power that this capacity holds. There are descriptions in *At the Heart of Hell* that are seemingly of moments of empathic connection. Gradowski writes, for example, of a wizened woman in Birkenau who is not reflecting on her own predicament but whose spirit is with her children who were taken from her the day before (2001, p. 65). Later he writes of a young man who has been separated from his betrothed: 'he felt, he saw with her eyes how she waited for him, pining for him, how she suffered in the throes of death' (p. 67). Immediately after this, he refers to a youthful father in the depths of despair who suffers alongside the wife he has been split from: 'they knew [as one], they felt, their looks pierced the many barriers of the prisons that separated them' (p. 67). In these moments, individuals experience the consciousness of others, join them from a distance. There is potentially a comparable phenomenon at work within the description of the undressing scene. Gradowski writes that some of the women want members of the Special Squad to touch and caress them so that they can feel as if their lover, their husband, is stroking and fondling them in a fit of passion (p. 85). Here the intimate motions of a stranger are interpreted as imaginatively becoming the tender caresses of a spouse. This explanation, however, is one that requires Gradowski to have entered into the minds of the women. He feels that this is what they feel or he deceives himself into understanding what unfolds between the men and women in this way.

It is also possible for the reader to empathize with Gradowski. It is conceivable to inhabit the motions of the pen, the palpable energy, underlying this composition. The mind, the emotions, behind the words is available to access if the reader is willing to imagine in terms similar to those employed by Didi-Huberman when confronted by Alex's photographs. This passage of prose, however, is not pregnant with anxiety and urgency but with excitement and arousal. The throb of the prose, invites, incites desire. Detail is taken to the level of obscenity. The testimony is carnal, pornographic. Its inducement occurs via its pulsating detail. This is a lush form of writing. It is not, however, the words alone that prompt empathy. It is their impact coupled with the knowledge of their craftedness. There is a delight in the act of composition present here, a frisson accompanying the embellished descriptions, that betrays the writer's joy in his subject. If Wiener can be condemned for moving too close to murders he was witnessing, Gradowski is equally open to censure for working so hard on this, at times, highly sensuous account of the women's fate. In *The Last Resistance*, Jacqueline Rose discusses the taint of temptation that accompanies reading literature about atrocity, the potential excitement in the face of horror: 'in the throes of identification – with victim *or* executioner – there is no limit to how far people are willing to go' (p. 145). Gradowski's account, the textual envisioning it prompts of the undressing room and, accompanying this, the insights it permits at the level of empathy, may bear out this assessment.

Filling in the gaps

Peter Schwenger has investigated at length how works of fiction can prompt an envisioning of the characters, places, events and sensations that are described in them in the reader. It is also possible, however, to extend the idea of envisioning to non-fiction works. All descriptive writing conjures images for the person who reads it. For Schwenger, the reader supplements the thin pages they turn with a depth of simulacra generated by their individual knowledge and memories. This supplementation is usually not consciously willed, it emerges from out of the unconscious which 'clothes words with vision' (Schwenger, 1999, p. 6). Schwenger's locating of this capacity to fantasize, to imagine, in the unconscious, in unwilled actions, potentially aligns it with Didi-Huberman's conception of empathy. Schwenger writes of writing's empty spaces that 'every book has these gaps, these blanks that are filled in reading' (p. 7). This resonates with Didi-Huberman's observation that we must necessarily imagine when we bear witness, 'listening to what testimony tells us by way of its silences' and looking for what a document shows us 'by way of its gaps' if we are to lift the veil on destruction perpetrated by the Nazis (p. 109). When the four photographs taken by Alex are treated as narrative by Didi-Huberman, he fills in the gaps surrounding the instants caught by the camera, imaginatively reconstructing the cameraman's actions, motions and mood. This forms a comparable kind of envisioning to that described by Schwenger. Envisioning appears close in spirit to Wolfgang Iser's (1978, p. 140) idea of reading in which, through image building undertaken by the reader, texts 'take us out of our own given reality'. This image building is conceived of as a process of filling in the 'gaps' or 'blanks' in common frames of reference between text and reader (pp. 166–169).

The narratives provided by the Scrolls of Auschwitz, often literally interrupted by gaps where text has been damaged or completely obliterated, also encourage textual envisioning or image building. One of Gradowski's accounts actively encourages such a practice with repeated urgings for the reader to accompany the narrator as he recounts situations he has witnessed. He writes at one point: 'Come, my friend, let us descend into the camp [...]. Hush and listen, my friend, to what is happening here' (Gradowski, 1985, p. 176). Later on, he entreats:

> Come, my friend, today a transport is about to arrive. Let us go out to the road into the camp. We will stand at the side of the road, to have a better view of the terrible and gruesome vision. Do you see, my friend, there in the distance? On the white road, barely moving, is a bent black mass, with black shadows surrounding it, continually bending toward the crawling mass and beating its bowed heads. (p. 177)

There are repeated appeals to the reader to see, and occasionally hear, what the narrator has experienced and, as the anthropomorphized shadows in the last quotation indicate, to perceive things as he has perceived them. The reader is encouraged to project into these experiences, filling them with mental images, forms, motions and moods.

Leib Langfuss's writings pose a similar demand on the reader to sense experiences yet without the explicit entreaties that can be found in Gradowski. This is clear, for example, in a draft composition scribbled on a scrap of address book that describes what happened to the bodies of a group of Polish Jews who had been transported from the ghetto of Maków Mazowiecki after they were all murdered in the gas chambers at Birkenau. Langfuss writes: 'The frying and roasting of people made the air in the entire area greasy, so that as soon as people got out of the cars, they already smelt burning people.'[5] The passage is loathsome, the visceral description unsparing. It is needfully indelicate. It also, however, holds the attention, troubles, demands consideration. The testimony is overwhelmingly one of olfactory and tactile sense impressions. These are captured by Langfuss with carefully worded precision. The stench of mass death clings to, cloys the prose. The descriptions turn the stomach. The reader feels as the new arrivals do, exiting the cattle cars at the heart of hell. The reader answers the account's call to imagine, to empathize.

The reader of Gradowski and Langfuss, however, is not absorbed by these bids, or, as Didi-Huberman understands them, ethical imperatives, to imagine. Schwenger is right to emphasize as part of his discussion of envisioning that there is 'some critical distance in any act of reading' (p. 9). The envisioning is not so powerful that the reader loses their grip on reality. Schwenger states that 'the visionary worlds created in fiction do not have to succeed in taking us over completely; their liminal status (both here and not-here) is enough to remind us of language's reality-making properties' (p. 17). This observation, which can be extended to non-fiction works such as the Scrolls, is reminiscent of Stein's conception of empathy as a being in feeling with an elsewhere, another, without being them. There is something real about any envisioning, the sickening feeling in the stomach, the sting of smoke, the physical excitement generated by a desirable body, something corporeal, tangible, yet there is also always the accompanying knowledge that this is not that world, a simultaneously comforting and discomforting awareness of distance and haziness, of distortion. The reader strives to bring greater clarity to this envisioning. There are, however, limits to how much these efforts can bring past experiences to focus. Words can only carry a reader so far.

This lack of focus, however, this haze, acts as a barrier against imaginative voyeurism. Imagination, as an empathic exercise, acquires a fragility and precariousness that works against settled insight. This elusiveness is captured well in Schwenger's description of imagination, as it occurs during reading, as 'flickers at the edges of the mind' (p. 92). The erotic tinge to Gradowski's account of the women undressing, for example, is inescapable yet the naked bodies that cause his excitement remain vague forms in the background of any empathic encounter. The violent factuality and savage clarity of the Wiener footage makes it impossible not to collaborate in his odious conduct. This is because he leaves no room for imagining. The kind of empathy made possible by the film is of a different order to that permitted by the Scrolls and also Alex's fragmentary photographic testimony. It is empathy at the level of brutal fact rather than of the ductile kind that accompanies registering and then filling in the gaps in a piece of testimony. Marion Milner's differentiation between fact and imagination is instructive here:

> outline [represents] the world of fact, of separate touchable, solid objects; to cling to it [is] therefore surely to protect oneself against the other world, the world of imagination. (1957, p. 17)

Wiener's witnessing is too harsh and unyielding. Testimony that is restricted to the world of fact, that is hard-edged, is often too graphic, pornographic, as is the case with Wiener's film or too abstract as frequently occurs in histories of the Holocaust where mass murder is reduced to unemotive names, dates and places. Factual testimony is testimony that leaves no room for imagining. It may induce empathy, as in the case of Wiener's film, or provide no possibility for such a response. If it does generate an empathic response then this reaction suppresses the sense of distance identified by Stein as characteristic of empathy. Stein writes that one who empathizes with another enters into their standpoint yet without relinquishing their own standpoint: both positions are retained at the same time (p. 64). The viewer of the Wiener film or similarly intractable testimony, however, becomes absorbed by such accounts. Their inhabiting of two positions at once, of two spatial and/or temporal places in the world, is rendered obscure. The jump cuts in Wiener are unlike the missing actions in the Sonderkommando photographs, the gaps between shots, or the fissured invitations to share experience in the Scrolls, in that they do not adequately distance the viewer from the act of looking. They do not sufficiently disassociate the one who watches from what appears on screen so that they become an onlooker rather than a participant. The bi-positionality inherent in all empathy is concealed. The graphic at-the-scene actuality possesses no enabling gaps through which the imagination can be exercised.

Restoring what remains

Hiatuses in testimony, such as the events and experiences that are only sketchily figured in the Scrolls, or the missing segments of action in the photographs taken by Alex, provide space for the kind of imaginings, empathic encounters, envisaged by Didi-Huberman. The accounts of events, and also the traces of gestures and thoughts that produced those accounts, carry those who meaningfully engage with these testimonies back to Birkenau yet without stifling the here and now. They embody a vital resistance from within the event of mass murder to Nazi efforts to destroy all traces of it. The motions of writing the Scrolls, measured yet rapid, surreptitious, the furtive compression of the shutter release on the camera, form kinetic resistances to the aggressive disciplining of bodies practised by the Nazis. To inhabit these gestures is therefore to index their defiance. It is a kind of witnessing that enables, and operates alongside, the descriptions of acts of rebelliousness that occur in the Scrolls, such as Gradowski's mention of the two women who chastised their murderers or Zalman Loewenthal cataloguing Sonderkommando efforts at resistance (Loewenthal, 1985, pp. 216–235).

This testimony can only be accessed through living in the gestures of another. Stein uses the hand as an example of a part of the body that can encourage empathy. She writes that in response to seeing another's hand pressed against a table her own hand is moved, not in reality but 'as if': 'It is moved into it and occupies its positions and attitude, now feeling its sensations, though not primordially and not as being its own.

Rather, my own hand feels the foreign hand's sensation "with," precisely through [...] empathy' (Stein, p. 58). The hand behind Leyb Langfuss's *Der Geyresh*, for example, is different from that of the reader yet familiar enough to draw them into its ambit by way of its distinct script. The encouragement to empathize with the original manuscripts is therefore particularly powerful in this context. The extant documents are compelling not simply for what they say, for the words on their pages, but also for the physical actions they register, preserve and communicate.

Gradowski recognized in *In the Heart of Hell* that there are often no traces, no cinders, to attest to the mass murders. He wrote of the disposal of the transport of murdered women: 'in a few minutes there will be no vestige left of them' (Gradowski, 2001, p. 115). His account at this point, in its stubborn substantiality, cannot figure the absence, the void caused by the acts of murder he has detailed. His words, like the word 'cinder' as Jacques Derrida conceives of it in *Cinders*, consume what they refer to. For Derrida (1991, p. 33), a cinder is both a phenomenon and a place. He writes 'il y a là cendre', 'there be cinders' (or, as Ned Lukacher translates it, 'cinders, there are'), signalling both position and thing. The cinder functions as a trace, figures the trace. Derrida writes of it as that which 'remains unpronounceable in order to make saying possible although it is nothing' (p. 73). The phrase 'there be cinders', however, is not quite nothing. It is unintelligible yet perceptible, received as a dream, compared by Derrida to a waft of tobacco smoke (p. 32). Cinders are ethereal yet pressing. The wording of cinders evacuates them of their actuality: 'the colour of writing resembles the only "literality" of the cinder that still inheres in a language' (p. 49). The word for cinder is a cinder of the cinder itself. Language burns its issue. The trace of the thing, the place, is reduced to the chromatics of writing: the grey characters on a printed page form its spectral vestiges.[6]

Gradowski's account of the women who undress and are then murdered form a remnant of remnants, motivated by, reliant upon, events it cannot presence or hold in the present. There is, however, a dreamlike aspect to the cinder as it is conceived of by Derrida that, whilst not readily grasped is not to be dismissed and is informative when it comes to reading the testimony. In the section about the transported women, in the moments before their murder, Gradowski (2001, p. 87) writes 'another image plays before my eyes, I see a companion pushing a wheelbarrow of cinders over there in the big pit'. Cinders are referred to within a section in which Gradowski engages in an imaginative act. These cinders are, however, not understood as substance. They signal the reality that 'there will be no trace of all those who are here'.

The cinders are not conceived of as traces, rather they are somewhere between absence and presence: a bodiless matter. They are what Pollock has referred to as 'the gap, the abyss, [which] truly defies representation' (p. 287).

In *Cinders*, Derrida writes: the name 'cinder' figures because there is no cinder here, not here (nothing to touch, no colour, no body, only words), but above all because these words, which through the name are supposed to name not the word but the thing, they are what names one thing in place of another, metonymy when the cinder is separated, one thing while figuring another from which nothing figurable remains (p. 71).[7]

In the Scrolls, acutely those for which the original manuscripts still exist, however, words and things are not easily separable, words as things have a testimonial power that retrospective accounts cannot possess. The characters in Langfuss's *Der Geyresh*, for instance, in their varying curls and densities, embodying distinct motions and forces, form mnemonic traces of physical actions. These actions, admittedly themselves inscriptions, metonyms, index collaboration and defiance, embody the perverse reality that resistance could only emerge from out of unconscionable privilege.

The vicissitudes that these carefully composed texts endured subsequent to their concealment, the taint of the grime and stains they accumulated, also attests to Birkenau. The texts were buried amidst the cinders. They carry literal vestiges of the dead within their pages, are scored by barbarism and tragedy. It is this, their most horrific, sickening aspect, which lends them their unbridled power, the reality that there is something to touch. This is a corpus made up of far more than words. It is this facet that current efforts at restoration threaten to efface. Schweidler wrote, as part of a discussion of the conservation of prints, that their character and tone have to be preserved at all costs. This requires that the restorer work with empathy (Schweidler, p. 109). Stein did not believe empathy could exist except between human beings. Schweidler, however, as mentioned earlier, personifies paper. He is therefore inviting the aspiring conservator to treat sheets like people. Paper, like a person, has 'character' (Schweidler, p. 109). It is this character, with his or her warmth or lack thereof, that the conservator must discover and empathize with.

One of the dangers of restoring the Scrolls without this empathic understanding is that important facets of their capacity to elicit imagining will be destroyed. The grime was not placed on the pages of each manuscript by members of the Sonderkommando. It is, however, a side effect of their concealing of the documents. It registers that concealment, the need behind it and the actions that enabled it. The queasy knowledge of what this 'dirt' is composed of also prompts envisioning despite the fact that it is 'mute' material. Paper, as a support for writing, is associated with civilization (Hunter, 1978, pp. 3–7). It permits the recording and diffusion of culture. The transmission of the cultured compositions produced by the authors of the Scrolls of Auschwitz, however, is interrupted by the barbarous acts of the Nazis. The taint of this barbarism, the barbarism Benjamin refers to in the epigraph to this chapter, is literally embodied in the physical condition of the paper, in the illegible and obliterated words and in the 'crud', the remnants of worlds, of people, that surrounds them. The stains and dirt form gaps of the kind envisaged by Didi-Huberman, openings for the imagination, imperatives to imagine. If these gaps are attended to and what they attest to is recognized, they permit invaluable insight into the death camp at Birkenau. They cause the reader to be in unsettling feeling with that horrible place.

Notes

1. Translation amended.
2. Emphasis is in the original. All emphases present in the original unless otherwise stated. Translation is my own. All translations are my own unless otherwise stated.
3. For an authoritative overview of this history see Susan Leigh Foster's chapter on the term in *Choreographing Empathy* (2011), pp. 126–173.
4. Greif detects embarrassment and shame in these passages and downplays the significance of Gradowski's descriptive ardour despite its testimonial import (p. 30).
5. This unpaginated scrap of paper is inserted in the leaves of a notebook in which Langfuss's testimony *Der Geyresh* (a manuscript currently not published in English translation) is written.
6. The brilliant blue lettering contained in much of Langfuss's *Der Geyresh*, for instance, is not even haunted by this residuum. At times, however, the composition lapses into a more ashen script, approaching this shade of semblance.
7. Translation amended.

Works cited

Benjamin, W. (1999) 'Theses on the Philosophy of History', in H. Arendt (ed.) *Illuminations* (London: Pimlico), pp. 245–255.
Bronfen, E. (1992) *Over her Dead Body* (Manchester: Manchester University Press).
Chare, N. (2011) *Auschwitz and Afterimages* (London: I.B. Tauris).
Cohen, A. (1993) *The Tremendum* (New York: Continuum).

Derrida, J. (1991) *Cinders* (Lincoln: University of Nebraska Press).
Didi-Huberman, G. (2003) *Images malgré tout* (Paris: Éditions de Minuit).
Felman, S. & Laub, D. (1992) *Testimony: Crises of Witnessing in Literature, Psychoanalysis and History* (New York: Routledge).
Foster, S. (2011) *Choreographing Empathy* (Abingdon: Routledge).
Gradowski, Z. (1985) 'Writings', in B. Mark, *The Scrolls of Auschwitz*, S. Neemani (trans.) (Tel Aviv: Am Oved), pp. 173–205.
Gradowski, Z. (2001) *Au coeur de l'enfer* (Paris: Éditions Kimé).
Herman, C. (1973) 'Letter of Chaim Herman', in Bezwińska J. & Czech D. (eds.) *Amidst a Nightmare of Crime* (Oświęcim: Publications of State Museum at Oświęcim), pp. 181–190.
Hirsch, J. (2004) *Afterimage: Film, Trauma, and the Holocaust* (Philadelphia: Temple University Press).
Hunter, D. (1978) *Papermaking: The History and Technique of an Ancient Craft* (New York: Dover).
Iser, W. (1978) *The Act of Reading* (London: Routledge).
LaCapra, D. (2001) *Writing History, Writing Trauma* (Baltimore: Johns Hopkins).
Levi, P. (1989) *The Drowned and the Saved*, S. Woolf (trans.) (London: Abacus).
Loewenthal, Z. (1985) 'Writings', in B. Mark, *The Scrolls of Auschwitz*, S. Neemani (trans.) (Tel Aviv: Am Oved), pp. 216–240.
Milner, M. (1957) *On Not Being Able to Paint* (Los Angeles: Jeremy P. Tarcher).
Nyiszli, M. (1973) *Auschwitz* (London: Granada).
Pollock, G. (2011) 'Death in the Image: The Responsibility of Aesthetics in *Night and Fog* (1955) and *Kapò* (1959)', in G. Pollock & M. Silverman (eds.) *Concentrationary Cinema* (Oxford: Berghahn), pp. 258–301.
Rose, J. (2007) *The Last Resistance* (London: Verso).
Schweidler, M. (2006) *The Restoration of Engravings, Drawings, Books, and Other Works on Paper* (Los Angeles: Getty Publications).
Schwenger, P. (1999) *Fantasm and Fiction* (Stanford: Stanford University Press).
Stein, E. (1989) *On the Problem of Empathy* (Washington: ICS).
Stone, D. (2001) 'The Sonderkommando Photographs', *Jewish Social Studies* 7:3, 131–148.
Stone, D. (2010) *Histories of the Holocaust* (Oxford: Oxford University Press).
Venezia, S. (2009) *Inside the Gas Chambers* (Cambridge: Polity).
Viñas, S. (2005) *Contemporary Theory of Conservation* (Oxford: Elsevier).
Wyschogrod, E. (1985) *Spirit in Ashes* (New Haven: Yale University Press).

3
'The Dead Are My Teachers': The Scrolls of Auschwitz in Jerome Rothenberg's *Khurbn*

Dominic Williams

As Dan Stone notes (this volume), the Scrolls of Auschwitz have received remarkably little attention from historians of the Holocaust. In addition to the limited number of discussions in the historiography, however, an extraordinary literary response to these documents can be found in Jerome Rothenberg's long poem *Khurbn* (1989), two sections of which name authors of the Scrolls and quote some of their words directly. This essay argues that Rothenberg's incorporation of the Scrolls into his own work brings to the fore aspects of these texts that historians have had much greater difficulty coming to terms with.

I consider the significance of Rothenberg's engagement with the Scrolls in a number of ways. First, I compare the ways in which the place of the literary in testimony has been theorized to the concerns of one of the Sonderkommando texts. I then discuss examples from the wider set of texts Rothenberg drew upon for *Khurbn*, which demonstrate a wide variety of literary qualities. The essay goes on to address the passages of the Scrolls which Rothenberg cites in his poem. A literary element is shown to be at work in all of the Scrolls, apparent not only in the narrative devices and patterns of imagery used by Zalman Gradowski, but also in the emotional responses aimed at by Leib Langfuss's writings and even in the rhetorical repetitions in Zalman Loewenthal's testimony. In his reworkings, Rothenberg does not make the literary quality of *Khurbn* a simple repetition of that found in the Scrolls. Rather, as a piece of writing that calls upon the resources of post-war American poetry, the poem is able to highlight not only the rhetorical aspects of the Scrolls but also the material and bodily circumstances in which they were written.

Holocaust, literature

For many of the most significant writers on the Holocaust, the difficulties of bringing together the subject with the realm of literature has been a central concern. Theodor W. Adorno's assertion that poetry after Auschwitz was unable to escape the collapse of the dialectic of culture and barbarism is well known. However, a role for literature still exists for Adorno, as resistance not only against the society in which it exists, but also against itself in its failure to be differentiated from that society (1983 [1949]; 1992 [1962]; 1973 [1966]). In a more straightforward way, the same idea features in Berel Lang's suggestion that 'imaginative writing about the Holocaust often, even typically, eschews standard literary devices or figures in favor of historical ones'. Such a foregrounding of the historical has to be brought about by literary means. The impression of truth-telling thus achieved is not so much an illusion as a way of focussing attention on the historicity of the material, with the literary element more or less cancelling itself out (Lang, 2000, p. 117). Even in what may appear to be polar opposite positions, we can observe a suspicion of the literary. Primo Levi argued that writing should not 'lend itself to equivocal interpretations' (1991, p. 158), and criticized Paul Celan's 'obscure writing' as little more than an outlet for private grief. Writing needed to make sure that 'every word reaches its target' (p. 162). As Hayden White has shown, this position does not preclude Levi giving his writing a form, but it is a form that is essentially functional, enabling the message to be conveyed as effectively as possible (2004). Champions of Celan, such as Shoshana Felman, see him as breaking with an 'aesthetic project' from which pleasure or meaning could be too readily derived and stripping poetry of its mastery. What is left instead are the 'sounds' which 'testify [...] to a knowledge they do not possess, by unleashing, and by drifting into, their own buried depths of silence' (1992, pp. 33–37). In all of these cases, complex as some of the positions are, the form is seen at the service of some kind of content: if that content can be communicated, the form must do as little as possible to obscure it; if it cannot, writing should break from all familiar forms to embody that incommunicability.

Of course, within these positions, there is room for the idea that a victim might need to find some way to express their suffering. But in these cases, the question of literary form is not even given consideration. Adorno (1973, p. 362) compared some poetry to the screaming of a tortured man, by implication an uncontrolled expression of pain. Primo Levi (1988, p. 35) touched briefly upon the existence of the Scrolls of Auschwitz, describing them as 'diary pages which were written feverishly for future memory and buried with extreme care near the crematoria'. It is significant here that Levi considered only the packaging and concealment of these texts to be careful, whereas the writing is feverish: pressed for time of course, but also suggesting the uncontrolled 'liberating outburst' that he believed was all that survivors of the Sonderkommando could produce (1988, pp. 36–37).

What an examination of the Sonderkommando manuscripts shows, however, is that literary form, deemed to be problematic after the event, and impossible during it, is precisely what they were giving to their writing. The language of Zalman Gradowski in particular is highly rhetorical. In one of his texts, telling the story of a transport from the ghetto in Grodno to Auschwitz, nearly a sixth is taken up with an anaphoric, incantatory address to the reader. This is a part that contains no real information; in fact the Auschwitz Museum's edition of the text leaves it out completely (Gradowski, 1973). But the rhetorical patterning shows quite clearly that care, effort, and probably time, have been put into the section, perhaps even more than in the narrative itself.

> Come to me you happy citizen of the world, who lives in that land where there still exist happiness, joy and pleasure, and I will tell you how modern-day common criminals have turned a people's happiness into unhappiness, changed its joy into everlasting mourning – destroyed its pleasure for ever.
>
> Come to me you free citizen of the world, where your life is assured by human morality and your existence guaranteed by law and I will tell you how these modern-day criminals and common bandits have crushed the morality of life and annihilated the laws of existence.
>
> Come to me you free citizen of the world, whose land is encircled by modern-day Great Walls of China, where the claws of these pitiless demons were not able to reach, and I will tell you how they have locked a people in their demonic arms and clamped their pitiless claws with sadistic brutality into their throats till they have choked and annihilated them.
>
> (1977, p. 288)[1]

In these first three paragraphs there appear sequential repetition of terms in the first paragraph ('happiness', 'joy', 'pleasure'), inversion of terms in the second ('life', 'morality' and 'existence', 'law'), and chiasmus in the third ('claws', 'pitiless', 'demons': 'demonic', 'pitiless', 'claws'). Between the paragraphs as well, terms are repeated, varied and built upon: 'happy citizen', 'free citizen', 'modern-day common criminals', 'annihilated'.

The self-consciously literary patterning carries out a complex function. Gradowski seems to be concerned with calling up a response in the reader, creating a state of psychological preparedness, an understanding of the state of the writer and the people whose fate he is describing, even a connection between reader and writer. In using, and reversing, the same terms to describe his life and the reader's, he shows how one is almost the exact reverse of the other. But the repeated use of the same terms actually starts to suggest that reader and writer share something. The repetition itself builds up to a climax: destruction of pleasure, annihilation of law, annihilation of a people – a rhetorical effect of course, building up suspense until the final revelation of what has happened – but it also seems to indicate a greater readiness for the writer to 'speak' and for the reader to 'hear'.

By the end of the address he writes:

> My friend, I believe that you understand us very well now, and even share our feelings in the present tragic circumstances.
>
> (1977, p. 299)

So it could even be said that the introduction is a form of spell. In its ritualistic quality it is invoking, summoning up, the very existence of a reader (a witness who is not there as Gradowski is writing), and even the converse: expecting to be dead by the time his text is found, Gradowski has to summon himself up before the reader.

For Gradowski, as for the other writers of the Scrolls, the content that his document communicated was not just a set of facts that need to be conveyed, but the reality which they were part of and needed to resist. Giving the content form was part of the process of resistance. Their words do not point backwards from a present shared by writer and reader to a historical past. Writing from within the event, the author must conjure up a future reader at whom he aimed his document. According to such writers as Adorno and Felman, after the Holocaust, writing must be resisted (or resist itself) in order to be true to the event. For the writers of the Sonderkommando, the event itself had to be resisted in order for there to be writing at all. The care Levi attributes to the manuscripts' burial had to extend to the way in which they were written. As something that shaped, even contained, the facts being written down, form was absolutely vital to the existence of the writing in the same way as the writing materials which needed to be *organized* and the containers in which the manuscripts were sealed and buried.

Aesthetics, then, had a vital, material existence for the writers of the Scrolls. I want to suggest that Jerome Rothenberg's poetic response to the Scrolls, one of a set of collections of testimony that he makes use of in *Khurbn*, offers ways of thinking about how formal responses might encode the material and bodily circumstances in which the Scrolls were produced. This is only in part what Lang or Levi might call 'the literary'. While Rothenberg does mobilize a history of writing in order to make sense of the scrolls, it is not based upon their influences. Instead of Dante or classic Yiddish writers, he presents them as anticipated by the Marquis de Sade and the Comte de Lautréamont, and feeding into the post-war art of Charles Olson and Tatsumi Hijikata. These figures form a counter-tradition that he mines for concerns that mainstream literary conventions have often excluded: the material, the bodily, the oral, a dislike of metaphor, an interest in documentation. In doing so, he provides us with a sense of why the Scrolls are such significant documents and why we must take their aesthetic strategies seriously.

Khurbn

Khurbn was published in 1989, nearly 30 years after Jerome Rothenberg's first collection of poetry. During the 1960s he had established himself as a poet and anthologist, in the lineage of the avant-gardes of Europe and America, but known especially for his ethno-poetic engagement with the rituals, language and practices of non-Western peoples. The two anthologies *Technicians of the Sacred* (1968) and *Shaking the Pumpkin* (1972) in particular brought these two interests together, drawing upon avant-garde procedures in the arrangement and translation of non-Western forms. As a translator he had shown some interest in Jewish writers and themes from early on, publishing some of the first versions of Celan in English and a selection of Martin Buber's Hasidic tales. But it was the 1970s that saw him take a sustained interest in Jewish themes in his poetry and anthologies: *Poland/1931* (1974), *A Big Jewish Book* (1978) and *Vienna Blood* (1980) (cp. Rothenberg, 2008, xvi). Although references to the Holocaust had appeared in some of these collections, in the main they 'fell just short of the Holocaust, of that which was still not to be spoken' (Rothenberg, 2000, p. 141). By his own account, it was during a visit to Poland in 1987 that he began work on *Khurbn*. After visiting Auschwitz-Birkenau and noting the number of tourists there, he was struck at Treblinka by the presence of only a handful of other visitors.

> The absence of the living seemed to create a vacuum in which the dead – the dibbiks who had died before their time – were free to speak. It wasn't the first time that I thought of poetry as the language of the dead, but never so powerfully as now. [...] The poems I began to hear at Treblinka are the clearest message I have ever gotten about why I write poetry. They are an answer also to the proposition – by Adorno & others – that poetry cannot or should not be written after Auschwitz. Our search then has been for the origins of poetry, not only as a willful desire to wipe the slate clean but as a recognition of those other voices & the scraps of poems they left behind them in the mud.
>
> (Rothenberg, 2007, pp. 153–154)

In his description of how the poems came to him, Rothenberg's ongoing interest in 'primitive' practices clearly comes to the fore: the idea of poetry as being possessed by the dead as well as the need to return to the origins of poetry. *Khurbn* begins with the present: the memory of the word *khurbn* (the Yiddish for destruction in general and the Holocaust in particular) as spoken by Rothenberg's relatives and the Polish landscape emptied of Jews.

> IN THE DARK WORD *KHURBN*
> all their lights went out
> [...]
> a disaster in the mother's tongue
> her words emptied
> by speaking
>
> (p. 155)

In Rothenberg's voice, the R-coloured vowels of 'dark' and 'word' match that of *khurbn* and echo through the rest of the section – in the repetitions of 'word', but also in words such as 'disaster' and 'mother', and even 'her' and 'your'.[2] Perhaps just because it is alien to my own accent, I become aware of what the mouth is doing as it forms these sounds: tightening at the back of the throat, of tongue and epiglottis (as described in Ladefoged, 2006: 92). Something feels held back, constricted, affecting the throat but also held safe in it.

> how I would take it from your voice
> & cradle it
> that ancient and dark word
> those who spoke it in the old days
>   now held their tongues

(p. 155)

Here, the obvious meaning of 'stayed silent' for the last line becomes coloured by the idea of the tongue being preserved or the particular way in which the tongue is held in the mouth.

The repeated sense of a word as a material thing, something that has tangible qualities and can be physically passed on from one body to another, and something that requires a particular bodily posture to be adopted, sounds through the first sections of *Khurbn*, where tongue, teeth and mouth are referred to again and again. Mining the word *khurbn*, and the resources of the Yiddish language in general, the poem sinks down into an underworld, part dream, part historical past, where other voices appear and speak through the poet. The climax of the entire poem is the point at which the voice of Rothenberg's uncle, who escaped Treblinka but later committed suicide, is given in Yiddish.[3]

In the section 'Dos Geshray (The Scream)', the poet prepares to be overtaken by the voices of the dead.

> 'practice your scream' I said
> (why did I say it?)
> because it was his scream & wasn't my own

(p. 161)

In addition to the paradoxical ideas that screaming could be rehearsed, or that one could produce someone else's scream for them, there are other, subtler, peculiarities. The poet speaks first and only later seems to understand what he has said. And it is uncertain whether his words are addressed to himself or to the original screamer. The poetic self being put into play here is not unified, which itself makes it possible for the scream to be passed from one owner to another. However, the scream he goes on to describe, of a 'jew | locked in his closet', has 'no sound' and is not heard directly. Rather, it makes

> the shoes piled in the doorway
> scatter their nails things testify
> – the law declares it –
> shoes & those dearer objects
> like hair & teeth do
> by their presence
>
> (p. 161)

A scream, a sound that is produced by a body without being articulated by a mind, imprints itself on objects and it is these which testify. In the absence of a whole body, body parts become objects too, albeit 'dearer' ones. An embodied self, not fully unified, responds to these physical cues.

> it is his scream that shakes me
> weeping in oshvientsim
> & that allows the poem to come
>
> (p. 163)

The shamanic 'possession' enacted here refers to a Jewish framework in its evocation of the figure of the *dibbuk*, but it also has a material basis: in the sites of Treblinka and Auschwitz, and in the documents which Rothenberg uses in a modernist collage. Other voices that speak through the poet are provided by a variety of documents, quotations from which are lifted and mixed together. Sources and quotations are attributed or demarcated, although not consistently. Quotation marks appear around some of the phrases used, not round others. What words are the poet's, and what are others', is not always easy to determine and this too suggests possession, or a breakdown between self and other.

Rothenberg makes use of a number of collections of testimony, of very different kinds. Abraham Krzepicki's '18 Days in Treblinka', an account recorded in the Warsaw Ghetto after his escape from Treblinka, sits alongside Jean-François Steiner's *Treblinka*, a best-selling documentary novel of the 1960s. Passages are taken from Terrence Des Pres's *The Survivor*, a literary study of survivor testimony; pastiches are given of the *yizker-bukh* for Ostrów Mazowiecka, especially those parts written by Rothenberg's uncles.[4] Already in these choices can be seen a different set of concerns than that which might operate for the historian. Testimony from Krzepicki – about as contemporaneous a witness as is available for Treblinka – is very different from that novelized by

Steiner from interviews with survivors. But it is not easy to identify the concerns in choosing sources as simply or straightforwardly literary. Take Steiner's *Treblinka*, for example. It is certainly not a text which has historical standing. A recent summary of the state of historical research on Treblinka dismisses it as '[w]issenschaftlich unbrauchbar' ('no use to scholars') (Benz, 2008, p. 404, n. 1). But it has an uneasy literary position too. Sidra DeKoven Ezrahi calls Steiner a 'middlebrow writer' (1980, p. 34) and laments the fact that his book has become 'a component in the cultural perception of major events, ultimately resisting the application of literary standards just as it resists the judgment of historical accuracy' (p. 35). James Young describes it as 'first-rate storytelling', notwithstanding its slapdash handling of source material (1988, p. 60). Pierre Vidal-Naquet straightforwardly denounces it as part of 'a vast subliterature representing a truly obscene appeal to consumption and sadism' (1992, pp. 14, 149–150, n. 24).

The peculiar status of this now little-cited text (most fully explored by Samuel Moyn (2005)) might itself have attracted Rothenberg. Unconstrained by literary taste, it added rather more prurient touches to its witness accounts. While there were testimonies from Treblinka which mentioned the commandant temporarily keeping a few adolescent boys as servants (Grossman, 2012; Wiernik, 1979, p. 176), Steiner included a sexual element that had not been explicit in his sources.

> The handsome Max Bielas had had a harem of little Jewish boys. He liked them young, no older than seventeen. In a kind of parody of the shepherds of Arcadia, their role was to take care of the camp flock of geese. They were dressed like princes and possessed several suits of clothes, but they had to wear the same thing at the same time, so that they would still be in uniform. Bielas had a little barracks built for them that looked like a doll's house because of its size and prettiness.
>
> (1994, pp. 157–158)

Rather than reproducing Steiner's coolly objective prose, Rothenberg takes it on as a sexually-charged fantasy, a breathless unpunctuated sentence, loosely tacked together with ampersands, that tumbles headlong over its line endings.

> the assignators even here breathing thru the lungs of the
> ill-fated Max Bielas handsome man who had a harem
> of little jewish boys & dressed them to the delight of

all who visited in perfect white blouses & dark blue hosen
over tummies & butts so round & firm he trembled yawned
sent them to tend the flock of geese a row of pretty boys
dressed up like princes & had a fabled dream house
built for them
[...]
they were his dwarfs & he
their gentle snow white swooning when they pressed around him
when he touched a tiny hand or let his thumb slide down
the young back proffered to him redfaced eager to
become a victim to his victim
the bright pornography of death implicit in each breath
each word the mind imagines it is desire that compels him
directs the flow the force engulfing him & them
all in the name of love that has delivered many to this place

(2007, p. 176)

Steiner's use of the conventions of genre fiction, especially his reliance on a simplistic schema for the characters' motivations was frequently criticized (Ezrahi, 1980, p. 32). But these conventions, with their appeal to obscenity and sadism, enabled Steiner to engage with sexual aspects of the genocide when 'higher' literary forms approach the question with more caution. As Cathy Gelbin's essay in this collection shows, it has taken a long time for the issue of sexual violence to be addressed by historians and scholars of the Holocaust. By allowing Steiner's voice to possess him, Rothenberg's nightmarish hallucination takes on retrospective sexual fantasies of the Shoah as a means to understand the fantasies which gave rise to the Shoah.

Steiner's book, which at the very least risks being a form of Holocaust kitsch, also provides Rothenberg with details of aestheticization or kitsch quality that took place in Treblinka itself. In one lengthy section (pp. 173–178), as well as Max Bielas and his harem, he refers to Artur Gold's orchestra and its elaborate uniforms (Rothenberg, p. 174; Steiner, pp. 289–290), the Treblinka song (Rothenberg, pp. 175–176; Steiner, pp.166–167) and the fakery of the Obermaidan station (Rothenberg, p. 178; Steiner, pp. 208–209). These are all part of the 'domain of the total',

in the monstrous minds of the masters   those who give themselves authority
over the rest of life   who dole out life and death   proportioned

> to their own appetites as artists   they forge a world   a shadow
>   image of our own
> & are the artists of the new hell
>
>   (p. 173)

Artistry, therefore, stands for both the deceptions that were part of the crime and the temptations that writing must avoid: 'the poem [...] must resist | even the artistry of death' (p. 171).

The kind of resistance that Steiner's book is concerned with is the revolt of 2 August 1943, which does not feature in *Khurbn*. Rothenberg is interested in resistance – both against the crime and against aestheticized ways of representing it – but his model is not so much an armed uprising as writing itself. Eschewing the 'artistry of death', he ends the section by citing Allama Prabhu's rejection of literary devices.

> o god of caves (the stricken fathers cry) if you are light
> then there can be no metaphor
>
>   (p. 178)

The Scrolls of Auschwitz

It is at this point that he turns to the writings of the Auschwitz Sonderkommando, which mark the final stage of his descent into the underworld, coming just before a litany of curses which erupt into the uncle's voice. Rothenberg draws upon the edition of the Scrolls prepared by Ber Mark and Esther Mark, published in Yiddish in 1977, and in English translation (of a Hebrew translation) in 1985. The Marks identified three authors for the documents they published and Rothenberg makes some use of all three. The words of Zalman Gradowski, Leib Langfuss and Zalman Loewenthal are cited in two sections of the poem: 'Di Magilas fun Aushvits (The Scrolls of Auschwitz)', and 'Der Vidershtand (The Resistance)'.[5]

The prose section 'Di Magilas fun Aushvits'[6] (pp. 179–180) is a set of ten paragraphs, indented so that each begins immediately below where the previous line ended. Some of them deal with the world of the spirits or the activities of dibbukim. Others offer bare factual descriptions. And yet others quote or refer to named individuals: especially Tatsumi Hijikata and Zalman Gradowski. The strange pairing of these two figures, a Japanese choreographer and a member of the Sonderkommando at Auschwitz-Birkenau, is all part of the disconcerting slippages of tone which take place between paragraphs or mixings of register within them. Beyond the citing of names, the range of voices also suggests other people being quoted or the words not belonging entirely to the poet. Bizarre or fantastic elements told in a quasi-objective way, with one object often transforming into another, or what appears initially to be metaphorical becoming concrete, add to the dreamlike quality.

The section can be divided by two 'rooms' – introduced in paragraphs 1 and 7. The first is the more dreamlike: 'a room no bigger than a giant's hand'. The second has some elements that might allow the reader to identify it as a gas chamber: perhaps even just the fact that it is described in some detail in a flat, objective way.[7] These two parts shift in tense from past to present to future, climaxing each time with quotations from the Scrolls: one from the section 'The 3000 Naked Women' by Leib Langfuss, the second from Zalman Gradowski.

Only Gradowski's name is given and his words are quoted rather more extensively than Langfuss's.

> [Gradowski's Testament] A black and white world, sky and earth. The court of angry shadows. These. Broken into. The open mouth of earth prepared to swallow us alive. The last. His world a tinted film. A bent black mass. Black shadows. Swallowed up in railway cars. Gradowski's testament. Along the white road. Thousands crawling on all fours. Two women at the roadside, crying. People shrunk to half their size. A finger moves across her throat. 'Take interest in this document. Keep looking. You will find still more.'
>
> (p. 180)

Rothenberg's filmic reference seems particularly appropriate, as the sentence fragments present a succession of images between which he cuts: a two-shot, an extreme long shot, a close-up. Examining the original, we can see that he also splices different time frames together. He makes particular use of one passage before the train journey starts.

> Come, my friend, today a transport is about to arrive. Let us go out to the road into the camp. We will stand at the side of the road, to have a better view of the terrible and gruesome vision. Do you see, my friend, there in the distance? On the white road, barely moving, is a bent black mass, with black shadows surrounding it, continually bending toward the crawling mass and beating its bowed heads. The nature of this mass cannot be perceived. Are these cattle being driven, or men shrunk to half their size? But look at them as they draw nearer: they are thousands, thousands of Jews, young and old,

> making their way to their new home. They are not marching but crawling on all fours. So decreed the young murderer who holds their lives and existence in his hand.
>
> (1985, p. 177)

Gradowski is far more concerned with producing a conventionally literary piece of writing, with a clear narrative element, a relationship between narrator and reader, and a consistent use of imagery. The need to guide a reader through what is happening, both to point out the strangeness of the events and to explain them is evident. The move from mystery to understanding is achieved through narrative.

In addition to this passage Rothenberg refers to several other moments on the journey. The image of a finger passing across a throat (although a well-known one from other sources) appears in a part when the train passes by the turn-off for Treblinka,

> which, according to the information in our possession, has swallowed up and eliminated most of the Jews of Poland, as well as Jews from abroad [...] How terrible: two young Christian girls are standing down there; they look up at the train windows and pass their hands across their throats. The onlookers have understood the hint; shuddering they turn silently aside.
>
> (p. 185)

In the original context, the gesture is a clear signal. The passengers know what happens in Treblinka and understand what the girls mean because of their knowledge. The approach to the turn-off therefore represents a clear threat, causing a build up of narrative tension, which is released when the train carries on along the main line.

The crying women appear in a passage close to the end of Gradowski's writing, when they are in the vicinity of their actual destination, Auschwitz. At this stage, much further away from their point of departure, the passengers are in much greater ignorance: less familiar with the area, lacking knowledge about Auschwitz and unable to make sense of what the women are doing.

> Between the trees stand two women; they look at us and wipe away their tears with handkerchiefs. There is no one there except for them, and no one knows why they are crying. Why has our appearance shocked them so? Why do these sad women cry?
>
> (p. 189)

Both of these images, therefore, work as part of a dramatic structure in Gradowski's original. The narrative creates tension, dissipates it and then builds it up again. It follows the passengers as they move from a modicum of knowledge to complete uncertainty, positioning readers so that they share something of the passengers' feelings while also being aware of their ultimate fate. Gradowski's use of conventional literary means speaks to the needs of his document. His constant references to the reader as his friend are a way to construct some kind of relationship between him and whoever may find his manuscript. His story-telling is a way of conveying what has happened, when he is completely uncertain how much information his future reader will have.

Rothenberg's repetition of 'black' and 'white' and of the verb 'swallow' retains something of Gradowski's own patterning (1985, pp. 174, 185, 191) and his use of filmic technique echoes with the sentence: 'It seems as if they are imprisoned in a mobile fortress, watching a film of this world in all its colors' (p. 183). But he calls more attention to the strangeness of Gradowski's writing, what might be called its ghostliness, than its conventional narrative elements. Cutting between the images cinematically allows them to become part of a kind of dream, with a set of surreal juxtapositions, switching time and place, between big and small in an unsettling way. The emphasis is placed upon images as images, which flash in and out of consciousness. In part it evokes the poet/shaman himself, having a vision inspired by Gradowski, but it also responds to a feature of the original text. The ghostliness of Gradowski's writing is a strategy of representation as well as a sign of his being marked for death. He must conjure up the reader to himself, and himself to the reader. The very fact that reader and narrator are something like ghosts to each other enables him then to have them both roam over Europe, or between one train carriage and another, or into the 'Hell' of the camps, in order to understand as fully as possible the extent of the atrocities.

The use of Langfuss's text might seem initially to be rather less engaged with the original. Aside from the words '3000 naked women', all that he quotes is a sentence from a young girl. Rothenberg seems to have alighted on these two striking phrases and used them as a frame to his own writing.

> In the dream 3000 naked women cry in pain. It is impossible to count them but he does. Their bodies will be used for kindling, their blood for fuel. No one will cry or turn away, but sometimes the wind will force a tear out of his eye, & his tongue & teeth will follow, flying

from his mouth. 'Ah,' the young girl will say, her legs twisted behind her back. 'The tear of a live Jew will go with me to my death.'[8]

In addition to the sentence's first words telling us that this is a dream, the number itself seems surreal, too large to be counted, and yet in its relative precision showing that they have been counted. The paragraph moves from unreality, the impossibility of coming to terms even with a fraction of the numbers involved in the deaths, to the reality of one person mourning another.

Langfuss's three-page narrative tells the story of the last hours of 3,000 women dumped in the grounds of Crematorium 2 after being imprisoned and starved for a week. Langfuss describes the physical state of the women, mostly unable to stand, move or protect themselves before some of them regain voices and go on to tell their story in a number of lengthy speeches. The words Rothenberg quotes are part of one girl's reaction to a member of the Sonderkommando bursting into tears.

> They examined our faces looking for an expression of sympathy. One stood in a corner and looked deep into the depths of these poor helpless souls. He could no longer control himself and burst out crying. A young girl then said 'Ah! I have been privileged to see before I die an expression of sorrow, a tear of sympathy at our sad fate, in this camp of murderers, in which so many are tortured, beaten and killed, in which people see so many murders and interminable horrors, in the camp where our senses become dull and petrified at the sight of the worst horrors, where every human emotion dies to the extent that you can see your brother or sister fall and not even sigh. Yes, here, can there be a man who will feel our disaster who will weep for our fate? Oh! What a wonderful vision, how unnatural! The tear of a live Jew will go with me to my death, the sight of a sensitive man. There is still someone who will mourn us, [and I] had thought that we would leave this world like miserable orphans. I find a bit of comfort in this young man; among people who are all murderers and criminals, I have found before my death a man with feelings.'
>
> (Langfuss, 1985, p. 213)

The man is moved and therefore able certainly to mourn her, but also to bear witness to her (a more literal translation of the Yiddish would be: 'I thought we would disappear from this world like abandoned orphans'). The kind of witness being demanded here is not simply being able to attest to the facts. It is evincing an emotional response, a response that in this context is *un*natural: human feeling beyond normal human capacities in these circumstances. It is not a case of simply being one typical human response to another's suffering, but something miraculous, impossible, wonderful and terrible at the same time. The man is broken by what he observes and, it seems, must be in order to be able truly to bear witness to the girl after her death. Thus, paradoxically, a modicum of moral agency is gained by losing self-control, even if it puts the self at risk.

Out of Langfuss's scene, Rothenberg conjures up images of bodies subject to impersonal forces, or taking on the values of objects. Bodies are burnt, twisted, exploded in ways that come across as surreal and dreamlike, while evoking the actual tortures, murders and desecrations that victims' bodies underwent. Body parts are used as objects whose function as 'kindling' and 'fuel' is to erase themselves and other bodies. Crying is one more process that works at nothing other than the physical level, although semi-surrealized in being the prelude to a body exploding. Tongue and teeth suggest language through which testimony might take place. While their flying out of the mouth can certainly be read as inability to testify, perhaps, if it is not too redemptive a reading, it might also suggest that testimony is produced, but not under conscious control. Such a reworking of Langfuss does not simply make new meanings out of his text, but responds to something in the text itself. Presenting crying in a non-psychologized way, as something that causes or is part of the disintegration of a body, catches something of how Langfuss shows the member of the Sonderkommando responding to the women.

The question that both Rothenberg and Langfuss are addressing, then, is how one person can be a witness for another. For Rothenberg, most pressingly, it is the question of how one of the living can speak for the dead. For Langfuss too there is the question of how the Sonderkommando could respond to the suffering of other victims. Although they might be seen to be in a physical condition which gave them the luxury of empathy, they, more than anyone else, saw death on an industrial scale and had to harden themselves to it. The Langfuss text suggests that it is in risking loss of control, and the registering of a bodily response, that witnessing must take place. This can serve as a model for Rothenberg's own performance of possession and is also brought into dialogue with Tatsumi Hijikata's statements about the dead being his teachers.

> Hijikata writes: To make the gestures of the dead, to die again, to make the dead enact their deaths again, this is what I want to feel. The dead are my teachers and live inside me.
>
> (p. 179)

In the original notes to *Khurbn* Rothenberg identifies Hijikata as a 'Japanese dancer/choreographer/ writer, founder, post-Hiroshima of expressionistic-traditional Butoh dance'. *Butoh* is thus implicitly identified as a response to one of the horrors of the war, which Rothenberg sees as one of the drivers of his own poetry. '[W]hat I feel retrospectively drove me into poetry was the experience of Holocaust. And not just what happened in the death camps, although that was an extremity, but you know, the other, particularly once we got away from the war itself. And what happened at Hiroshima began to sink in first' (Rothenberg, 2010).

Indeed, the words that Rothenberg quotes from Hijikata also draw upon the choreographer's own personal mythology of wartime suffering. The dead person living inside his body is his sister, who he claimed was sold into prostitution during the war.[9]

> I would like to make the dead gestures inside my body die one more time and make the dead themselves dead again. I would like to have a person who has already died die over and over inside my body. I may not know death, but it knows me. I often say that I have a sister living inside my body. When I am absorbed in creating a butoh work, she plucks the darkness from my body and eats more than is needed. When she stands up inside my body, I unthinkingly sit down. For me to fall is for her to fall.... She's my teacher; a dead person is my butoh teacher.
>
> (Hijikata, 2000, p. 77)

Sondra Fraleigh and Tamah Nakamura interpret Hijikata's desire to be inhabited by the dead as a programme for dance movements based on bodily disunity, struggle with uprightness and downward orientation. A 'low level of bodily unity' brings dancers closer to their body (2006, p. 52). Being inhabited by the dead, therefore, is not simply about being haunted by the past. It is also a means to explore a body that is fragile, fallible and not under one central controlling mind, taking it as the ground for a new aesthetic of movement. In Hijkata's own dancing, he often seems to be rediscovering and exploring new possibilities for his body as much as experiencing its breakdown.

The idea that suffering might provide a basis for a new aesthetics needs to be approached with some caution and some readings of Hijikata's practice are certainly too redemptive to be applied to the writings of the Sonderkommando. However, even Ichikawa Miyabi's argument that 'severely tormenting the body' allowed it to resist violation by institutions makes some sense in this context.

> [O]ur modern institutions infiltrate every nook and cranny of people's bodies. Having been thoroughly violated by this institutionalizing process, people must turn on their own bodies a violent hatred in order to be able to stand on their feet again. Hijikata's work from the early 1960's reveals a strong interest in making dances that were violent, in dealing with the theme of homosexuality, and in severely tormenting the body, even going so far as to attempt to dismember it.
> (1988, pp. 70–71)

Being able to respond to and to gain some idea of the pain of one girl is torment for the member of the Sonderkommando, the cause, and result, of his losing control over an institutionalized body, maintained and adapted to work in a factory of death. Such a loss of control and sense of being inhabited by death turns, as Michael Hornblow suggests, into a way of being open and responding to other bodies.

> To 'die alive' is no longer undertaken only in terms of one's own body and the turning of its own being in relation to innateness (ontogenesis). In a dead and hollow-body this turns into an affective communication with other beings, through a form of continuity or becoming as infinite opening (morphogenesis). [...] For Hijikata, it is also where the impersonal aspect of death (that part that knows him even if he doesn't know it), offers the chance to experience so many deaths, and to have these other deaths transfigure him.
> (2006, p. 35)

Nothing in Hijikata's personal history, not even in the rather embellished version he tended to relate, can be compared to the life surrounded by death inflicted on Langfuss and the other members of the Sonderkommando. Nonetheless, by bringing these two figures together, Rothenberg does suggest how we might draw upon Hijikata's art in moving towards some understanding of Langfuss's writing. An awareness of this kind of aesthetics should not preclude consideration of the Sonderkommando's necessary efforts at shaping and controlling their language. But it also offers ways of reading their lack of mastery too: over their own bodies and feelings, as well as over the materials with which they wrote.

Resistance

Such a form of writing without mastery is most evident in the text by Zalman Loewenthal, to which Rothenberg refers in the following section of the poem. 'Der Vidershtand (The Resistance)' quotes at some length from Loewenthal's commentary on a diary from the Łódź Ghetto, a document he appears to have found in a victim's effects.

> the words of zalman lowenthal of poland
> who had been dragged into the woods who saw
> 'the damned plays of liquidation' – incredible (he wrote)
> the ocean seeping across the empty field
> inside his head how like a sump how grungy
> the world reduced to yellow flesh & mud
> the man in black whose hands are in black gloves
> has killed them the red one
> still standing at the gates of warsaw
> waits & the other at the gates of paris holds
> the dark rule now past the 8th month 1944
> a game of shootings hangings gassings burnings
> written down between the walls of the black building
> from the time he searched for reasons
> for his suffering & wrote
> about himself 'what happened to that jew?'
>
> (p. 181)

Loewenthal's text, in its English version, is also laid out as if it were a poem (not actually a feature of the Yiddish edition). Dashes indicate wholly missing parts, with reconstructions of partly missing words placed within square brackets.

> – – – we are now in Ger[man] ha[nds] – – –
> – – – [Jew] helpless and unarmed – – –
> [wh]y? Those black hands
> [which] kill – – –
> [the] Jewish women and children, the same hand

> bringing it [to] extinction – – –
> now! For three weeks the red one has been standing
> by the gates of Wars[aw] – – – for several
> days he has been standing by the gates of Paris
> and he is still maintaining
> the dark rule and continues
> the diabolical game of shootings, hangings,
> gassings, burnings, everything [that] can
> be destroyed.
>
> (Loewenthal, 1985, p. 237)

Even though Loewenthal's writing is clearly less self-consciously composed than Langfuss's or Gradowski's, Rothenberg quotes longer continuous sections, remaining truer, as it were, to the form that Loewenthal gave it. I would suggest that even here there are elements that might be called literary, elements to which Rothenberg is attuned. Loewenthal's piece gives the impression of being written at speed, with little time for correction. For example, loose use of pronouns causes confusion between the 'red one' standing at the gates of Warsaw and the figure maintaining his 'dark rule' (presumably the Germans). But there is a rhetoric at work nonetheless in his writing: repetition of (dark) hand ('*di zelbe lape*' in the Yiddish original: 'the same paw') and parallels of 'for three weeks', 'for several days'. I read these rhetorical structures not simply as a means of patterning or making sense of the experience, but as a scaffolding which enables the construction of sentences. Having such structures gives a form into which words can be fitted as quickly as possible. Rhetoric here, I suggest, is essential simply to being able to testify, necessary precisely in Loewenthal's circumstances of being restricted and pressed for time. Rothenberg has picked up on the striking succession of images as if it were a form of automatic writing.

> it is by chance that this
> is buried by chance that it comes to light
> the poetry is there too
> it is in the scraps of language
>
> (Rothenberg, 2007, p. 182)

The first line and a half are derived from Loewenthal, with the enjambment mirroring that in the Am Oved edition: 'it is by chance that [this] | is buried in several places' (Loewenthal, 1985, p. 240). The rest is

Rothenberg's expansion and commentary. The writing was buried and discovered by chance, but its form as 'scraps' is also the result of further chance processes: reacting with the earth and the material of its container, the time taken to find it, the processes of deciphering and translation – indeed, we might see the lineation as a further chance operation. It is precisely here that Rothenberg finds its poetry, because it fits with some of the procedures and approaches to writing that he previously championed: chance operations, automatic writing, shaman-style actions, performance (cp. Rothenberg, 1995, p. 289). Here the fragmented nature of the scrolls is not simply a loss – although it is of course this. It is also a form that can be interpreted with the aesthetic resources at Rothenberg's disposal.

Treating the signs of extreme deprivation (lack of materials, pressure of time, need to conceal what one is doing) as if they were aesthetic features might seem rather perverse, if one were not taking aesthetics seriously. For Rothenberg, these procedures are the most suitable means that can be used to respond to the atrocity, because they attend to what was at stake in it.[10] The writings of the Sonderkommando are action at the same time as they are representation and are aware, and make their readers aware, of material and bodily realities that are not part of a notionally unified, organized self.

It is Charles Olson especially, whose post-war theorizations of poetry were so influential for poets of Rothenberg's generation, who provides the terms through which Rothenberg approaches this aspect of the Sonderkommando's writings. 'Der Vidershtand (The Resistance)', as well as calling to mind the Sonderkommando's revolt of 7 October 1944, takes its title from one of Olson's essays.

> DER VIDERSHTAND (THE RESISTANCE)
> began with this in olson's words it was
> the pre/face so much fat for soap
> superphosphate for soil fillings & shoes for sale
> such fragmentation delivered by whatever means
> the scrolls of auschwitz buried now brought to light
>
> (p. 181)

'Olson's words' are taken from 'The Resistance (for Jean Riboud)' (1953) and 'pre/face' refers to the title of Olson poem 'La Préface' (1946). The dedicatee of the former was a survivor of Buchenwald, the latter was written to accompany an exhibition of drawings by Corrado Cagli, one of the soldiers who liberated the camp. These two key texts in Olson's career are direct responses to the Holocaust (Fredman, 1993, pp. 47–49; Maud, 1998, pp. 79–80). As Rothenberg summarizes it, the 'ground against which Olson, writing in the late 1940s, set his own poetry of 'resistance' was the too familiar ground of Auschwitz & the death camps of World War II' (2000, p. 139).

Similarly to Hijikata, Olson's essay argues for a poetic practice rooted in the body.

> When man is reduced to so much fat for soap, superphosphate for soil, fillings and shoes for sale, he has, to begin again, one answer, one point of resistance only to such fragmentation, one organized ground, a ground he comes to by a way the precise contrary of the cross, of spirit in the old sense, in old mouths. It is his own physiology he is forced to arrive at. And the way – the way of the beast, of man and the Beast. [...] It is his body that is his answer, his body intact and fought for, the absolute of his organism in its simplest terms, this structure evolved by nature, repeated in each act of birth, the animal: man; the house he is, this house that moves, breathes, acts, this house where his life is, where he dwells against the enemy, against the beast.
>
> (1997, p. 174)

As with Hijikata, Olson's emphasis on the body thinks through both its weaknesses and the possibility of grounding an aesthetic in it. From the concept of a body as a resistant stand to its environment, he developed his idea of projective verse, with line length being determined solely by breath and with the page acting as a score for vocal performance. Such an approach is part of his quest to find new roots for poetry after the war. 'La Préface' quotes from what appear to be graffiti scratched on the walls of huts in Buchenwald.

> 'I will die about April 1st...' going off
> 'I weigh, I think, 80 lbs...' scratch
> 'My name is NO RACE' address
> Buchenwald   new Altamira cave
> With a nail they drew the object of the hunt.
>
> (Olson, 1987, p. 46)

The most natural reading of these lines, I think, would be that Buchenwald is a 'new Altamira cave', where victims scratched on the wall with a nail in the same way people painted images of their prey on cave walls. Buchenwald is Altamira because it represents culture reduced to its zero degree, or the furthest point back it is possible to go, or a zero point from which culture now needs to go on. Thus, by saying that resistance begins with the Scrolls of Auschwitz, Rothenberg is not simply saying that they were a way of fighting against the Germans, but also that they anticipated, and found their logical endpoint in, the post-war revaluation of culture undertaken by people such as Olson.

Finding a connection between the Scrolls of Auschwitz and avant-garde poetry is, therefore, not simply a one-way process, by which the avant-garde provides a method to extract more meaning from the texts. It attends to the way in which the Sonderkommando aimed their writing outside, at the future. In 'Di Magilas fun Aushvits', Rothenberg ends each of his quotations from them with verbs in the future tense, and calls them, and Abraham Krzepicki's testimony, a prophecy. Not, I think, in order to mystify these voices from the dead, but to focus on the demands that they make of the reader, not just to be there, or even to read, but to take action. 'Take interest in this document. Keep looking. You will find still more' (Rothenberg, 2007, p. 180): an amalgamation of Gradowski's first words and Loewenthal's last.

What appears to be one of the last paragraphs that Leib Langfuss wrote, although not one cited in *Khurbn*, shows how his position as writer, the risks he was running and the gamble he had to take with his writing reconfigure the positions of both author and reader.

> I ask that all my various descriptions and notes, signed Y. A. R. A., which were buried in their time, be collected together. They are located in various boxes and jars in the courtyard of Crematorium 2. Also 2 longer descriptions one entitled 'The Expulsion' it lies in a pit of bones at Crematorium 1. Another a description entitled Auschwitz it lies among bones strewn across the south-west side of the same courtyard. Afterwards I rewrote and expanded it and buried it elsewhere in the ash by Crematorium 2. Put it into order and publish it all together under the name
> 'Amidst the Horrors of Murder'
>
> (1977, p. 361)

It is clear that Langfuss is concerned that his message be found and understood, but he wants more than this. There are straightforwardly literary matters: making sure that his texts are unified and organized as he wanted them, that his (anonymous) authorship is recognized. But there are also a set of concerns that are less simply literary. Copying has become a vital part of the process of writing (it doubles the chance of the information being found) and although one version he discusses is enlarged, it does not really seem to take priority over the other. It is also about letting us know where other writings are located. Authorship is not simply about originating the words, but about increasing their possibility of being read and is therefore a collective process. As survivors from the Sonderkommando attest, there was equally a network of responsibility for the writing in the first place: the need to *organize* the materials with which to write. One prisoner supplied the paper, another pen and ink. Light too was a scarce resource: a bunk had to be arranged that was near a window. Materials that would preserve the texts once buried were also needed and there was a constant search for wax to seal them in their containers: the jars and boxes that Langfuss mentions (Greif, 2005, pp. 165, 247).

Because of the vulnerability of these texts, there is also a network of responsibility delegated to his readers: they – we – are asked to find the different parts, bring them together, establish an order for them and to help disseminate them. His readers are asked to participate in the process of authorship. The significance of using Hijikata's claim that 'the dead are my teachers' lies in this relationship between the writers of the Scrolls and their readers. In rewriting the Scrolls, Rothenberg is not simply their interpreter, but becomes their heir, taking on something that they have bequeathed to the future.

Notes

1. Where the 1977 Yiddish edition is given, translations are my own. I have mostly used the 1985 English edition, because this is the one Rothenberg quotes from.
2. A recording of Rothenberg reading part of *Khurbn* is available at: <http://media.sas.upenn.edu/pennsound/authors/Rothenberg/Xavier-2011/Rothenberg-Jerome_12_In-the-Dark-Word-Khurbn_Xavier-U_4-13-11.mp3>.
3. Other readings are provided by Christine A. Meilicke (2005, pp. 224–253) and Norman Finkelstein (2001, pp. 106–110).
4. Among the texts that are explicitly referred to in some form or other are the writings of Tatsumi Hijikata, Allama Prabhu, Charles Olson and *The Scrolls of Auschwitz*. The sources that I have identified and that have no explicit reference in the poem are: Jean-François Steiner, *Treblinka* (1994 [1966]); Rachel Auerbach, 'On the Fields of Treblinka' and Abraham Krzepicki, '18 Days in Treblinka' (both in Donat, 1979); Terrence Des Pres, *The Survivor* (1976).
5. The Auschwitz Museum assigns the authorship of these passages differently, but this essay will follow the Marks's attribution. It was the Marks's edition

that Rothenberg used and I believe them to be correct. For a discussion of this issue, see Chare & Williams (forthcoming).
6. Rothenberg's retranslation from English to Yiddish – the original was Megiles Oyshvits.
7. This paragraph is actually taken verbatim from Abraham Krzepicki's description of a gas chamber in Treblinka (1979, p. 105).
8. The third sentence in this paragraph is based on Rachel Auerbach (1979, p. 38).
9. This claim was often reported as fact in earlier texts on Hijikata, but the current consensus appears to be that there was a large element of invention in this story (Barber, 2012).
10. This also fits with interpretations of automatic writing as itself bound up with hysteria, trauma and the shock of war (Lyford, 2007, pp. 18–19; Rainey, 1998, pp. 130–132).

Works cited

Adorno, T. (1973) [1966] *Negative Dialectics*, E. Ashton (trans.) (London: Routledge).
Adorno, T. (1983) [1949] 'Cultural Criticism and Society', in *Prisms*, S. and S. Weber (trans.) (Cambridge, MA: MIT Press), pp. 19–34.
Adorno, T. (1992) [1962] 'Commitment', in R. Tiedemann (ed.) *Notes to Literature: Volume 2*, S. Weber Nicholson (trans.) (New York: Columbia University Press), pp. 76–94.
Auerbach, R. (1979) 'In the Fields of Treblinka', in A. Donat (ed.), *The Death Camp Treblinka* (New York: Holocaust Library), pp. 17–74.
Barber, S. (2012) *Hijikata: Revolt of the Body* [Kindle edition] (Elektron Books). Available at: <www.amazon.co.uk>.
Benz, W. (2008) 'Treblinka', in W. Benz and B. Distel (eds.) *Ort des Terrors* Vol. 8 (Munich: Beck), pp. 407–443.
Chare, N. & Williams, D. (forthcoming) *Matters of Testimony: Interpreting the Scrolls of Auschwitz* (Berghahn).
DeKoven Ezrahi, S. (1980) *By Words Alone* (Chicago and London: University of Chicago Press).
Des Pres, T. (1976) *The Survivor* (Oxford: Oxford University Press).
Felman, S. 'Education and Crisis, or the Vicissitudes of Teaching', in S. Felman & D. Laub (eds.), *Testimony Crises of Witnessing in Literature, Psychoanalysis, and the History* (New York: Routledge), pp. 1–56.
Finkelstein, N. (2001) *Not One of Them in Place: Modern Poetry and Jewish American Identity* (Albany: State University of New York Press).
Fraleigh, S. & Nakamura, T. (2006) *Hijikata Tatsumi and Ohno Kazuo* (New York and London: Routledge).
Fredman, S. (1993) *The Grounding of American Poetry: Charles Olson and the Emersonian Tradition* (Cambridge: Cambridge University Press)
Gradowski, Z. (1977) 'Fartsaykhenungen', in B. Mark, *Megiles Oyshvits* (Tel Aviv: Yisroel Bukh), pp. 290–352.
Gradowski, Z. (1985) 'Writings', in B. Mark, *The Scrolls of Auschwitz*, S. Neemani (trans.) (Tel Aviv: Am Oved), pp. 173–205.

Greif, G. (2005) *We Wept without Tears: Testimonies of the Jewish Sonderkommando in Auschwitz* (New Haven: Yale University Press).
Grossman, V. (2012) 'The Hell of Treblinka', in C. Rajchman, *Treblinka: A Survivor's Memory* [Kindle version] (London: MacLehose) Available at: <www.amazon.co.uk>.
Hijikata, T. (2000) 'Wind Daruma', *The Drama Review* 44:1 (Spring), 71–81.
Hornblow, M. (2006) 'Bursting Bodies of Thought: Artaud and Hijikata', *Performance Paradigm* 2 (March), 26–44.
Kassow, S. (2007) *Who Will Write Our History? Rediscovering a Hidden Archive from the Warsaw Ghetto* (London: Penguin).
Krzepicki, A. (1979) '18 Days in Treblinka', in A. Donat (ed.) *The Death Camp Treblinka* (New York: Holocaust Library), pp. 77–146.
Ladefoged, P. (2006) *A Course in Phonetics*, 5th ed. (Boston, MA: Thomson Wadsworth).
Lang, B. (2000) *Holocaust Representation: Art within the Limits of History and Ethics* (Baltimore: Johns Hopkins University Press).
Langfuss, L. (1977) 'In groyl fun retsikhes', in B. Mark, *Megiles Oyshvits* (Tel Aviv: Yisroel Bukh), pp. 353–378.
Langfuss, L. (1985) 'The Horrors of Murder', in B. Mark, *The Scrolls of Auschwitz*, S. Neemani (trans.) (Tel Aviv, Am Oved), pp. 206–214.
Levi, P. (1991) 'On Obscure Writing,' in *Other People's Trades*, R. Rosenthal (trans.) (London: Sphere), pp. 157–163.
Loewenthal, Z. (1985) 'Addendum to the Łódź Manuscript', in B. Mark, *The Scrolls of Auschwitz*, S. Neemani (trans.) (Tel Aviv: Am Oved), pp. 236–240.
Lyford, A. (2007) *Surrealist Masculinities: Gender Anxiety and the Aesthetics of Post-World War I Reconstruction in France* (Berkeley: University of California Press).
Mark, B. (1977) *Megiles Oyshvits* (Tel Aviv: Yisroel Bukh).
Mark, B. (1985) *The Scrolls of Auschwitz*, S. Neemani (trans.) (Tel Aviv: Am Oved).
Maud, R. (1998) *What Does Not Change: The Significance of Charles Olson's 'The Kingfishers'* (Madison & Teaneck: Fairleigh Dickinson University Press).
Miyabi, I. (1988) 'A Preface to Butō,' Susan Blakeley Klein (trans.), in Klein (ed.), *Ankoku Butō: The Premodern and Postmodern Influences on the Dance of Utter Darkness* (Ithaca, NY: East Asia Program, Cornell University), pp. 69–71.
Meilicke, C. (2005) *Jerome Rothenberg's Experimental Poetry and Jewish Tradition* (Bethlehem: Lehigh University Press).
Moyn, S. (2005) *A Holocaust Controversy: The Treblinka Affair in Postwar France* (Waltham, MA: Brandeis University Press).
Olson, C. (1987) *The Collected Poems of Charles Olson: Excluding the Maximus Poems*, in G. Butterick (ed.) (Berkeley & London: University of California Press).
Olson, C. (1997) *Collected Prose*, in D. Allen & B. Friedlander (eds.) (Berkeley and Los Angeles: University of California Press).
Rainey, L. (1998) 'Taking Dictation: Collage Poetics, Pathology, and Politics,' *Modernism/Modernity* 5.2: 123–153.
Rothenberg, J. (2000) 'Nokh Aushvits (After Auschwitz)', in E. Selinger (ed.), *Jewish American Poetry: Poems, Commentary and Reflections* (Hanover, NH and London: The University Press of New England for Brandeis University Press), pp. 137–145.

Rothenberg, J. (2008) 'Pre-Face', in Rothenberg & S. Clay (eds.), *Poetics and Polemics 1980–2005* (Tuscaloosa: University of Alabama Press), pp. xv–xviii.

Rothenberg, J. (2010) Transcription of part of interview between Al Filreis and Jerome Rothenberg, [online] Available at: <https://jacket2.org/node/187> [accessed 3 December 2012].

Steiner, J.-F. (1994) *Treblinka*, H. Weaver (trans.) (New York: Meridian).

Vidal-Naquet, P. (1992) *The Assassins of Memory: Essays on the Denial of the Holocaust* (New York: Columbia University Press).

Vigodsky, Y. (1977) [5737] 'A vort fun a gevezenem asir in Oyshvits', in Z. Gradowski, *In harts fun geheynem: A dokument fun Oyshvitser zonder-komando, 1944* (Jerusalem: Haim Volnerman).

White, H. (2004) 'Figural Realism in Witness Literature', *Parallax*, 10:1, 113–124.

Wiernik, J. (1979) 'A Year in Treblinka', in A. Donat (ed.) *The Death Camp Treblinka* (New York: Holocaust Library), pp. 147–188.

4
Chain of Testimony: The Holocaust Researcher as Surrogate Witness

Anne Karpf

Affect and research

On first learning that the Scrolls of Auschwitz, the testimony of the Sonderkommando found buried near the crematoria at Birkenau in the extermination camp itself, were to be analysed as literary documents, my reaction was an involuntary but resounding 'no'. Here, in its own way, was surely 'the surfeit of memory' that Charles Maier (1993) had talked about. Not only did it seem almost impossible to view the Scrolls as texts when their very materiality was so charged, but I also could not help but wonder how Nicholas Chare and Dominic Williams could mobilize their cognitive skills without also letting loose a school of other, less welcome, sensibilities. The Scrolls, I found myself initially thinking, belonged more in a reliquary than academic seminar. In the event (2010), Chare and Williams's meticulous scholarship and deep sensitivity rendered such misgivings redundant and I dismissed my own first instincts as those of someone, a child of survivors, with a heightened engagement with testimony. Yet as I began to reflect more on the question, it seemed to me that such instinctual responses should not immediately be evicted but were themselves material that merited analysis because they touch on powerful ideas about how Holocaust research can and should be conducted, and speak of the existence of an underworld of unruly feelings that, by being exposed to the light of scrutiny and discussion, can help deepen and enrich Holocaust scholarship.

Debates about the role of affect in researching and writing about the Holocaust are not new: it is almost 15 years since Dominick LaCapra (1998, p. 17) talked of the need 'to examine one's implication in the problems one studies – issues that are pronounced with respect to extremely traumatic phenomena in which one's investment is great'. Since then positivist assumptions and practices – that history can be studied dispassionately and objectively – have been so robustly challenged by postmodern critiques that it might seem as if the battle has been won and no self-respecting scholar could embark on Holocaust research with a sense of themselves as disinterested observer intact. And yet, in reality Holocaust historiography remains dominated by a positivist historical method (Stone, 2012) and in practice it is common to find historical accounts where the idea that studying trauma might also produce it remains quite foreign. Historians rarely reflect on their own affective investment in the material they study; indeed, there is often an inverse relationship between the traumatic intensity of the event being studied and their readiness to discuss their own emotional involvement or the affective sources which led them to take up that research field in the first place. More than that, any leakage of feeling into research often still seems to be a source of shame, a transgression of the ideal type researcher. What appears to be demanded of the historian, in such cases, is the blank canvas of the psychoanalyst, upon which history itself can project its own feelings. This kind of history has its roots, according to Hayden White (1978, p. 123), in the 'profound hostility to all forms of myth' in historiography after the French Revolution, which required the historian to expunge from their apprehension of reality any intuitive processes.

In reality, of course, analysts themselves have feelings, and those treating Holocaust survivors have described the anxieties stirred up in them when they have encountered the horrors of the concentration camps experienced by their patients. In such cases, the psychoanalyst has to confront their own resistances in order to help produce an effective analysis. Ilse Grubrich-Simitis (1981, p. 442) has argued that the 'ability to empathise with sufferers is a precarious cultural acquisition' and is threatened by the defences activated by the analyst to protect themselves against the revival of the infant's feeling of extreme helplessness in the face of existential threat. By identifying with the survivor patient 'are we not in fact afraid that [...] we might experience, albeit in an incomparably weaker form, something of that which the survivors actually lived through?' (p. 444). In order to be able to help the analysand, the analyst has to achieve their own 'successful' work of mourning the Holocaust (Grubrich-Simitis, 1984).

Historians are not psychoanalysts, yet neither can historical method seal them against the transference and counter-transference set off by Holocaust research. Researchers, no less than psychoanalysts, experience resistances and defences of their own in working with traumatic material. Dealing with testimony, LaCapra (1998, p. 11) argues, 'raises the issue of the way in which the historian or other analyst becomes a secondary witness, undergoes a transferential relation, and must work out an acceptable subject-position with respect to the witness and his or her testimony'. The refusal of some historians to engage with testimonial literature, according to Federico Finchelstein, 'is also a mechanism of defense, of neutralizing one's own subject-position vis-a-vis the traumatic charge that seems to emanate from victims' testimonies' (Laub & Finchelstein, 2010, p. 59). The role of secondary witness places a heavy burden of responsibility on the researcher and positions them in a relay of memory – a chain of testimony in which they act as a medium for the transmission of first-hand accounts to future generations for whom the Holocaust will be nothing but history. In the case of testimony left by victims rather than survivors, the burden is even heavier and the researcher becomes not only a secondary witness but in some sense also a surrogate one, charged with speaking on behalf of those who no longer can.

One might argue that this is the case with historical documents of any kind – preserving and transmitting 'thick' description and memory left by preceding generations is the very nature of the historical task – and yet when the testimony concerns such a comprehensive and unprecedented attempt to extirpate memory itself, its retrieval enlists the researcher (albeit in footling fashion) in the project to challenge both Nazi ideology and the whole National Socialist enterprise. Rare must be the researcher in whom an alternating sense of impotence and omnipotence, inadequacy and awe are entirely absent. These sentiments, I want to suggest, are legitimate material for debate and discussion, and not extrinsic to the historical events themselves. We are tempted, perhaps, to write them off because, in the crude Freudianism that is current and widespread, psychic responses are thought to result almost entirely from individual subjectivity: they reside in the personal unconscious and appear autonomous. Although cultural studies have been deeply informed by psychoanalysis, bringing psychoanalytic theories into contact with Holocaust research (or, even worse, the Holocaust researcher) still seems to represent a dangerous turn away from historical and sociological analysis, running the risk of banalizing the Holocaust and narcissistically replacing the perpetrators, victims and bystanders as the focal point of research with the researchers themselves.

In reality, 'structures of feeling' (Williams, 1986) are as culturally produced and historically contingent as the notion that you can do history without feeling, and our affective responses to the encounter with Holocaust material are themselves a historical resource. By keeping these emotions latent we not only deny ourselves another dimension through which to understand the Holocaust and its aftermath but also endow them with the power to destabilize the research. It must be stressed that we are engaged here in a project not of psychohistory (which often hovers intolerably close to exculpation) or any kind of speculative psychological profiling of either perpetrators or victims but rather the adopting of a reflexive stance about the researcher's own practice:

> Without at least the awareness of what defence mechanisms are and what they do, the historian is at the mercy of her own repressions. These repressions and resistances will determine, to a certain extent, what it is the historian chooses to write about or not write about. What gets excluded from history, then, has as much to do with what it is historians can psychically handle.
>
> (Morris, 2001, pp. 54–55)

Dirk Rupnow (2012) has argued, for example, that historians have been reluctant to describe in detail what happened in the gas chambers in part through self-protection and their inability to bear those details. On the other hand, the blithe confidence of Hugh Trevor-Roper, author of 'The Last Days of Hitler', when he wrongly authenticated the forged diaries of Hitler, may have owed something to a sense of grandiosity developed when studying Hitler's final months in the bunker (Rosenbaum, 1998).

My concern here is with what gets excluded from history but also with the psychological freight that history has to carry. My starting point is my own psychic load as the daughter of Holocaust survivors. I have described elsewhere (Karpf, 2008) my experiences growing up with survivor parents and the dawning realization that much of what I'd assumed to be a purely personal pathology was actually common to members of the so-called 'second generation'.[1] Since the book's original publication in 1996, the circles of impact have widened further still and I have become aware that some of the reactions that I had assumed were confined to children of survivors are, in fact, shared by those without direct personal connections to the Holocaust: they are part of what Marianne Hirsch calls 'postmemory'. Although Hirsch coined this phrase to describe children of Holocaust survivors and of parents who had suffered other collective traumatic experiences, it seems to me to bear application more generally also to those born after the Holocaust and grappling with it in various ways, since she defines postmemory as 'a powerful and particular form of memory precisely because its connection to its object or source is mediated not through recollection but through an imaginative investment and creation' (1997, p. 22).

Impulses and phantasies

Freud (1958a) identified the rescue phantasies that some men have for women. Children of Holocaust survivors, overwhelmed by the stories they have heard or gleaned about their parents' experience of extreme brutality and the prospect of annihilation, commonly entertain retrospective rescue phantasies of their own. I want to suggest that Holocaust researchers and commentators, while they remain sufficiently in touch with reality to know that the victims of Nazism remain dead and that pivotal events that helped survivors to survive took place decades earlier, may have their own version of the rescue phantasy, but in this they help rescue the survivor or, more poignantly, the victim not from death but from oblivion. They are tasked with pulling memory from the rubble of the past, of reviving memories and descriptions that have been almost obliterated, to claim a place for victims and survivors in collective memory. In the case of the Scrolls of Auschwitz how much more compelling might rescue phantasies be since the testimony literally had a humus of crematoria ashes and decomposed bone clinging to it. How hard it must have been, one imagines, for Chare and Williams, and the Scrolls researchers who preceded them, to resist the idea that these artefacts represented an unmediated past, a synecdoche, a frayed remnant of the Holocaust itself. Or to eschew the phantasy that in some way they might be imaginatively resuscitating its authors...

Claude Lanzmann has made explicit his own rescue phantasies, as expressed in his film *Shoah*, where he fixates on the loneliness of the death of Holocaust victims and retrospectively inserts himself into their narrative to keep them company:

> The idea that always has been most painful for me is that all these people died alone [...] A meaning for me that is simultaneously the most profound and the most incomprehensible in the film is in a certain way [...] to resuscitate these people, to kill them a second time, with me accompanying them.
>
> (Qtd. in LaCapra, 1998, p. 133)

Interestingly, even in phantasy, Lanzmann cannot entertain such omnipotence as could reverse time (for some, this may be the only way of engaging with the Holocaust; it was given fictional form in Martin Amis's novel *Time's Arrow*, 1992), although the impulse to somehow defeat or overcome time is certainly a common response to the Holocaust. In *The War After* I described how tenaciously in my imagination I had clung to an old and mythologized Poland until I actually visited the country. Even then I viewed the present through the lens of the past, imbuing each receipt and postcard with a sense of 'lostness' far in excess of what it might actually sustain, 'as if they were archaeological relics encoded with meanings and potential clues' (p. 297). After visiting both Płaszów and Birkenau, where my mother was an inmate, I came to realize how thoroughly I had

> confused time and place, history and geography, as if coming in person to the site of terrible events which occurred fifty years ago could somehow yield them up for us to transform them – they might actually extrude through the stones and the earth and be mitigated by modern sorrow. But it is time which has enfolded and buried those events, not place, and it was their contemporaries on different continents who had the possibility of intervening, not those of us standing here now.
>
> (p. 300)

This attempt to erase the distance between past and present is not, I've come to believe, particular to children of survivors, even though we may experience it particularly acutely, but embeds itself in the undertow of much historical research and cultural debate. Implicit in the project of recording is the impulse to prevent the kind of 'second murder' committed by time itself: time becomes not just the agent of forgetting but an active accomplice in the task. Research and writing, by contrast, act as an antidote, a countervailing force, seeming to confer immortality. Pierre Nora has argued that our 'hallucinations of the past', the result of discontinuities and distance from events, stoke our sense of wanting to retrieve the past's secrets. 'The most fundamental purpose of the lieu de memoire is to stop time, to block the work of forgetting, to establish a state of things, to immortalize death, to materialize the immaterial...to capture a maximum of meaning in the fewest of signs' (1989), even though, as James Young (1993) has pointed out, 'once we assign monumental form to memory, we have to some degree divested ourselves of the obligation to remember'.

Lanzmann has acknowledged how the recurring desolate images of rolling trains in *Shoah* expressed a yearning for the erasure of time:

> These disfigured places are what I call nonplaces of memory (non-lieux de memoire). At the same it is nevertheless necessary that traces remain. I must hallucinate and think that nothing has changed. I was conscious of change but, at the same time, I had to think that time had not accomplished its work.
>
> (Qtd. in LaCapra, 1998, p. 133)

We must guard against pathologizing such phantasies but rather recognize them as one way of dealing with trauma and the painful feelings of impotence that it can excite in the secondary or surrogate witness. Another way of dealing with such secondary trauma is through what LaCapra calls 'archival fetishism'. The anguished exhortation of the historian Simon Dubnow, murdered by the Nazis, 'Shreibt un farshreibt!' ('Write and record!') (Marrus, 1997, p. xiii), seems to have been infused with almost magical properties, so fiercely and religiously have researchers adhered to it, recording whatever minutiae of life and death under Nazism can be recovered. It sometimes seems as though every receipt or timetable, each log or inventory, has evidentiary potential, as if, with sufficient determination and graft on the part of the researcher, some new constellation of information might be revealed.

It is impossible not to be moved by the scrupulousness of much of this research and its pressing agenda of recovery. In part it is a belated response to survivors' need to bear witness and be listened to, a need mostly unmet in the aftermath of the war and for years to come. Primo Levi (1987, p. 227) found that speaking and not being listened to was almost as grievous to him as his camp experiences and represented a second abandonment by the world after the first abandonment during the war.

And yet, on occasion, when it comes to documentation, there is an almost palpable excess in operation and the boundary between a thing and a person, a document and the individuals who produced it, is at risk of becoming dissolved or at least made tenuous. Even Raul Hilberg, the archetypal 'rational' historian, found himself in thrall to the magical aura of some of his sources. In *Shoah*, he hinted as much when he tried to explain to Lanzmann why documents were so fascinating to him:

Well, you see, when I hold a document in my hand, particularly if it's an original document, then I hold something which is actually something that the original bureaucrat held in his hand. It's an artifact. It's a leftover. It's the only leftover there is. The dead are not around.

(Qtd. in LaCapra, 1998, p. 132)

The care extended to Holocaust documents is all the more poignant because these are traces, leftovers, remnants (Agamben, 2008). Each time we handle attentively a Holocaust testimony or the records of a victim, it brings into consciousness, or to its rim, the lacunae that cannot be filled, the documents that will not be found and, most unspeakably, our knowledge of the lack of care and humanity allowed to its subject. Or as Helga Satzinger put it, 'So much effort put into preserving records of people, and so much effort put into their murder.'[2] Testimony is always in dialogue with silence and absence; the more heedfully and thoughtfully we treat it, the more painful it becomes.

Traces

Phantasies of comprehensiveness and completeness dog most archival researchers at one time or another, whatever their field, yet in the case of Holocaust research these are particularly charged, because of the Nazis' declared intention to remove all traces of their crimes and produce a genocide without witnesses or traces, leading to claims of 'memorycide'. Thus behind archival fetishism lies an even larger project, one in which remembering and retrieving are endowed with almost prophylactic capacities, and the potential to somehow avoid a recurrence of atrocity, if only every shred of evidence is exhumed and preserved. As Rupnow (2012, p. 63) has argued, 'Destruction and forgetting on the one hand and remembrance and justice on the other hand are usually seen as not simply arbitrarily linked but as inseparable in their character.'[3] It is as though historical memory carries some sort of retributory charge and the very act of memorializing is not only a retrospective act of preservation but also, somehow, a prospective one too – a reversal of time's arrow indeed.

For the Jewish researcher in particular, recovering traces and witnesses can thus become a small but significant act of retrospective resistance, which can all too easily slide into a compulsion. The case of Edmund de Waal is one such example. In The *Hare With Amber Eyes*, his fine account of how he tracked, through the biography of the netsuke bequeathed him by his great uncle, his ancestral Jewish family's experiences in Europe under Nazism, de Waal relates how he tries 'to hunt down' every picture that hung in his ancestor Charles Ephrussi's room in nineteenth-century Paris. He starts to list all the museums in which the paintings now hang, to trace how they got there and contemplates how long it would take him to go to them all, to see 'if I can see what his eyes saw' (2007, p. 87), before he realizes the impossibility of the task. But the impulse is there and de Waal's obsession with the tiniest detail of his ancestors' lives, his copious chronicling of the provenance, placing and afterlife of their artefacts, gives the measure of his grief.

The compulsion to chronicle copiously is a reparative one: it tries to re-humanize those who were dehumanized in the Holocaust. Perhaps, too, it acts as a kind of obsession-compulsion that helps to keep at bay the horror. If one is always engaged in research one never has time to stop and let the subject matter overwhelm one. As Griselda Pollock, writing about Charlotte Salomon's 'Leben? oder Theater?', put it:

> What is a subject in catastrophic circumstances when all that 'I' appear to be under is the condition of subjective dissolution and politically encompassed annihilation? Charlotte Salomon used love and philosophy. They did not save her. But she has a name. We must honor it by reading her work with care.
>
> (2011, p. 14)

De Waal observes, of his own obsessive chronicling, 'I think [...]of all the listings of families in the manifests, for deportations. If others can be so careful over things that are so important, then I must be careful over these objects and their stories' (p. 348).

Maike Rotzoll, a German psychiatrist, has researched the murder of institutionalized German psychiatric patients at six killing centres under the Aktion T4 euthanasia programme. Together with colleagues, she used the discarded files of 3,000 of these patients, found after the fall of the Berlin Wall, to discover on what basis they were selected for the gas chambers. Most of these patients have, until now, had no name. Indeed, until recently there was little interest in them: although there was a card index of perpetrators, none existed of victims. At the very least Rotzoll and her colleagues are trying to rescue them from anonymity and name them; where possible they have also attempted to reconstruct their life stories. Patients such as Karl Ahrendt, killed at 87, 33 years after he was first hospitalized: 'After his admission', Rotzoll (2011) notes, 'Ahrendt didn't exist any more – he vanished behind official forms'.

The treasure trove of paintings by the incarcerated that they also found, such as drawings by Wilhelm Werner, 1898–1940, a victim of compulsory sterilization, reveal the human subjectivity behind the number. His work is among that exhibited at the Prinzhorn Collection Museum in Heidelberg.[4]

As Baudrillard (1994) put it, 'Forgetting extermination is part of extermination, because it is also the extermination of memory, of history, or the social.'[5] Naming thus becomes important not just as a historical tool but also as an act of memorializing. The gathering of names takes on the flavour of a commemorative book; it is a small gesture of *Wiedergutmachung*. Perhaps because of the nature of the material, and also because she is a German psychiatrist working on files in which her predecessors are implicated, Rotzoll is sensitive to her own investment in the project. 'We're psychiatrists and seeing every day patients who would have been murdered under the Nazis. Reading a file you seem to be in contact in some way with that person. The most difficult moment is to put the file away: you don't know if, in the future, anyone will ever look at it again.'[6] Like Lanzmann, Rotzoll has tried to 'accompany' her subjects, but has had to painfully acknowledge the moment that they part.

Sacralization

The suggestion that Holocaust researchers and writers should scrutinize their own engagement with trauma might be thought to bring risks of its own, most notably that, in rejecting a positivist methodology, we embrace an over-identification with the victim, something of which LaCapra rightly accuses Lanzmann (1998). In Lanzmann's case he went so far as to publicly humiliate an Auschwitz survivor who planned to screen a documentary with which he disagreed and to excoriate anyone who attempted to seek explanations as to why the Holocaust took place. In appropriating the terrible dictum of an SS guard to Primo Levi – 'Hier ist kein warum' (here there is no why) – and perversely recasting it as his own slogan, Lanzmann loses not only any sense of humility but also hubristically marks out the acceptable field of study in his capacity as surrogate survivor-in-chief (Rosenbaum, 1998).

Self-aggrandizement is not particular to Lanzmann. Daniel Goldhagen (1997, p. 3), author of *Hitler's Willing Executioners*, claimed to be 'reconceiving central aspects of the Holocaust'. He deliberately 'eschews the clinical approach' in his account of 'blood, bones and brains flying about' (p. 22). Though his emotional description of the killing of little girls by members of the Einsatzgruppen, according to LaCapra (2001), veers perilously close to kitsch, Goldhagen, whose father was a refugee from Europe, was highly resistant to attempts to explore the origins of his approach to the Holocaust, and regarded allegations of 'displaced, unacknowledged revenge impulse' as intrusive (Rosenbaum, 1998). Yet in trying to avoid objectifying the victims, Goldhagen might be said, like Lanzmann, to have over-identified with them. (Shalom Auslander's (2012) comic novel, *Hope: a Tragedy*, brilliantly satirizes, through the character of the hero's grandmother, this impulse of post-Holocaust generations to insert themselves retrospectively into the narrative.) In reality the researcher or critic is more, and not less, likely to produce a sentimentalized, sacralized representation of the survivor or victim if they fail to be attentive to their own projections. Let me give you a cautionary tale from my own experience.

In January 1998, *The Guardian* sent me to interview Binjamin Wilkomirski, author of the already acclaimed supposed Holocaust memoir *Fragments* (1996). I was moved by both book and author, despite two fleeting concerns. (It is hard to recover these on exactly the scale that they struck me at the time, so tempting is it to place oneself retrospectively in the 'doubters' camp, but I shall try.) Firstly, Wilkomirski told me that he didn't know how old he was but that 'my doctors guess that I might have been born at the end of 1938 or the beginning of 1939' (Karpf, 1998, pp. 2–3). In the interview, though, he also mentioned that 22 January was his birthday. I phoned him later to ask him to clear up the contradiction and he elaborated that he celebrated 22 January as his birthday because this was the date that he emerged from Birkenau. Consequently I started my article with the sentence, 'It was only after I'd left Binjamin Wilkomirski in his hotel room that it occurred to me that he was a man without a birthday' and then went on to talk about the substitute birthday that he'd fashioned for himself. In other words I did some of the interpretive work on Wilkomirski's account in order to resolve the contradiction: I placed the two comments together in a mutually supportive sequence.

Secondly, I was struck by how lachrymose Wilkomirski was. I grew up in a community of survivors and hardly ever saw one cry: most of them had learnt to armour themselves against tears during the Holocaust and those I knew well were at the steely end of the emotional spectrum. Wilkomirski's tears flickered somewhere on my gauge of discrepancy but I never pursued this. Moreover, when I recounted the contents of both book and interview to my mother, she immediately retorted that there were no child survivors of Majdanek, and certainly not one so young.

I dismissed her reaction. What is intriguing in hindsight is that I was more able and willing to discredit my mother's response than I was able to discount Wilkomirski's. Why did I – admittedly, not alone – prove so gullible, especially since Lawrence Langer, among many others, has protested that, from his first reading, he 'assumed that Fragments was a fictional narrative' (2006, p. 50)?

One's reading of any text is shaped by many factors: in this case, mine could be said to have been over-determined. The book arrived already lionized as a memoir, which seemed a guarantor of its facticity. Its very fragmentariness seemed to mimic the broken nature of memory and in particular a child's memory, lending it further authenticity. It was the Holocaust story, perhaps, that was yearned for as the century in which the Holocaust took place was drawing to a close – the story of the child who survived what Anne Frank did not, who could take the 'late born' into the next century, and the perfect 'postmodern' text, fragmentary, without strict chronology. But there were also personal reasons that predisposed me to believe Wilkomirski and allow my reservations only whispering room. My reactions were shaped primarily, I now think, by my relationship with Holocaust testimony, specifically that of my mother, which had occupied a central, incontestable place in my life. While I could challenge my mother's reaction to Wilkomirski's book – that, after all, was simply her opinion, albeit a highly informed one – I could no sooner dispute his apparent testimony than that of my own parents. My own excess became clear in my feelings when his duplicity was unmasked: a deep sense of rage at the deception, at his appropriation of a story that was more 'mine' than 'his' (in reality, it belonged to neither of us) and at the exploitation of my own readiness to believe that had been forged so painfully in my childhood.

Fractures

Most survivor families are highly sensitive to the rupture of the family line and find different ways of trying to come to terms with it, but the recognition of and response to the fragmentation of the subject (which Wilkomirski so unerringly identified in the title of his work) is a key issue in Holocaust narrative generally. While Freud (1958d) compared the joint work of analyst and patient to an archaeologist's excavation of a destroyed or buried building, Foucault stressed the discontinuities and fractures, thresholds and limits present in historical analysis: he argued for the questioning of 'ready-made syntheses' and their replacement by the idea of 'dispersed events' (1989, p. 24). Nevertheless, Dori Laub claims, the Holocaust researcher can synthesize the traumatic testimony of survivors into a unified narrative: 'the historian is now in a position to witness those fragments that have come together and to integrate them with facts that she has from other sources' (Laub & Finchelstein, 2010, p. 57). Yet surely the researcher must resist the temptation to reconstitute the shards of testimony into something too whole: 'unbroken' is an adjective, describing a pristine state – there is no verb to 'unbreak'. (This should not be confused with the argument that the Holocaust is essentially unrepresentable and incomprehensible – an argument that Rupnow (2012) expertly dismantles.) Indeed the Scrolls of Auschwitz, as described by Chare and Williams, are themselves material metaphors of Holocaust memory – buried, uncovered, recovered, restored but always fragmentary. It seems fitting that they were discovered in different decades – the 1940s, 1950s, 1960s and 1980s, like different sedimentary layers of memory and understanding, a palimpsest, a reminder that retrieval of Holocaust evidence can never be complete and will always inevitably be refracted through the time of its finding. Chare (2011), in his understanding of the problematics of restoration and the risks of normalizing the Scrolls, seems exquisitely able to tolerate their brokenness.

Chare and Williams have also acknowledged what so many researchers have found unbearable: the enforced complicity of the Scrolls' authors – members of the Sonderkommando and thus of what Primo Levi called 'the Grey Zone' (1989) – in mass murder. As a result, following James Young (1988), they can summon the cool historicity to view the Scrolls as literary documents and are able to wrest deeper, more extraordinary meanings from them: that the penmanship of one of the Scrolls' authors, Leyb Langfuss, suggests 'that he saw himself as a self. This is not the writing towards disintegration' (Chare, 2011, p. 85); that even in such close proximity to the crematoria, precision of expression was so highly valued. This helps us understand that, in such conditions, precision of expression becomes not a creative flourish or literary self-indulgence but an existential imperative.

Chare sets himself against 'a perceived quasi-spiritual revelation of the truth of the object', in favour of a deep theoretical engagement with the Scrolls and their materiality, and argues that they demonstrate 'a faith in the testimonial capacity of language under the most extreme conditions' (pp. xx–xxi). Yet this is no easy, redemptive uplift, of the kind that takes place at the end of *Schindler's List*, where the survival of a handful of Jews seems to have begotten an entire nation, seemingly a replacement for those who have died. Or the sort of redemption found all too often in writings about Anne Frank, whose ruthlessly decontextualized few lines about still believing that people are good at heart that have become so famous (the ones about people's innate 'urge to destroy [...]to kill [...] murder and rage' have curiously never found equal fame) have turned her into an emblem of forgiveness, as though she were in some sense anticipating her own death and absurdly exonerating those responsible. Even as generally sensitive a critic as Francine Prose colludes with this trope, arguing that Anne Frank lives on in the vitality of her writing, just as she always wanted to (2010). But Anne Frank isn't alive: she died a horrible death (Karpf, 2010). Gabriel Josipovici (1999, p. 323) has argued that 'when communal memory, dialogic memory, breaks down or disappears, myth rushes in to fill the gap'. Little exemplifies this more than the mythologizing of Anne Frank.

So how can the Holocaust researcher steer a path between a positivist refusal to reflect on their own implication in what they study and an over-identification with the victim that produces such intolerable anxiety that they must vaporize it with consoling messages or the illusion of having reunited the shards of testimony? Saul Friedländer suggests that 'the voice of the commentator' should be clearly heard and it should 'disrupt the facile linear progression of the narration, introduce alternative questions' (qtd. in Eaglestone, 2004, p. 187) but 'without giving in to the temptation of closure' (1994, p. 261). LaCapra calls for 'empathic unsettlement' (2001, p. 41), a receptivity to other people's traumatic experiences without their appropriation, and the undergoing by the historian of 'muted trauma' (1998, p. 40).

Both Friedländer and LaCapra's proposed stance are variants of what Freud called 'working through', rather than 'acting-out'. In the latter, the patient repeats in the form of an action a trauma that they have repressed – repeats instead of remembering. In working through, by contrast, the patient attains a reconciliation with their repressed material through the medium of the transference, which allows it to change (Freud, 1958b). Similarly while mourning results in the patient's eventual return to vitality, its pathological form, melancholia, involves a narcissistic identification with a lost object (Freud, 1958c). Indeed we could see archival fetishism as a refusal to mourn the lost object: by choosing instead a melancholic attempt to preserve it, this kind of research paradoxically keeps it lost. Working through and mourning are related to what Melanie Klein called the 'depressive position', in which the persecutory anxieties to be found in the split paranoid-schizoid condition become more muted as the infant learns to tolerate ambivalence and reaches the stage where the internal object can be simultaneously loved and hated (Klein, 1986). For Holocaust scholars and commentators, the depressive position can serve as a foil to omnipotent phantasies, an encouragement to accept those limitations that the 'completism' of archival fetishism denies. Hannah Arendt (1993, p. 20), though she was famously hostile to psychoanalysis, adopted a stance not dissimilar to the depressive position when she maintained that, as regards the Holocaust, 'the best that can be achieved is to know precisely what it was, and to endure this knowledge, and then to wait and see what comes of this knowing and enduring'.

The Hare With Amber Eyes exemplifies the work of mourning and a hard-won attainment of the depressive position. The book ends with de Waal's journey with his younger brother, Thomas, to Odessa, the city where the Ephrussi family started. They find the family house only to learn that it has just been renovated, its remaining original contents despoiled and discarded only a month before. 'I am too late', de Waal laments, his mania for chronicling artefacts finally left unsatisfied. But as he looks out of the window at the vista to the Black Sea he realizes that traces of his ancestors are still, in some sense, there, in the stories of Isaac Babel and in the charitable endowments they left behind. This understanding seems to free him to 'Let it go. Let it lie. Stop looking and stop picking things up [...] Just go home and let these stories be' (2010, p. 346). De Waal's compulsion to document, though it results in an eloquent book, trapped him in a quest for infinite detail, one carrying a powerful emotional charge and libidinal energy. It is only once he works out what has been killed off and what remains – an essential task of mourning – that he is able to let go and allow the past to be past.

On the other hand, we could argue that the task of integrating the Holocaust into Jewish life and history without melancholia is too psychically and culturally great to be achieved either individually or – so relatively soon after the events themselves – historiographically. Perhaps the depressive position is only occasionally attainable. Josipovici counsels that 'We must accept that we cannot respond as we ideally should, and that sometimes we cannot respond at all. We should ask ourselves how often our involvement with the details of the Holocaust has more to do with our own pathology, with our suppressed guilt and our suppressed masochism' (pp. 326–327).

The case of the historian Otto Dov Kulka demonstrates both the limitations of history from which all affect has been evicted and the impossibility of achieving a neat synthesis of documentation and reflexivity. Kulka's example is an extreme one, in that he is both a historian and a child survivor. Now based in Jerusalem, he was born in 1933 in Czechoslovakia, from where, aged ten, he was deported with his mother first to Theresienstadt and thence to the 'family camp' in Auschwitz. Kulka has, as a historian, described this camp and its liquidation in an article based on documents he found in German archives, an article in which 'I use the third person, as one who is describing a distant historical reality' (Kulka, 2013, p. 18). Indeed, he assumes that

> readers of my historical publications will have identified me unequivocally with an attitude of strict and impersonally remote research, always conducted within well-defined historical categories, as a kind of self-contained method unto itself. But few are aware of the existence within me of a dimension of silence, of a choice I made to sever the biographical from the historical past.
>
> (p. xi)

Eventually, however, this professional exile from his biographical past became unsustainable.

> That rigorous 'pure scientific' writing is fraught with tremendous 'meta-dimensional' baggage and tensions [...] The fact is that in all my research I never had to deal with the stage, the dimension, of the violent end, the murder, the humiliation and the torture of those human beings. I left, or skirted that dimension.
>
> (pp. 82–83)

In a slim new volume he faces it directly. Saturated with affect and a recovered subjectivity, alongside dreams and speculation, his memoir ends with a near-disintegration of the rational, which is replaced by an almost messianic, quasi-religious vision. An appendix reprints his article on the family camp, from which Kulka qua inmate is banished. The contrast is astonishing – a colossal psychic split made manifest within the covers of a brief book. Kulka, even now, understands only too well the rationale for his former stance: 'had I not found that "safe passage" I could not have borne those tensions and anxieties' (p. 93).

While most contemporary Holocaust researchers and commentators do not have to carry the 'meta-dimensional' baggage that Kulka does, developing an understanding of the routes that they have taken to ensure their own 'safe passage' can only enhance their work.

Notes

I am grateful to Dan Stone and Daniel Pick for their invaluable comments on this chapter.

1. A term I dislike precisely because it places children of survivors in too close a relationship with their parents' experiences, presuming an identification which it should be problematizing.
2. Personal communication, 21.10.11
3. Rupnow, op cit, p. 63. Rupnow has challenged the concept of 'memorycide', arguing that, in reality, the Nazi politics of memory was much more ambivalent and contradictory, and amounted to an attempt to 'Aryanize' the representation of their crimes.
4. See also *Die Namen der Nummern* (Berlin: Fischer, 2007) in which Hans-Joachim Lang identifies the 86 victims gassed by the Nazis in August 1943 in Natzweiler-Struthof concentration camp.
5. This is also the title of a book by Rotzoll and her colleagues (Fuchs et al., 2007).
6. Personal communication, 21.10.11.

Works cited

Agamben, G. (2008) *Remnants of Auschwitz*, D. Heller-Roazen (trans.) (New York: Zone Books).
Amis, M. (1992) *Time's Arrow* (London: Penguin).
Auslander, S. (2012) *Hope: a Tragedy* (London: Picador).
Arendt, H. (1993) *Men in Dark Times* (Orlando: Harcourt Brace).
Baudrillard, J. (1994) *Simulacra and Simulations – III. Holocaust*, S. Glaser (trans.) [online] Available at: <http://www.egs.edu/faculty/jean-baudrillard/articles/simulacra-and-simulations-iii-holocaust/> [accessed 6 August 2012].
Chare, N. (2011) *Auschwitz and Afterimages* (London: I. B. Tauris).
Chare, N. & Williams, D. (2010) 'The Scrolls of Auschwitz: Visual and Literary Analyses', paper for workshop *Witnesses to the Holocaust: The Scrolls of Auschwitz and the Matter of Testimony*, University of Reading, 26 March 2010.
Felstiner, J. (1995) *Paul Celan: Poet, Survivor, Jew* (New Haven: Yale University Press, 1995).
Eaglestone, R. (2004) *The Holocaust and the Postmodern* (Oxford: Oxford University Press).
Foucault, M. (1989) *The Archaeology of Knowledge* (London: Routledge).
Freud, S. (1958a) 'A Special Type of Choice of Object Made by Men', in *The Standard Edition of the Complete Psychological Works of Sigmund Freud*, James Strachey (trans.) (London: Hogarth Press), vol. xi.
Freud, S. (1958b) 'Remembering, Repeating and Working Through', *Standard Edition*, vol. xii.
Freud, S. (1958c) Mourning and Melancholia', *Standard Edition*, vol.14.
Freud, S. (1958d) 'Constructions in Analysis', *Standard Edition*, vol.23.
Friedländer, S. (1994) 'Trauma, Memory, and Transference', in G. Hartman (ed.) *Holocaust Remembrance* (Oxford: Blackwell).

Fuchs, P., et al. (2007) *Das Vergessen der Vernichtung ist ein Teil der Vernichtung selbst: Lebensgeschichten von Opfern der nationalsozialistischen 'Euthanasie'* (Goettingen: Wallstein Verlag).

Grubrich-Simitis, I. (1981) 'Extreme Traumatization as a Cumulative Trauma: Psychoanalytic Investigations of the Effects of Concentration Camp Experiences on Survivors and Their Children', *Psychoanalytic Study of the Child*, 36, 415–450.

Grubrich-Simitis, I. (1984) 'From Concretism to Metaphor: Thoughts on Some Theoretical and Technical Aspects of the Psychoanalytic Work with Children of Holocaust Survivors', *Psychoanalytic Study of the Child*, 39, 301–319.

Hirsch, M. (1997) *Family Frames: Photography, Narrative, and Postmemory* (Cambridge, MA: Harvard University Press).

Josipovici, G. (1999) 'Memory: Too Much/Too Little', in E. Timms & A. Hammel (eds.) *The German/Jewish Dilemma: From the Enlightenment to the Shoah* (Lampeter: Edwin Mellen Press), pp. 317–327.

Karpf, A. (1998) 'Child of the Shoah', *The Guardian*, 11 February, 2–3.

Karpf, A. (2008) *The War After: Living With The Holocaust* (London: Faber).

Karpf, A. (2010) 'Review of F. Prose', *Anne Frank: The Book, the Life, the Afterlife*, *The Guardian*, 21 August, [online] Available at < http://www.guardian.co.uk/books/2010/aug/21/anne-frank-francine-prose> [accessed 3 December 2012].

Klein, M. (1986) 'A Contribution to the Psychogenesis of Manic-Depressive States', in J. Mitchell (ed.), *The Selected Melanie Klein* (London: Penguin).

Kulka, O. (2013) *Landscapes of the Metropolis of Death* (London: Allen Lane).

LaCapra, D. (1998) *History and Memory After Auschwitz* (Ithaca: Cornell University Press).

LaCapra, D. (2001) *Writing History, Writing Trauma* (Baltimore: The Johns Hopkins University Press).

Langer, L. (2006) *Using and Abusing the Holocaust* (Bloomington: Indiana University Press).

Laub, D. & Finchelstein, F. (2010) 'Memory and History from Past to Future', in Y. Gutman et al. (eds.) *Memory and the Future* (London: Palgrave Macmillan), pp. 50–65.

Levi, P. (1989) *The Drowned and the Saved*, R. Rosenthal (trans.) (London: Abacus).

Levi, P. (1987) *If This is a Man and The Truce*, S. Woolf (trans.) (London: Abacus).

Maier, C. (1993) 'A Surfeit of Memory? Reflections on History, Melancholy and Denial', *History and Memory*, 5:2 (Fall–Winter), 136–153.

Marrus, M. (1987) *The Holocaust in History* (London: Penguin).

Morris, M. (2001) *Curriculum and the Holocaust: Competing Sites of Memory and Representation* (Mahwah, NJ: Lawrence Erlbaum Associates, 2001).

Nora, P. (1989) 'Between Memory and History: Les Lieux de Mémoire', *Representations*, 26 Special Issue: Memory and Counter-Memory (Spring), 7–24.

Pollock, G. (2011) *Allo-Thanatography or Allo-Auto-Biography: A Few Thoughts on One Painting in Charlotte Salomon's 'Leben? oder Theater?', 1941/42* (Ostfildern: Hatje Cantz).

Prose, F. (2010) *Anne Frank: The Book, the Life, the Afterlife* (London: Atlantic Books).

Rosenbaum, R. (1998) *Explaining Hitler* (London: Macmillan, 1998)

Rotzoll, M. (2011) 'The Nazi Patient killing "Aktion T4"', paper given at 'Science, Medicine and the Holocaust: Recent Research and Memorial Practices in Germany', Wiener Library, 21 October.
Rupnow, Dirk. (2012) 'The Invisible Crime: Nazi Politics of Memory and Postwar Representation of the Holocaust', in D. Stone (ed.) *The Holocaust and Historical Methodology* (Oxford: Berghahn Books).
Stone, D. (2012) Introduction, *The Holocaust and Historical Methodology* (Oxford: Berghahn Books).
de Waal, E. (2007) *The Hare With Amber Eyes* (London: Vintage).
White, H. (1978) *Tropics of Discourse: Essays in Cultural Criticism* (Baltimore: The Johns Hopkins University Press).
Wilkomirski, B. (1996) *Fragments* (London: Picador).
Williams, R. (1986) *The Long Revolution* (London: Penguin).
Young, J. (1988) *Writing and Rewriting the Holocaust* (Bloomington: Indiana University Press).
Young, J. (1993) *The Texture of Memory* (New Haven: Yale University Press).

5
What Remains – Genocide and Things

Ulrike Kistner

Walter Benjamin on his work on *The Arcades Project:*

> Method of this project: literary montage. I needn't *say* anything. Merely show. I shall purloin no valuables, appropriate no ingenious formulations. But the rags, the refuse – these I will not inventory but allow, in the only way possible, to come into their own: by making use of them.
>
> (1999c, p. 460)

A key
A comb
A fork, a spoon
A razor handle
A mug handle
The bottom of a pot
The base of a bottle
A pair of tongs and a spoon
A pair of scissors
An enamel mug
An enamel pot
The base of a beer bottle
A beer bottle top
Medicine bottles – (Figure 5.1–5.17)

Equipment (*Zeug*) that is put to use to particular effect, that serves a purpose, is embedded in a network of arrangements and actions (Heidegger, 1953, p. 83).

A key – to open which door enclosing a household left behind, to which room housing personal belongings or other household items and

105

Figure 5.1–17 Photographs of material remains at Auschwitz-Birkenau taken by Ulrike Kistner.

Figure 5.2

Figure 5.3

Figure 5.4

Figure 5.5

Figure 5.6

Figure 5.7

Figure 5.8

Figure 5.9

Figure 5.10

Figure 5.11

Figure 5.12

Figure 5.13

Figure 5.14

Figure 5.15

Figure 5.16

Figure 5.17

valuable objects? A key – possibly from the camp's metal workshop, also site of a resistance group, for gaining access to locked offices, sorting barracks and rooms storing food and medical supplies.

Comb and razor, a bottle of shaving lotion or perfume – for personal grooming. Enhancing one's personal appearance, soliciting respect from others, means moving along the permeable boundary separating the drowned from the saved, improving the chance of getting past the selections, therefore a matter of survival.

Fork, knife, spoon, pot, plate, mug, cup – eating utensils – are vital means of subsistence left up to the prisoners, stripped of all personal belongings, to *organize* for themselves. For without pot or bowl, without plate, mug or cup, there is no way of receiving the daily ration of soup, which, together with bread, forms the staple in the camp.[1] Tongs, scissors, knife – utensils that can restore given, found and appropriated objects for renewed use or modify them to different ends. Pending the availability of *organized* goods and materials, they are put to use in the limited manufacture of other objects which in turn are useful in being exchangeable for foodstuffs, either for one's own consumption or for purposes of further exchange for other objects;[2] also for purposes of resistance, especially in preparation for the Sonderkommando uprising of October 1944.

Beer and medicine bottles: pure luxuries. Personal belongings are confiscated from deportees on their arrival. Clamouring for such wares are mainly SS personnel, Sonderkommando members and Kapos, and the *Lager Prominenz*. Medicines, in demand from all sides, are taken from prisoners by SS personnel. The few medicines circulating in the camp enter either the labyrinths of barter or the limited medical care administered to sick prisoners by medical doctors, orderlies and assistants, on whose organizing capacity the sparse equipment and supplies for medical treatment depend (Setkiewicz, 2008, pp. 149–151, 228–229).

The network of arrangements and actions surrounding this 'stuff' (*Zeug*) – its use, expropriation, re-use and disposal – stretches across the whole of Europe: an imprint at the base of a pot names the town of Bielsko in Poland as its place of manufacture; the plug of a bottle, filled and sealed in 1936, reveals as its place of origin the town of Satu-Mare, Apa, Hungary (close to the Romanian border); a bottle is marked with the date of 1937 and with the brand of export beer from Italy.

Rather than expressing any stable use value, any determinate purpose, any sense of personal belonging, any claim to possession, any point of origin or destination, the network of transactions surrounding these objects is characterized by theft, robbery, misappropriation, smuggling and barter. At their source, these objects are snatched in danger-defying forays, through bribing guards, initiating contact with persons and middle men who, in their turn, take calculated risks in entering the spoils into further circuits of exchange feeding the systematically deregulated market with ill-gotten gains (Langbein, 2004, p. 134). Every favour, concession and exemption from threatening actions on the part of functionaries and orderlies exacts its price in payments of bribes or services on the part of camp inmates whose struggle for preservation of life and limb at that moment puts them at the mercy of those who at that moment emerge as their superiors.

Strictly guarded and severely punishable, robbery, theft and illicit transactions involving pilfered goods are nevertheless positively sanctioned, in an implicit acknowledgement of their role in providing for basic needs and in drawing the lines of social distinction on which camp social life turns. Goods and services, concessions and exemptions obtained through illicit transactions create limited possibilities of social mobility within a fixed ranking system – through relative gain or loss of prestige and status according to the capacity to seize opportunities as they arise, to take risks and *'organize'* (Levi, 1987, pp. 83–92); and according to the relative capacity to withstand hunger, hardship, misery, illness and desperation.

On arrival, deportees had to hand in everything they had brought along on the trip to an unknown destination – clothes, food, utensils, tools, medication, personal belongings and valuables; in return for the latter, they were sometimes granted a few items of clothing (Langbein, 2004, p. 138).[3] Some were promised non-specified compensation at a later date (Strzelecki, 2000, p. 10). But promises, agreements and all manner of symbolic exchanges, turn out to be meaningless; not grounded in any form of consensus, they do not carry any socially or legally binding force. In a levelling operation that reduces the means of payment in their role of general equivalents to the function of bartering for the necessities of life, transactions reported by survivors include a diamond ring for a few sips of water, a diamond for an apple (Langbein, 2004, p. 138), a winter coat for bread, a wedding dress and ring for bread (Browning, 2010, p. 161)[4] Transactions of this nature are doubly incommensurable: while giving practical expression, literally, to the 'diamond-water paradox' of classical political economy,[5] they level the incomparability between two kinds of values (utility and value in exchange), raising another imponderability: that of the demise of the work of culture in a context of commoditization and alienability without remainder.[6]

Scheduled at more or less regular intervals was a random change of clothes (*Wäschetauschen*): an exchange of underwear worn for at least two weeks for a disinfected set of underwear piled up in heaps of clothes collected from prisoners on arrival. Any further shirts were obtainable only through bartering transactions in exchange for rations of bread and soup obtained from starving inmates who gave their only shirt, their last belongings, for half a ration of bread.

On the black market, foodstuffs pilfered from kitchens and store rooms – turnips, carrots and potatoes – were offered to prisoners in exchange for the last of their meagre possessions. Foodstuffs also entered the black market from outside of the camp, mostly through barter of valuables which prisoners had painstakingly saved from theft and confiscation. Circuits of exchange terminated through consumption of foodstuffs leave no cultural or social traces, thus failing to create lasting values. Consuming the necessities of life is devoid of merit, except in comparison with those who do not attain the subsistence minimum (Veblen, 2000, p. 103).[7]

Jewellery, valuables, clothes and household utensils – as objects marking social distinctions – are out of reach for most inmates after their deportation and imprisonment, while vital food rations obtainable only under harshest sanctions are devoid of any social, world-forming and cultural value.

Any prospect of determining and regulating exchange values through money as general equivalent was rendered out of sight. In the autumn of 1943, a scrip system was introduced, allegedly to award bonuses in recognition of special effort. When the purported incentives failed to produce the desired effect, the coupons were distributed 'in small amounts and at utterly capricious ratios' (Kogon, 2006, p. 122). The few coupons in circulation could be exchanged for different foodstuffs in continuously fluctuating supply, quantity and quality.

Three or four bread rations, on average, were obtainable in exchange for one's own gold teeth, whose repeated exchange afforded the less hungry new owner of the gold at least 20 bread rations in turn. One kilogram of gold was requisitioned, in one recorded case, for sparing a human life (Browning, 2010, p. 211).

Contraband forms the currency of illicit deals. Exchange transactions are based on misappropriation, robbery, theft, smuggling and extortion. Hard currency taken away from prisoners is deposited quarterly, in accordance with regulations, into a special account of the Administration of Concentration Camps within the SS-Economic Administration Head Office (SS-WVHA) (Strzelecki, 2000, p. 10). Conditions in the camp render smuggling and organizing activities necessary for survival; yet being caught at it incurs heavy penalties.[8]

Inmates admitted to the infirmary are stripped of their last belongings. Orderlies grab clothes and shoes of those separated out in selections and they barter the few precious medicines on the black market for food items. Nurses swop spoons from the patients for any other desirable items.

Complex, all-round exchanges, in relations of value devoid of any proportionality, symmetry or equivalence – incommensurate, irregular, arbitrary, momentary and contingent, in continuous motion and subject to continuous fluctuations in supply, demand, quality, quantity, price and value. Everything is subject to continuous valuation, devaluation and revaluation.

Clothes are searched for valuables sewn into seams, pockets, belts and collars; then sorted, bundled and distributed to SS personnel, to ethnic Germans or industrial workers, or channelled into the Reich. Worn clothes are stitched, patched, repaired and issued for re-use or sent as rags to the Reich textile industry for reconditioning and recycling (Strzelecki, 2000, pp. 11–12, 34). Alcohol, preserves, cocoa and chocolate are stored for consumption by the SS (Strzelecki, 2000, p. 32). Jewellery, valuables and valuta are dispatched, first to the relevant camp authorities, then to Office D KZ: Concentration camp administration (*Amtsgruppe D*), and finally, in the last instance, to the Reichsbank.

Full utilization of every object, without remainder, is considered imperative. Nothing may be left to disintegration and dissolution; nothing may be wasted. Everything has to be used, repaired, re-fitted, re-conditioned and re-used.[9] Everything is alienable, nothing remains inalienable: no trace of the person of the owner or user is left on the object. In general exchangeability without remainder, all personal, affective and cultural investments in objects once held to be inalieanable, are destroyed – and with them any continuity, tradition and symbolic-cultural value once materialized in those objects.[10]

All objects entering into circuits of exchange – even those originally highly valued for their symbolic or aesthetic qualities – attain the character of depersonalized commodities; the possibility of gifts forming, expressing and maintaining social relationality is excluded. Under these conditions, 'many social habits and instincts are reduced to silence' (Levi, 2004, p. 93).

Among the camp inmates, a certain measure of mutual support is vitally necessary and yet beset with great danger. Values conducive to reciprocity and reliable communication are systematically undercut and destroyed. Showing solidarity, developing trust, expressing gratitude means engaging in risky business.[11]

Destructive impulses, on the other hand, find favourable conditions in camp life. Not 'beyond good and evil', but 'this side of good and evil' is where Primo Levi (1987, p. 92) situates this hell:

> We [...] invite the reader to contemplate the possible meaning in the Lager of the words 'good' and 'evil', 'just' and 'unjust'; let everybody judge, on the basis of the picture we have outlined and of the examples given above, how much of our ordinary moral world could survive on this side of the barbed wire.

The history of an object circulating under these conditions does not involve social relations and networks, but atoms emerging from dissolute, destroyed sociality.

While the camp is tightly enclosed and fenced off, locked-up and guarded, the relations spanning it from one end to the other, are not entirely separated from surrounding networks. Barter is not an isolated economic system of exchange characterizing the camp internally; rather, it forms an element in the economic and political systematicity of the Nazi regime, and that of the occupied territories in particular, in so far as they are enjoined to bear the costs of their occupation (Gross, 1979, p. 46).

The economies of the occupied territories were subordinated to the economy of the German Reich. Enterprises in the occupied territories were required to meet the Reich's demand for consumer goods, foodstuffs, raw materials, compulsory labour and other services. The occupation subjected them to dispossession of freehold land and of state-owned assets and enterprises, closure of industries perceived to be in competition with German interests, mandatory payments of dividends and profits to the currency bank and other corporations of the occupying force, and arbitrary fixing of exchange rates (Neumann, 2009, pp. 179, 181–182) – with disastrous social and economic consequences for the inhabitants of the occupied territories, whose subsistence base was thereby eroded.

The Four-Year Plan promulgated in 1936 provided for price controls on basic foodstuffs, on agricultural and industrial products, and on transport of all kinds of goods. Price controls forced the closure of enterprises thereby rendered economically unviable, thus exacerbating shortages of consumer goods (Neumann, 2009, pp. 305–306). But the appearance of a regulated economy is deceptive. Centrally decreed price controls are not equivalent to limitations on market expansion and corruption. Quite the contrary: uncoordinated expansion and corruption become generalized (Neumann, 2009, p. 354):

> the basic correlations of prices undergo permanent changes, permanently adjust themselves to the permanently changing conditions of production and marketing. The visible general readjustment taking place in the market after a general slump within a competitive system is replaced under the totalitarian regime by a steady subterranean current of readjustments modifying the system of price equations through scarcely visible convulsions every hour and every minute. The market, instead of being abolished by regimentation, functions invisibly underground and maintains, within the framework of regimentation, legions of unco-ordinated economic decisions that scorn planning and control [...]. [I]t is precisely the incessant excess of

demand over supply that provides a powerful stimulus for expansion and higher profits. This is the motivating force of the National Socialist economy.

(Neumann, 2009, pp. 314)

Irregular business practices became widespread to the extent that businesses were forced to cut their deals on and through the black market. Severe limitations or proscriptions on the free exchange of information and commodities, tight circumscription of economic exchanges in certain locations (e.g. the ghettos) and disruptions in supplies created conditions conducive to speculation, profiteering and arbitrary price determinations (Gross, 1979, pp. 109, 111–112). Pervading all economic transactions under Nazi occupation were deregulated forms of exchange, illicit deals and corruption. Corruption flourished in the absence of socially regulating and mediating instances, institutions and norms (Gross, 1979, pp. 148, 154).

The influx into the camp's informal market of goods obtained through theft, robbery and plunder becomes palpable in the availability and variety of goods, the speed of their circulation, and inflationary and deflationary tendencies in price determinations. Delegation to outside work commandos becomes an attraction to the extent that it holds out the possibility of limited contact with the outside world and with it the possibility of obtaining goods, passing on information and engaging in all manner of organizing.

What does a relational network integrally tying human lives and objects together in formless, indeterminate, ever moving and changing relations mean for the broader context of sociality, constituted through culturally significant actions, affective relations and political reference points? Reflecting on this question, Franz Neumann (2009, p. 524) lists some factors: terror; an economy characterized by predatory expansion; the destruction of institutions and organizations; the proscription of civic initiative, of interest groups and political parties; and the atomization of all human relations.

Confronted by such conditions, historians, anthropologists, sociologists, political scientists and philosophers hit the limits of their theorizations and explanations. For Franz Neumann (2009, p. 386), national-socialist totalitarianism destroys all human relations within the arena of economic and social exchanges. The remaining transactions escape conceptualization. A 'natural' economy with fortuitous barter, so Marcel Mauss tells us, has never determined a form of sociality (1969, pp. 3, 80–81). If at all, a limited form of barter occurs only between absolute strangers or potential enemies (Graeber, 2001, pp. 153–154).

A society in which all goods are held to be utilizable without remainder, and reducible to alienable (non-)possessions, in which everything can be exchanged for everything else, is humanly and culturally unthinkable, according to anthropologist Igor Kopytoff (1986, p. 70).[12] It would exclude the very possibility of commonly held values or valorizations, thus annihilating pivotal functions in the constitution of culture and society. Things thus fall to what is rendered invisible in the process of enculturation. Cast aside as 'dirt-cheap', they are separated from the cultural matrix, leaving the universe of civilized things as 'refuse' (Böhme, 2006, p. 130).

Things valueless and useless, rusted, broken, full of holes, shards, fragments, scraps of metal (including remains of the extermination machinery), partly sorted in rubbish heaps, partly scattered all over the place. Things whose network of transactions has been untied, whose personal counterparts are no longer with us, whose value and distinction have evaporated, whose shelf life has long expired.

A traditional historiography, focused on historical actants, would have no place in theory for scattered inert material remains. From such perspective, history winds its course around humans acting on ahistorical nature and ahistorical inanimate objects (Latour, 2002, p. 190). In the absence of human actors, things lose historical significance and human interest.

To apprehend the relationship between objects and those who once held them, shaped them, coveted them, used them, held them back or gave them in exchange, we would have to break with traditional historiography of the above description. We would then recognize a chiastic change of positionality enacted by things in their after-life: while death renders humans indifferent from and to lifeless things, apparently lifeless things retain a trace of life, past and present. 'That is what makes things so uncanny and strange: not being given to dying' (Böhme, 2006, pp. 123, 124).

It is this uncanny persistence that explains the double anxiety of philosophers (as compared to the 'simple' inexplicability registered by anthropologists, political scientists, historians and sociologists). The thing stands as intransigent *factum* in relation to the concept. In this particular case, it does not lend itself to capture by categories of material culture or value, nor by categories of purpose or function; nor do the fields of action and relational networks in which it circulates, yield any explanation of determinate or inherent aim, end or purpose.

Confronted by the after-life of lifeless things devoid of any criteria for their categorization, devoid of value und function, extracted from their erstwhile networks of circulation through which they once did attain tenuous, precarious and unstable value and function, the theorist finds her- or himself at a loss. Historiography, anthropology, philosophy, sociology and political science tend to respond to such loss with reservation in the face of such facticity, and justifiably so, as any attempt to determine origin, function and destination of these things would be misdirected (Ebeling, 2008).

Searching for a way out of this *aporia* is a contemporary form of commemorative culture that dedicates itself to conservation, valorization and aesthetic presentation of select objects to be exempted from unkindly disposal. The obverse that is nevertheless integral to this commemorative labour, namely the degradation to waste, is excluded from the purview of memorialization; all other objects scattered on and around the ground of the site, and the site itself, are sacralized,[13] thus proscribing, countering or limiting historical inquiry, or re-directing it to ritualized commemorative practices, in the same move as that by which those objects are blithely being left to rot.

Instead, the museal custodians of history direct their diligence primarily at those objects that can singularly demonstrate a synecdochal relation to an implied overarching whole and thus fulfil an integrative function (Stockhammer, 2010, p. 86). It is through a search for totality and integrated unity that commemorative culture functionalizes the found objects in its own image, thus pre-forming a commemorative performativity. Most suitable for commemorative musealization are specific personal items, which are presented as representative of the fate of all victims, whose life histories are recreated in a totality unknown to themselves: suitcases marked with the names and places of residence of their owners, sometimes also with birth and deportation dates of individual prisoners, piled on top of one another; single shoes, each one bearing the imprint of an individual wearer, differing in size, shape, colour and degree of wear and tear, in a huge heap; spectacle frames of different forms, fitted for each individual user, in a dense tangle of wire.

Photo exhibitions piece together individual family histories and lineages, with the ambition of providing a complete picture.

Stations of suffering are marked and signposted, along a predetermined path retraced by the visitors to the site, led by expert guides.

The focus is on the mass victim in a focalization that solicits an inescapable identification based on a feeling of collective, inherited guilt, transmitted by language, the family telescoped across generations, the educational system and the media, rather than a sense of collective responsibility (Offe, 1997, p. 79).[14]

Conflictual social relations, forms of organization and material exchanges, differences and erasures in memory shared and divided, the relationship between determination and agency, between socially and geographically bounded spaces and interstices, between functionalization, refunctionalization and dysfunctionality, between valuations, devaluations and revaluations – all of these issues are largely bracketed, if not excluded, from commemorative musealization, thus foiling a struggle for understanding.

One possibility of reaching for understanding lies in the gaze of the empty-handed collector, the collector without aspiration to possession.[15] This is an important specification here, distinguishing the gaze of the collector as historical researcher, physiognomer of the world of things (Benjamin, 1991, p. 217), from the collector whose project is possession of a complete series of objects with the ambition to achieve systematic classification, causal connections and total integration (Arendt, 1999, pp. 48, 52; Baudrillard, 1996, pp. 86–87; Benjamin, 1991, p. 216). The gaze of the fragment-picking collector focused on the particular in an incommensurable relation to an intuition of the universal harbours the impetus of research – albeit one that the custodians of 'authenticity' in memory may consider sacrilegious. For the collector 'gathering fragments from the debris of the past' (Arendt, 1999, p. 50), things attain significance in their dispersal.

Remembrance fastens onto objects, especially fragmented, broken objects discredited and discarded. 'Without remembrance and without the reification which remembrance needs for its own fulfilment [...], the living activities of action, speech, and thought would lose their reality at the end of each process and disappear as though they never had been' (Arendt, 1957, p. 95). The thing-character of use values affords a sense of worldliness and worldliness becomes palpable through things. Things maintain a relation to the world that outlasts the lives of those who produced them (Arendt, 1957, p. 96). Thus divested of use, they speak of social relations, even and precisely as they lose definition and function of what they once were.

In assembling and juxtaposing things, the collector develops a sense for their arrangement, which raises further questions and contradictions, reveals hitherto invisible connections and interactions. The collector seeks to grasp not only the object, but also its past which would account for the process of its formation (Benjamin, 1991b, p. 217). But it is not simply an inert past that the collector is intent on preserving; collecting circumscribes a past marked by discontinuities.

Material objects act as conduits of past lives and their arrangement provides a glimpse of their transformations and transitions. Material objects act as carriers of what Benjamin, along with Proust, calls 'involuntary memory' in confrontation with 'voluntary memory' – memory 'in service of the intellect' (Benjamin, 1999a, p. 154), which fails Proust's narrator until it is presented by some material object 'though we have no idea which one it is' (p. 155). Mindfully distant from involuntary memory embedding experience (*Erfahrung*) that is yet lost to the memory that seeks retain it (p. 184), the collector brings to light the historicity of things – where the relation between the particular and the universal is held in suspension as that which has been irretrievably lost, yet not given up.

Illuminating the affinities of things, the collector can trace their placement in time and thus gather them up for a lesson in history – albeit not a conventional one. To the gaze of the collector corresponds a historiography which tears the historical object from the continuities imposed on it (Benjamin, 1991a, p. 595), strips it bare and shows it in interstices and switched circuits. She or he reads what has been thrown together in a rhetorical location between synecdoche (which thinks the part together with the allusion to an implied whole) and metonymy (the switching of the name to another of what is enunciated) (Stockhammer, 2010, p. 85).

The collector Walter Benjamin (1991a, p. 275) shows a particular interest for what has gone to pieces, what has been abandoned and rejected – not in order to re-assemble and reconstitute it in its past honour, but in order to 'make history from the refuse of history' (1972, p. 218). He wishes to confront cultural history with it, while saving it from a tradition 'which is catastrophe' (1999c, p. 472):

> An object of history is that through which knowledge is constituted as the object's rescue. (p. 476) [...] What are phenomena rescued from? Not only, and not in the main, from the discredit and neglect into which they have fallen, but from the catastrophe represented very often by a certain strain in their dissemination, their 'enshrinement as heritage.' (p. 472) [...] To the process of rescue belongs the firm, seemingly brutal grasp.
>
> (p. 472)

The grasp of the collector is a destructive, decontextualizing one:

> The present determines where, in the object from the past, that object's forehistory and after-history diverge so as to circumscribe its

nucleus. (p. 476) [...] It is the inherent tendency of dialectical experience to dissipate the semblance of eternal sameness, and even of repetition, in history. Authentic political experience is absolutely free of this semblance.

(p. 472)

Rendering things and their arrangements palpable in their worldliness, even in their destroyed worldliness, the gaze of the collector becomes a task[16] – that of holding practical remembrance up to political judgement.

Notes

The reflections collected in this chapter emerge from research carried out together with Anthony Court whose insights, contributed to discussions in the course of writing, I would herewith like to acknowledge with gratitude.

1. Primo Levi describes the manufacture of these vitally important utensils:

    > The Lager does not provide the new arrivals with spoons, although the semi-liquid soup cannot be consumed without them. The spoons are manufactured in Buna, secretly and in their spare moments, by Häftlinge who work as specialists in the iron and tin-smith Kommandos: they are rough and clumsy tools, shaped from iron-plate worked by hammer, often with a sharp handle-edge to serve at the same time as a knife to cut the bread.
    >
    > (1987, pp. 100–101)

2. Christopher Browning mentions such handiwork:

    > The skilled craftsmen...produced not only high-quality customized products for the Germans on demand but also an array of consumer goods for sale to Poles on the black market. To be effective, this operation needed not only craftsmen but large numbers of scroungers to keep the craftsmen supplied with raw materials and smugglers to transport and sell the finished products.
    >
    > (2010, p. 165)

3. This and other expropriations were legally enshrined: German Jews living outside of the borders of the Reich were denationalized. The same amendment to the Reich Citizenship Act of 1935, which was promulgated on 25 November 1941, decreed the confiscation of property of those who were thus denationalized. This pertained especially to denationalized German Jews who were deported to the East. A further decree issued by the Business Administration Main Office (WVHA) on 7 January 1943 ordered the confiscation of all goods left behind by Jews, Poles and Soviet citizens (Strzelecki, 2000, pp. 19, 10).
4. A more radical revaluation and destruction of all values is hard to imagine: sacred, aesthetic and tradition-bound objects are degraded to commodities

and set into continuous circulation. In the process, socially and culturally drawn distinctions between different circuits of exchange and valuation are levelled, destroying the material bearers of culturally efficacious symbolic actions, along with tradition and cultural memory, and with it any socially consolidating and sustaining valuations.
5. The 'diamond-water' relation (arguably styled into a paradox by adepts of marginal utility theory; see White, 2002, pp. 660–661, 668), on which the distinction between use value and exchange value becomes inscribed, is characterized by Adam Smith as a 'frequently' inverse relation (*An Inquiry into the Nature and Causes of the Wealth of Nations*):

> What are the rules which men naturally observe in exchanging them [goods] for money or for one another, I shall now proceed to examine. These rules determine what may be called the relative or exchangeable value of goods. The word VALUE, it is to be observed, has two different meanings, and sometimes expresses the utility of some particular object, and sometimes the power of purchasing other goods which the possession of that object conveys. The one may be called 'value in use;' the other, 'value in exchange'. The things which have the greatest value in use have frequently little or no value in exchange; on the contrary, those which have the greatest value in exchange have frequently little or no value in use. Nothing is more useful than water: but it will purchase scarce anything; scarce anything can be had in exchange for it. A diamond, on the contrary, has scarce any use-value; but a very great quantity of other goods may frequently be had in exchange for it.
>
> (1976, pp. 44–45)

6. See n. 12
7. Anette Weiner extends this point:

> Of all objects [...], food is the most ineffectual inalienable possession because its biological function is to release energy rather than store it. Therefore, in its use to humans, food changes, deteriorates, or perishes. So significant is this loss to those without extensive durable things that, in some cases, attempts are made to transform food into more permanent words or things.
>
> (1992, p. 38)

See also Hannah Arendt:

> The least durable of tangible things are those needed for the life process itself. Their consumption barely survives the act of their production; in the words of Locke, all those 'good things' which are 'really useful to the life of man,' to the 'necessity of subsisting,' are 'generally of short duration, such as – if they are not consumed by use – will decay and perish by themselves.' After a brief stay in the world, they return into the natural process which yielded them either through absorption into the life process of the human animal or through decay; in their man-made shape, through which they acquired their ephemeral place in the world of manmade things, they disappear more quickly than any other part of

the world. Considered in their worldliness, they are the least worldly and at the same time the most natural of all things.

(1957, p. 96)

8. Examples are adduced by Hermann Langbein, who also refers to Primo Levi's elaborations: buttons on the clothes of prisoners, polished shoes, mended clothes, clean walls in barracks, wash rooms and infirmary were required to pass strict controls. The utensils, buttons, shoe polish and paint to meet these requirements of cleanliness and orderliness were, however, not freely available and had to be *organized* by the prisoners themselves in exchange for their food rations (Langbein, 2004, p. 134).

9. This is illustrated by a report of SS-Hauptsturmführer Kersten of November 1944. Indignant at the sight of the 'rubbishing' of items of clothing and textiles, he orders the surveillance of the handling of clothes in the camp.

> Rubbish removal is a special chapter. It turns out that all kinds of textiles are thrown into the rubbish bin and land on a compost heap outside the camp. This practice is still going on as we speak

(Qtd. in Strzelecki, 2000, p. 45).

(This and all further translations from the German in this essay are mine.)

10. Anette Weiner elaborates the concept of inalienability:

> Inalienable possessions are imbued with affective qualities that are expressions of the value an object has when it is kept by its owners and inherited within the same family or descent group. Age adds value, as does the ability to keep the object against all the exigencies that might force a person or a group to release it to others. The primary value of inalienability, however, is expressed through the power these objects have to define who one is in a historical sense. The object acts as a vehicle for bringing past time into the present, so that the histories of ancestors, titles, or mythological events become an intimate part of a person's present identity.

(1992, pp. 22–23)

> What makes a possession inalienable is its exclusive and cumulative identity with a particular series of owners through time. Its history is authenticated by fictive or true genealogies, origin myths, sacred ancestors, and gods. In this way, inalienable possessions are transcendent treasures to be guarded against the exigencies that might force their loss.

(1992, p. 33)

All the more significant are the attempts on the part of Sonderkommando members to withdraw from circulation the belongings of the prisoners passing through their hands. Withholding these objects, even burying them, means withdrawing them from continuous, interminable trafficking and bartering, rendering them inalienable, and thereby bestowing new value on them – the value of testimony, of transmitting signs to posterity, of commemorating (Bezwińska et al, 1996).

Other attempts to withdraw valuables from circulation and thereby bestow renewed value on them could be considered acts of resistance. This is how ex-prisoner Kitty Hart sees it:

> Even though being caught in the possession of such things was punishable by death, my three friends and myself never turned anything of value in. We'd rather use bank notes for toilet paper. We buried boxes with gold and valuables. We used every opportunity to hand such things over to male prisoners with whom we could get into contact. They in turn had contact with the underground movement outside of the camp, and handed the valuables to them. We were hoping that they could use the items of value to obtain arms and ammunition for a future uprising.
>
> (Qtd. in Strzelecki, 2000, p. 36)

11. Mietek Pemper (2005, p. 84) relates his experience of enforced thanklessness in Płaszów concentration camp: one could, he says, neither expect nor show gratitude.

12. Igor Kopytoff explains:

    > if the homogenizing process is carried too far and the perceived world begins to approach too closely [...] utter commoditization – culture's function of cognitive discrimination is undermined.
    >
    > (1986, p. 70)

    > In the sense that commoditization homogenizes value, while the essence of culture is discrimination, excessive commoditization is anticultural [.]
    >
    > (p. 73)

13. The overarching importance accorded to 'conservation' of the 'authenticity' of the Memorial of Auschwitz (to which about 4 million Euro are dedicated per annum) is authorized by reference to the need 'to protect it from profanation and deliberate destruction' (Cywiński, 2009, p. 5). Jarosław Mensfelt, spokesperson for the state-run Auschwitz Museum and Memorial, comments on the arrest of a visitor who took a piece of barbed wire from the memorial site: 'This was an act of desecration of a place of memory. Every object here is priceless' (Anon, 2011).

14. Offe concludes her critique with a caution and a postulate:

    > In fact, collective memory of the Holocaust might force upon those who remember (the descendants of the perpetrators) and those who are remembered (the victims) the very relationship it strives to overcome: a circularity that reproduces a homogenizing, mutually exclusive notion of identity as it was used by the perpetrators of the past to stigmatize the victims. But if collective memory is seen as a necessary basis for the reassertion of universal norms and democratic institutions, then this very circularity has to be broken.
    >
    > (1997, p. 80)

15. See Benjamin's method stated in the epigraph.

16. Calling it a 'task' calls to mind the 'Task of the Translator' (*Die Aufgabe des Übersetzers*) in a double sense of the verb *aufgeben*. It involves, among others, *Aufgeben* of any notions of authenticity, originality, accuracy, fidelity and preservation, to yield the *Aufgabe* of an interlinearity, 'in which literalness and freedom are united' (Benjamin, 1999b, p. 82).

Works cited

Anon (2011) 'Frenchman Arrested for Stealing Barbed Wire from Auschwitz', *Herald Sun*, 20 May [online] Available at <http://www.heraldsun.com.au/news/breaking-news/frenchman-arrested-for-stealing-barbed-wire-from-auschwitz/story-e6frf7jx-1226060009689> [accessed 3 December 2012].

Arendt, H. (1957) *The Human Condition* (Chicago & London: University of Chicago Press).

Arendt, H. (1999) 'Introduction', in W. Benjamin, *Illuminations* (London: Pimlico), pp. 7–58.

Baudrillard, J. (1996) *The System of Objects*, J. Benedict (trans.) (London and New York: Verso).

Benjamin, W. (1991) 'Lob der Puppe', in H. Tiedemann-Bartels (ed.) *Kritiken und Rezensionen* (*Gesammelte Schriften*, vol. III) (Frankfurt a.M.: Suhrkamp), pp. 213–218.

Benjamin, W. (1999a) 'On Some Motifs in Baudelaire', in *Illuminations*, H. Zohn (trans.) (London: Pimlico), pp. 152–196.

Benjamin, W. (1999b) 'The Task of the Translator', in *Illuminations*, H. Zohn (trans.) (London: Pimlico), pp. 70–82.

Benjamin, W. (1999c) *The Arcades Project*, H. Eiland & K. McLaughlin (trans.) (Cambridge, MA & London: The Belknap Press of Harvard University Press).

Bezwińska, J. & Czech, D. (eds.) (1996) *Inmitten des grauenvollen Verbrechens: Handschriften von Mitgliedern des Sonderkommandos* (Oświęcim: Staatliches Museum Auschwitz-Birkenau).

Böhme, H. (2006) *Fetischismus und Kultur: Eine andere Theorie der Moderne* (Reinbek: Rowohlt).

Browning, C. (2010) *Remembering Survival: Inside a Nazi Slave-Labor Camp* (New York & London: Norton).

Cywiński, P. (2009) 'Introduction', in *Report 2009: Memorial Auschwitz Birkenau State Museum*. (Oświęcim: Auschwitz-Birkenau State Museum), pp. 4–5.

Ebeling, K. 'Spiel/Zeug. Eine Archäologie des Homo ludens', Paper given at VII. Kongress der Deutschen Gesellschaft für Ästhetik: 'Ästhetik und Alltagserfahrung', Friedrich-Schiller-Universität, Jena, 29 September–2 October 2008. Available at <http://www.dgae.de/downloads/Knut_Ebeling.pdf>

Graeber, D. (2001) *Toward an Anthropological Theory of Value: The False Coin of Our Own Dreams* (London: Palgrave Macmillan).

Gross, J. (1979) *Polish Society Under German Occupation: The Generalgouvernement 1939–1944* (Princeton: Princeton University Press).

Heidegger, M. (1953) *Sein und Zeit*, 7th ed. (Tübingen: Max Niemeyer Verlag).

Kogon, E. (2006) *The Theory and Practice of Hell: The German Concentration Camps and the System Behind Them*, Heinz Norden (trans.) (New York: Farrar, Straus & Giroux).

Kopytoff, I. (1984) 'The Cultural Biography of Things: Commoditization as Process', in *The Social Life of Things: Commodities in Cultural Perspective* (New York: Cambridge University Press), pp. 64–91.

Langbein, H. (2004) *People in Auschwitz*, H. Zohn (trans.) (Chapel Hill & London: University of North Carolina Press).

Latour, B. (2002) *Die Hoffnung der Pandora: Untersuchungen zur Wirklichkeit der Wissenschaft*, G. Rossler (trans.) (Frankfurt a.M.: Suhrkamp Verlag).

Levi, P. (2004) *If This is a Man and The Truce*, S. Woolf (trans.) (London: Abacus).

Mauss, M. (1969) *The Gift: Forms and Functions of Exchange in Archaic Societies*, I. Cunnison (trans.) (London: Routledge & Kegan Paul)

Neumann, F. (2009) *Behemoth: The Structure and Practice of National Socialism, 1933–1944* (Chicago: Ivan R. Dee, in association with the USHMM).

Offe, S. (1997) 'Sites of Remembrance? Jewish Museums in Contemporary Germany', *Jewish Social Studies*, n. 3:2 (Winter), 77–89. Available at <http://www.jstor.org/stable/4467497> [accessed: 20 June 2011].

Pemper, M. (2005) *Der rettende Weg: Schindlers Liste: Die wahre Geschichte* (Hamburg: Hoffmann & Campe).

Setkiewicz, P. (2008) *The Histories of Auschwitz IG Farben Werk Camps 1941–1945* (Oświęcim: Auschwitz-Birkenau State Museum).

Smith, A. (1976) *An Inquiry into the Nature and Causes of the Wealth of Nations*, vol. 1 (1776), in P. Campbell, A. Skinner, & W. Todd (ed.) (Oxford: Oxford University Press)

Strzelecki, A. (2000) 'Der Raub des Besitzes der Opfer des KL Auschwitz', in *Hefte von Auschwitz* 21, 7–99.

Veblen, T. (2000) *Theorie der feinen Leute: Eine ökonomische Untersuchung*, 6th ed. (Frankfurt a.M.: Fischer).

Weiner, A. (1992) *Inalienable Possessions: The Paradox of Keeping-While-Giving* (Berkeley, LA & Oxford: University of California Press).

White, M. (2002) 'Doctoring Adam Smith: The Fable of the Diamonds and Water Paradox', *History of Political Economy*, 34:4 (December), 659–684.

6
Representing the Einsatzgruppen: The Outtakes of Claude Lanzmann's *Shoah*

Sue Vice

In this chapter, I will ask why literary and filmic representations of the wartime Einsatzgruppen are so much less common than those of the other experiences of the Holocaust years, such as living in hiding or in ghettos, and imprisonment in concentration and death camps. In an attempt to answer this question, I will consider whether Claude Lanzmann's reasons for excluding two Einsatzgruppen interviews from *Shoah* are justified on aesthetic and pragmatic grounds, and whether they possess a wider applicability.

Claude Lanzmann has often expressed regret in interviews and in his autobiography that he was not able to include in his 1985 film *Shoah* an interview with anyone from the wartime Einsatzgruppen units. These were the mobile security squads that followed in the wake of the invading Wehrmacht units to protect their security during the invasion of the Soviet Union and were responsible for the deaths of 1.4 million Jews and others, including Roma, the mentally ill, partisans and Soviet officials (Angrick, 2008, p. 78). Indeed, in his autobiography Lanzmann observes that he wanted one of the Einsatzgruppen leaders in his film 'at any cost' ('*à tout prix*') (2009, p. 477).[1] However, despite the fact that lack of material is often given as a reason for this absence, Lanzmann did track down and secretly film the former Einsatzgruppen members Heinz Schubert and Karl Kretschmer during a visit to Germany in 1976, and the cost of the effort alone turned out to be a significant personal and aesthetic one. Commentators mention the fact that Lanzmann's quest to interview former Einsatzgruppen members was not only fruitless but dangerous, since in the case of Heinz Schubert he was badly beaten by the man's family; remarkably, the footage of this interview was not lost and the prelude to the assault was itself recorded.[2]

The 'Holocaust by bullets'

Both the total number of victims and the methods of killing, which were characterized by what the historian Andrej Angrick calls the 'abandon[ment] of all civilised reservations' (2008, p. 79), are striking features of the Einsatzgruppen murders; indeed, it was partly because of concerns about the psychological toll taken on the killers, who shot at close quarters civilians including women and children, that other, more 'impersonal' methods of mass murder, such as killing by gas vans and then gas chambers, were developed. The activities of the Einsatzgruppen as part of Operation Barbarossa, the invasion of the Soviet Union, are seen as a 'watershed' in Nazi racial policy and its escalation into genocide (Earl, 2010, p. 8); and the legal defences of the Einsatzgruppen leaders mounted at their 1947 trial at Nuremberg turned on just the kinds of bathetic excuse that Lanzmann must have hoped to draw out in interview: that of superior orders, including those allegedly from Hitler; ignorance of the murders; having committed fewer murders than the prosecution claimed; military necessity, including the belief that all the Jews were saboteurs or Bolsheviks who had to be killed for the sake of German self-defence; that it was better to shoot the victims than risk their starvation; or that the massacres were conducted in a 'humane' manner.

The 'Holocaust by bullets' with its 1.4 million victims was perpetrated in the occupied Soviet Union, particularly Ukraine and Byelorussia, and the Baltic States, by four Einsatzgruppen detachments, often assisted by other SS units and local auxiliaries, between 1941 and 1942. This has been described as the 'ignored reality' of the Holocaust (Snyder, 2009),[3] since more has been heard from and known about the fate of Western European Jews, although recent work has helped to reverse this trend.[4] As Timothy Snyder argues, the numbers killed in the Soviet Union in these brutal, public mass shootings over two years are equal to the number of those murdered at Auschwitz, yet it is the latter that has come to be seen as 'an adequate or even a final symbol of the evil of mass killing' (Snyder, 2009, p. 14). Although *Shoah* does include aspects of the Holocaust other than Auschwitz, particularly the Operation Reinhard death camps, including Bełżec, Sobibór and Chełmno, where over 1.5 million Jews were killed in 1942–1943, it is only in the outtakes of the film that the absence of any interviews with those connected to the 'Holocaust by bullets' is made good. It was not until after what Lanzmann calls the 'Einsatzgruppen fiasco' – his failure to secure a fully-fledged interview with a perpetrator – that he tried to interview a survivor.

Although he succeeded in tracking down Rivka Yossilevska, who had survived an Einsatzgruppen *aktion*, at her home in Israel, she refused to be filmed (Lanzmann, 2009, p. 485). However, the focus on perpetrators pre-existed Lanzmann's interest in the Einsatzgruppen, since under the pseudonym of 'Dr Claude Marie Sorel' he sought interviews with former Nazis who had held a variety of roles, and it is not only the rarity of survivors of these mass killings that led to their absence from *Shoah*.

Secret filming and *Shoah*'s outtakes

Lanzmann has described his regret at the necessity to exclude from *Shoah* material from the 250 hours of extra footage, which includes what he calls 'magnificent things', as well as the more obviously dispensable 'silent shots, beginnings of interviews, things that were ruined' (Chevrie & Le Roux, 2007, p. 46). Yet the two fragments of Einsatzgruppen film fall into the former category rather than the latter, and their exclusion from *Shoah* must have been a hard decision, despite the fact that both are very short. It is hard to tell whether Schubert or Kretschmer, in their limited air time of, respectively, 99 and 44 minutes, is a 'character' of the kind Lanzmann chose to include in the final cut of *Shoah* and the opportunity for the 'resurrection' of the past that takes place in other interviews is necessarily limited.

These encounters are the preludes to fully fledged interviews. Lanzmann gets no further than Kretschmer's doorstep during their conversation, because the latter has builders in the house. In Schubert's case Lanzmann's pretence at discussing the possibility of an interview almost turns it into the early stages of the real thing. Both conversations were filmed secretly, using the microphone-sized paluche camera that became available in 1976 and was named after the French slang term for 'hand'. Instead of recording images on film, this camera contained a transmitter whose signal could be picked up within a small range by a magnetoscope, which would then record and retain the images (Lanzmann, 2009, p. 468). The Kretschmer footage is in colour and in three parts: a prefatory section in Lanzmann's hotel room; an initial conversation at which Lanzmann and Bernard Aubuoy, the sound-recordist, are present and which ends because Kretschmer goes back into his house; and a second conversation on the same day when Lanzmann returns to Kretschmer's home with his interpreter Corinna Coulmas. The first conversation is filmed by the paluche hidden in a bag positioned at ground level, resulting in low-level shots of Kretschmer from below. The second part is filmed from the VW van and shows clearly the difference between the accidental effects recorded by the paluche and the design of a cinematographer. By contrast, the footage of the Schubert encounter, like that in the secretly filmed interviews in *Shoah* with the perpetrators Franz Suchomel, Walter Stier and Franz Schalling, is of a grainy, flickering, black and white quality and includes frequent sections where either audio or the image disappears. The Schubert footage is shot from a static, although not always stable, position: the viewpoint itself never changes, but the bag containing the camera is moved around. There are no edited shots but a continuous stream of material in 11-minute sections.

Because of the technological constraints of the clandestine filming, which, as well as hiding the camera in a bag and the absence of a cinematographer, necessitated wiring up Lanzmann with a sound recorder, the mise-en-scène in both encounters seems to be outside the director's control. For instance, although we are aware of the presence of Heinz Schubert's wife throughout the conversation and hear her speaking, she can be seen only indistinctly; and in place of Lanzmann's customary presence in *Shoah*, his leg alone occasionally appears in view, depending on his movements and not those of the camera. The mise-en-scène is subject to constraint in both encounters. We see none of the tracking and panning shots for which *Shoah* is well known nor full close-ups. It might appear that the fixed paluche 'viewpoint' in the encounter with Schubert and some of that with Kretschmer constitutes a stark contrast to seeing the events of the Holocaust through the Nazis' lens, as we do in archive imagery. Here there is no human eye present at all. But the *effect* of a gaze, and one that judges and exposes, is nonetheless constructed by the paluche, accidental though the angle and set-up of its shots may be. It can only gesture towards the wish of critics such as Sandy Flitterman (1981, p. 245) who argue for a film-making that would 'render problematic the voyeuristic pleasures of cinema', whether these consist of the spectacle of femininity or Nazi atrocities. Rather, a counterpart to the Nazis' objectifying gaze is established and directed back at them. Despite the apparently impersonal nature of the paluche's filming, the exertion of directorial control is still possible and can be seen in such moments as Lanzmann's instruction to Coulmas to retrieve a 'precious document' from her bag, which Frau Schubert had just placed on the floor, so that he can ask Schubert about the defence he mounted at his trial – and also lift up the camera in its bag to focus once more on Schubert's face (Lanzmann, 2009, p. 480).[5]

In these instances of clandestine filming there seems to be no possibility of the kind of rehearsed and staged interview in a recreated setting that we see in *Shoah* in the case of Abraham Bomba, the barber from Treblinka, and Henryk Gawkowski, the former driver of trains to that camp, and, in the outtakes, in the case of Tadeusz Pankiewicz, who is interviewed wearing a white chemist's coat in what used to be the Cracow Ghetto pharmacy, where he was the only non-Jew living in the ghetto during the war. Even the minimalist staging in Suchomel's interview, in which Lanzmann provides the former guard with a pointer to indicate locations on a large wall map of Treblinka,[6] and in which the hiding place of the camera, and therefore the construction of the mise-en-scène, is stable and still, is necessarily absent from these Einsatzgruppen fragments. In the encounters with both Schubert and Kretschmer, Lanzmann speaks in German and, although Coulmas is present, she cannot, given the secret nature of the filming, fully take up her translator's role.

However, the very nature of the fragmentariness, and their tangential relation to the final version of the film, makes the two Einsatzgruppen interviews its crucial critical adjuncts. Some other sections of the outtake material have appeared separately in the three feature films Lanzmann has released since *Shoah*, two of which consist of footage from which there are no extracts in the film itself: *Un vivant qui passe: Auschwitz 1943, Theresienstadt 1944 (A Visitor from the Living* 1997), *Sobibór, 14 octobre 1943, 16 heures* (2001) and *The Karski Report* (2010), including more of Lanzmann's interview with the eponymous wartime Polish envoy. In these instances, and in the most recent example, *The Last of the Unjust* (2013), Lanzmann has issued films of single interviewees that give the viewer insight into the editing of *Shoah* itself, in which sustained interviews of this kind, for instance that with Simon Srebnik, are broken up and interspersed with others over the course of nine-and-a-half hours. In *Sobibór*, we hear from Yehuda Lerner about his part in the uprising at the Sobibór death camp, while in *Un vivant qui passe*, Lanzmann interviews Maurice Rossel, a Red Cross official who said of his visit to Theresienstadt that he must have seemed to the inmates like a 'visitor from the living', yet who declared conditions in the camp to be satisfactory. In *The Karski Report*, Karski describes his fruitless efforts during the war to convey to Roosevelt, and to the Supreme Court Associate Justice Felix Frankfurter, the enormity of the Jewish genocide to individuals who did not believe his words. The Einsatzgruppen films seem unlikely to have such separate release.

Although there are apparent reasons in both cases why none of the footage from the encounters with Schubert and Kretschmer appears in *Shoah*, and despite initial appearances that may suggest their dispensability, both are not only fascinating but also revelatory sequences. They show details of Lanzmann's method of clandestine filming and cast light on the foundational elements of *Shoah* itself, including such features as the exclusion of archive imagery, the staging of interviews, the importance of dialogue versus mise-en-scène, the construction of that mise-en-scène, Lanzmann's reliance on Raul Hilberg's *The Destruction of the European Jews*, which he has called his 'Bible', his performance as interviewer, and the imbrication of the past in the present. In both encounters, the disjunction between what we see in the mise-en-scène and the events of the past, to which viewers of *Shoah* will already be accustomed, takes place at an extreme pitch. We see Kretschmer and Schubert in the settings of mid-1970s German suburban life, outside the former's home and in the latter's living room. This can only emphasize the absence of any visible trace in these sequences of the actions that both men witnessed and undertook, as well as the comfortable post-war lives of these perpetrators. These domestic locations are far in place and time from the Crimea, where Schubert, as a member of Einsatzgruppe D, 'inspected' the murder of 1,400 people in December 1941; and Ukrainian towns such as Kursk and Zhytomyr, from which Kretschmer, as a member of Sonderkommando 4a from Einsatzgruppe C,[7] wrote letters home about taking part in mass shootings. It is easy to imagine a different filmmaker prefacing the Schubert and Kretschmer conversations with imagery of their deeds, to 'illustrate and validate' (Farr, 2005, p. 164) the interviews. Lanzmann's (1991, p. 99) famous statement, that he would destroy footage of death in the gas chambers if it were to come to light, is shown to be metonymic. Although *Shoah* does make industrial slaughter in the camps its focus, no such footage from the Holocaust years is shown, even where this exists, as it does in the case of the Einsatzgruppen murders.[8] Rather than show archive imagery, Lanzmann chooses to quote these perpetrators' words: in Schubert's case, central phrases from his trial and, in Kretschmer's, the letters he wrote to his family in autumn 1942 about the mass murders in which he was taking part.

Lanzmann's rejection of archival imagery has led to debate with other filmmakers, particularly Jean-Luc Godard, over the importance of such footage in Holocaust representation in general and the relative significance of dialogue – which Godard accuses Lanzmann of preferring – to imagery. Such an apparent paradox in the aesthetic choices of a film director is more nuanced than Godard suggests, given the importance that Lanzmann ascribes to the mise-en-scène in his work. Indeed, the different uses to which the two filmmakers put the paluche camera summarizes not only their differing filmic practice but their attitude to Holocaust cinema. Godard's film *Histoire(s) du cinéma* (1997–1998) reproduces not only wartime footage of Auschwitz and the liberation of Belsen but a fragment of *Shoah* itself (Saxton, 2008, p. 48). For Godard, the paluche is a means for a non-specialist to film spontaneously, a '*director's* camera' allowing that person to be 'somewhere *other* than the places normally prescribed by the traditional cinema' (Beauviala & Godard, 1985, p. 172). In *Shoah*, such a function is taken to an extreme: the unusual 'places' to which this camera allows Lanzmann access are those occupied by former perpetrators, their homes and their memories of the past. Beauviala and others, including the critic Raymond Bellour, and the film theorist and artist Thierry Kuntzel, liken the paluche to an extension of the hand rather than the eye, since it has no viewfinder and claim it as a literalization of the *caméra-stylo*,[9] which 'writes' a distinctive filmic narrative consisting of images. In the case of Lanzmann's Einsatzgruppen encounters, it is indeed the case that the hidden camera follows the hand rather than the eye, mimicking the format of an interview in which a microphone is offered to a speaking subject.

In the encounter with Schubert, the filmic elements of script, storyboard and image all become contingent, relying upon the vagaries of chance and technology. Will Frau Schubert move the camera in its hiding place in Coulmas' cloth bag – in the customized appearance of which she takes an unnerving interest – so that her husband's face is out of range? Will the interview take place in a room sufficiently close to the recording equipment in the van outside in the street for it to pick up a signal? Lanzmann (2009, p. 468) describes efforts to 'improvise' a mise-en-scène in situations where he could not predict the layout of a house and could only attempt to influence where the conversation took place, since the signal from the camera took precedence over the look of the scene, by manoeuvring the interviewee to a particular position. The paluche here is not a literalized *caméra-stylo* that writes but an independent device that records and exposes. While the mise-en-scène in the encounter with Kretschmer is partly chosen, that in the Schubert encounter has an arbitrary appearance necessitated by the concealed camera. This is particularly fitting in that the mise-en-scène can offer only a blurred black and white visual correlative, in Schubert's case, of a man sitting at a table, for the 'place' and actions of his past. Indeed, these outtakes are in a sense Lanzmann's (2007a, p. 112) ideal kind of filmmaking, constructed as they are without the *plans de coupe*, that is, storyboards of the set-ups necessary to ensure continuity in the final version, which he claims to detest.[10]

Staging the past

It seems that the Einsatzgruppen sequences in the outtakes of *Shoah* consist of a contingent and therefore documentary record. However, staging does take place in the Schubert and Kretschmer encounters, as well as in the other secretly filmed interviews in *Shoah*, just as it does in the Bomba and Gawkowski interviews. The persona of Dr Sorel constitutes a risky kind of staging. Although Lanzmann felt sufficiently unthreatened outside Kretschmer's house to let slip his mask, there is no possibility of his doing so in Schubert's living room. For instance, when Frau Schubert cannot recall the pretext of Lanzmann's original letter requesting an interview, which she thinks concerned making a film about the Third Reich, Lanzmann notes with affected indifference, 'many of those have already been made'.[11] Lanzmann describes his demeanour in the Einsatzgruppen encounters as that of a 'technician' and that he had an argument with his cinematographer William Lubtchansky, whose father had been killed at Auschwitz, because the latter objected to Lanzmann's apparently unruffled bearing, the ethics of taking Suchomel and his wife out to dinner, and his decision to pay the former Treblinka guard for his testimony.[12] The description that Lanzmann gives in his own defence, of his 'iron discipline' in maintaining a 'coolness' (*'froideur'*) and 'calm' as an integral part of the trickery (2009, p. 473), is equally applicable to his demeanour in Schubert's living room and allows for the latter's increasingly talkative manner.

Lanzmann is always in role in *Shoah* and we see a spectrum of his performances during the film. For instance, critics have responded in various ways to Lanzmann's insistent questioning of Bomba in the barber shop sequence, asking if he goes too far in demanding that the survivor tell his story. In the outtakes, however, Lanzmann's role is more obviously one of empathy with Bomba in an interview on the Tel Aviv coast, in which he holds his interviewee's hand – breaking the contact only to light a Gitane – to encourage him through the painful memory of his escape from Treblinka. As in the other staged encounters in *Shoah*, truth is approached via artifice in those with Schubert and Kretschmer. Raye Farr argues that the staging of the interview with Bomba in a barber shop 'undermines its own fiction' (p. 162), leading to what Lanzmann (2009, p. 453) describes as the 'moment' in which 'the truth is embodied' when Bomba breaks down and in the clandestine interviews with perpetrators this paradox is even more pronounced. Fiction is the necessary precondition for the encounters to take place at all and for their unusual kinds of success. In Lanzmann's conversation with Schubert, the latter moves from hesitantly and euphemistically referring to the co-defendants at the Einsatzgruppen Trial as 'other...former...er...gentlemen implicated in our...trial' to bluntly describing the 'emotional' difficulty of being faced with 'a circle of human beings...who must be executed'.

Heinz Hermann Schubert

Although Schubert was of relatively low rank and took an apparently bureaucratic role in Einsatzgruppe D, he was a defendant in the Nuremberg Einsatzgruppen trials and refers to himself in the conversation with Lanzmann as a 'central witness' in other post-war trials. At Nuremberg he was found guilty on all counts as charged – crimes against humanity, war crimes and membership of criminal organizations (the SS and SD) – and sentenced to death; however, this was commuted to a ten-year sentence and Schubert observes to Lanzmann that he was released from prison as early as December 1951, for 'time served'. Schubert was adjutant to Otto Ohlendorf, the commander of Einsatzgruppe D, that is, assistant with particular responsibility for communications. In his memoir of the Einsatzgruppen trial, over which he was the presiding judge, Michael Musmanno (1961, p. 208) argues that, although he was not a 'shooter', precisely because Schubert was an adjutant, he 'lived the whole gamut of this organisation's activities, since he handled its orders, assignments to executions, and reports to Berlin on the results attained'. As Schubert himself puts it, he did not simply 'hold Ohlendorf's coat'. Ohlendorf, who insisted on meticulous record-keeping, testified at the Einsatzgruppen trials that Schubert was sometimes asked to stand in for him at executions, in particular at what Musmanno calls 'the Christmas of Simferopol' (p. 209). This massacre of 14,000 Jews and others, including the 800 gypsies whose murder Schubert particularly described at trial (Musmanno, p. 211), took place between 11 and 13 December 1941 on the orders of Field Marshal von Manstein, who insisted that Simferopol be cleared of Jews 'by Christmas'. The detailed description Schubert gave at his trial of his activities at Simferopol, which included overseeing the transportation of gypsies, blocking the road from public view and gathering the victims' valuables in an orderly fashion before they were shot, was intended by his defence counsel to demonstrate his lack of culpability, but, of course, simply confirmed it.

As Lanzmann observes, the encounter with Schubert ends before they get much beyond preliminaries. Lanzmann's demeanour during this encounter is aimed at encouraging Schubert to speak freely and his interventions, particularly his refrain 'I understand' ('*das kann ich verstehen*'), are expertly double-voiced, to the point of sounding to the viewer like an ironized agreement. Lanzmann frequently responds, 'yes, that's important'; and 'yes, it's unbelievable'– as indeed it is – when Schubert describes von Manstein's claim at Nuremberg not to know who Ohlendorf was. This strategy is successful in that Schubert becomes sufficiently prolix and careless in what he says that Frau Schubert is prompted to intervene on several occasions. Frau Schubert acts as the present-day guardian of her husband's legal defence at Nuremberg, which consisted of Schubert's argument that, as Ohlendorf's adjutant, he was not involved in mass murder and that when asked to stand in for his superior at the Simferopol massacre he simply observed and did not participate. Frau Schubert's interventions paradoxically draw attention to the very moral and verbal sleights that resulted in the commuting of her husband's death sentence as part of the 'Christmas amnesty' under John McCloy, the US High Commissioner to Germany. She corrects several of her husband's remarks, including, for instance, Schubert's observation that Ohlendorf, in whose place he oversaw the killing at Simferopol, 'wanted to know, had things gone according to the orders given by me':

FRAU SCHUBERT: Just a minute...given by you, or by...by Ohlendorf?
SCHUBERT: Given by Ohlendorf.
FRAU SCHUBERT: Yes...be careful...[...] you didn't give any orders [...]
SCHUBERT: Well, but I'm not in front of a tribunal.
FRAU SCHUBERT: But, you know, that could be considered as a verbal memorandum (*Gedachtnisniederschrift*).

It is unclear here in the phrase 'to the orders given by me' whether Schubert has accidentally confessed here to his full involvement in the massacre or is quoting Ohlendorf's words. A moment later, Coulmas' promise to Schubert not to name the former adjutant is, just like Lanzmann's to Suchomel, broken at the very moment it is recorded and Schubert's slip is witnessed by a 'tribunal' of film-viewers, the transcript its 'verbal memorandum'.

However, Lanzmann's role under his pseudonym of Dr Sorel does not simply consist of monosyllabic facilitation. Schubert speaks at great length about the reasons for hesitating to grant Lanzmann an interview, in particular his anxiety about allegations that he has sullied the reputation of the Wehrmacht by describing its responsibility for mass murder, and how he is viewed by the contemporary German authorities. Lanzmann diverts Schubert from his course on three occasions. The first consists of Lanzmann's effort to make Schubert speak more concretely by asking about Pretzsch, the location of a training event for Einsatzgruppen leaders such as Ohlendorf in May 1941 to prepare for their 'security' role in Operation Barbarossa. This diversionary questioning takes place just after Coulmas goes out of the house to fetch a copy of Hilberg's *The Destruction of the European Jews* – which appears both in the form of the historical backdrop to and as an object in the mise-en-scène – and is also prompted by Frau Schubert's sudden interest in the bag containing the paluche, whose customized appearance she declares 'refined'. Later we will learn that this is not a coincidence. Frau Schubert has just passed on a phone call to her husband from neighbours who saw Coulmas check on the recording in the VW van. Lanzmann's more extended diversion concerns the phrases Schubert used at his trial and he interrupts the latter's veiled comments about the accuracy of the historical record on the Wehrmacht to ask about this. These diversions change the nature of the encounter from a discussion about whether the interview can take place at all to an interview *tout court*; they bring out into the open, and into this suburban living room, the reality of mass murder. In this way for the spectator the encounter is not 'conditional', in Lanzmann's (2009, p. 475) description of his unsuccessful attempt to film an interview with the SS officer Perry Broad, but a performance, enacting what it describes.[13]

Schubert's is the kind of denial of atrocity by twisted logic that underlies Lanzmann's (2009, p. 469) interest in interviewing two kinds of Nazi who appear in *Shoah*, the bureaucrats (such as Stier) and the criminal (such as Suchomel): Schubert combines elements of both. Lanzmann tells Schubert early in their conversation that if he were to interview him it would not concern the details of his trial, but rather 'something completely different': 'the atmosphere of the epoch' and its 'human relations'. However, both the 1947 trial and the possibility of another such trial (at which he assumes that he would expect to be a witness, not a defendant) frame Schubert's attitude to the past, in particular the fact that he does not seek to claim his innocence as much as his lack of guilt. This produces an overt clash of interests between Lanzmann's in 'human relations', that is, the fate of the Jews, and Schubert's in self-justification. Lanzmann provocatively claims, in the Hilbergian vein of focusing on alleged lack of resistance by the victims, that 'a large question-mark remains' on the subject of the Jews, concerning 'what these people knew, or didn't know, about German politics...how it was possible to bring these people along so easily, etcetera'.[14] The latter question appears to prompt Schubert to engage in moral reflection: 'It's very... today it's still very difficult' and 'it's a very dangerous chapter for me' – but he is thinking rather of his own post-war fate as a war criminal. The self-concern evident here is repeated bathetically at other moments in the interview. Of the Wehrmacht's 1941 order to clear Simferopol of Jews before Christmas, Schubert begins by apparently referring to the Einsatzgruppen's scruples: 'on our side we replied: we absolutely cannot do this', but concludes with the murderous pragmatism of the era: 'we haven't got vehicles or... er... er... we simply haven't got the necessary resources, it's impossible'. The massacre went ahead with equipment provided by the army. Throughout the encounter, Schubert claims that he is the one who has 'suffered' from the slur during his trial that he had denigrated the 'old German Wehrmacht' and insists that he and his family have paid a high price (*'sehr – sehr teuer'*) for his giving evidence against Wehrmacht generals such as von Manstein. Such back-to-front thinking is a direct continuation of Schubert's Nuremberg defence; and, far from getting away from the trial as Lanzmann wishes, Schubert's observation, 'I do not complain about my own personal fate' is an almost verbatim repetition of his final statement at trial: 'Yet, I shall never complain about my fate'.[15]

Even Schubert's claim to think differently in the present reveals in veiled form the double bind in which he finds himself:

> from today's viewpoint, much of what I believed...what I deeply believed...all of this I've had to reject today...because at such a distance, I don't see things in the same way as I did at that time...when I was right in the middle of things.

If Schubert repudiates his past beliefs, he is closer to admitting his guilt; yet he must do so or he risks, as he says to Lanzmann in the first few minutes of their conversation, being viewed as a 'neo-Nazi' by the German authorities. Not only this: Schubert's claim no longer to see things as he did makes him of less interest to Lanzmann and his project of 'reincarnating' the Holocaust than, for instance, Suchomel. The latter's rendition, not once but twice, of the Sonderkommandos' song from Treblinka constitutes just such a reincarnation of the past, as song often does in *Shoah*. Lanzmann describes how he experienced both 'horror' and the realization that Suchomel's was an 'extraordinary testimony' on seeing the 'sudden hardness' of the former guard's eyes as he sang: 'he was entirely taken over again by his past' (*'reassaisi'*) (2009, p. 475). By contrast, it seems that being taken over by the past in public, at a trial or in an interview, is exactly what Schubert fears. His caution blocks the possibility of a Suchomelian return of the suppressed memory of mass murder.

Karl Kretschmer

At first sight, there seems even less opportunity in the short encounter with Kretschmer than there was with Schubert for Lanzmann to stage-manage or provoke a return to the past. Kretschmer is laconic and vague – he claims to think Lanzmann wants to talk to him about the American miniseries *Holocaust*[16] – in contrast to Schubert's long-winded circumlocutions and he refuses the offer of payment for an hour's interview to provide a 'commentary' on his wartime letters to his family. However, Kretschmer's curiosity is sufficiently piqued by Lanzmann's visit that he remains on his doorstep for nearly 45 minutes, deflecting in a variety of ways the questions put to him, and these deflections offer their own links to the past. The role that Lanzmann assumes here is different from that with Schubert. Partly because of Kretschmer's offhand manner and to gain his interest, it is Lanzmann himself who effects a daring and parodic 'reincarnation' of the past based on Kretschmer's letters. This is all the more remarkable since the Kretschmer encounter took place after that with Schubert and its violent conclusion, and in the opening scene in a hotel room we hear Aubuoy speculate whether Schubert knows Kretschmer and may have warned him about a possible visit from 'Dr Sorel'.

Although Kretschmer is not mentioned in it by name, Hilberg's history again lies behind Lanzmann's choice of prospective interviewee. In *The Destruction of the European Jews*, Hilberg drily describes the problem posed for Einsatzgruppen leaders by the fact that the mass killings, which were conducted in broad daylight and often in full view of local people, became a 'sensation'. Not only did soldiers and civilians turn up to observe, but those involved 'took pictures, wrote letters and talked' (Hilberg, 1967, p. 212) with the result that the news spread throughout the occupied territories and into Germany itself. During 1942, Kretschmer wrote to his family in Berlin about Einsatzgruppe C's activities and in the letters raises the notion of gossip by the very fact that he asks his wife not to pass on news of the massacres to Frau Kern, a family friend. Kretschmer's letters, which ended up in the Ludwigsburg archives[17] and feature the underlining of incriminating passages by the Karlsruhe police, for whom he had worked before the war and with whom he unsuccessfully sought employment again in 1945,[18] could have resulted in his severe punishment. Yet, as Helmut Langerbein (2003, p. 122) points out, Kretschmer did not expect to be held responsible for the actions of his Sonderkommando and thus did not destroy the letters after the war, despite the time he spent in various forms of detention.[19] As Kretschmer reminds Lanzmann, he was acquitted at the Darmstadt Trial of 1967–1968 because his criminal involvement in Einsatzgruppe C's activities could not be proven.

Kretschmer's letters have been widely quoted, by reason of their breathtaking combination of everyday sentiment (a letter sent from Kursk on 15 October 1942 concludes, 'Lots of kisses and greetings for the children') and self-interest (he notes the difficulty of acquiring a '*Persianer*', an astrakhan fur coat, for his wife)[20] with professions of brutality and ideological cliché ('There is no room for pity of any kind') (Klee, 1991, pp. 168, 164, 165). Yet the precise significance of the letters is not self-evident and they have been cited to various ends. For instance, in his letter of 27 September 1942 Kretschmer writes to his wife that, 'As the war is in our opinion a Jewish war, the Jews are the first to feel it' (Klee, p. 163). Daniel Goldhagen views this phrase as evidence for his thesis that there existed a general German 'comprehension and endorsement' of Hitler's genocidal antisemitism, while David Redles reads the same statement as evidence for his argument that the Nazis entertained a 'millennial vision of evil Jewish Bolsheviks [...] locked in apocalyptic battle with Germany' (1996, p. 404).[21] Langerbein, on the other hand, notes that Kretschmer's phrase about the 'Jewish war' is followed by sentiments testifying to the fact that 'killing human beings was not an easy task' and that the apparent support of their addressee, Kretschmer's family, was crucial in allowing him to carry out such unpleasant actions (p. 123).[22] Kretschmer continues, 'Here in Russia, wherever the German soldier is, no Jew remains. You can imagine that at first I needed some time to get to grips with this' (Klee, p. 163). Lanzmann asks Kretschmer about both kinds of response. It appears that he wants to expose the contradictions between horror at, and commission of, mass murder, but it becomes clear that he is most interested, as he was in Schubert's case, in their complex intertwinement.[23]

Only scant details emerge during Lanzmann's conversation about Kretschmer's career, although he readily agrees that he was in Einsatzgruppe C from August 1942. This was the time of the 'second wave' of genocidal killings in Ukraine; as Wendy Lower puts it of an order by Himmler in July 1942, 'Four months later all of Ukraine's shtetls and ghettos lay in ruins; tens of thousands of Jewish men, women and children were brutally murdered by [...] SS police units and indigenous auxiliaries' (2005, p. 8). Kretschmer makes clear that he was not at Babi Yar nor at Chełmno,[24] describes the various trials at which he was a defendant after the war and gives his age as almost 72. Yet even these small facts suggest significant differences from Schubert, who had been a younger and more radical Nazi.[25]

In his performance as interviewer during this encounter, Lanzmann unexpectedly resembles recent confrontational documentarists such as Michael Moore, who plays himself, or the 'situationist-hoaxer'[26] Sacha Baron Cohen, who plays a variety of comic roles, while confronting their often unknowing subjects. During their encounter, Lanzmann asks Kretschmer everything a viewer will always have wanted to ask a former Nazi, including how small children could have been shot as 'saboteurs' and whether Kretschmer was a father at the time. At first, Lanzmann performs a role recognizable from *Shoah* by moving gradually from factual to subjective questions in the hope of gaining access to the interviewee's past, but Kretschmer's reluctance and reticence provoke in him a more confrontational style. It is one we do not see elsewhere in *Shoah*.

However, it is a phrase about wartime rations of black pudding that inspires Lanzmann's most faux-naif questioning and Kretschmer's least successful deflection. On 15 October 1942 Kretschmer wrote, 'People get used to the sight of blood, but Blutwurst [blood sausage] is not very popular round here' (Klee, p. 167) and Lanzmann demands to know what he meant by this joke (*Witz*). Lanzmann succeeds in prompting Kretschmer to describe it thus: 'It's a sausage made mostly with blood, and which looks black'. Lanzmann need hardly add:

LANZMANN: I think you mean that after a shooting, after an execution, it was impossible to eat Blutwurst.
KRETSCHMER: i-i-i-i-i...

It is here, in Kretschmer's incoherent stuttering, that the viewer witnesses and shares something of another 'resurrection' of the past, in the form of the perpetrator's visceral disgust at the mass murder which nonetheless went morally unquestioned. In a fictional version of the psychological impossibility of such consumption, Jonathan Littell's protagonist Maximilien Aue in his novel *The Kindly Ones* observes that, during a pause in the murders at Babi Yar, 'when the cases [of food] were broken open, the men, seeing rations of blood pudding, started raging and shouting violently' (2010, p. 127). This incident makes explicit the elements that underlie Lanzmann's questioning of Kretschmer. These include a return of the repressed knowledge of murder, one that works against what Aue describes as his fellow perpetrators' 'surprising way of never thinking about things' (p. 89). In *The Kindly Ones*, although at Babi Yar 'the canteen had been set up farther down, in a hollow from which you couldn't see the ravine', the 'blood pudding' makes the bloodshed in the ravine perceptible again. The rations prompt a bodily acknowledgement of murder, as Aue describes:

> Häfner, who had just spent an hour administering deathshots, was yelling and throwing the open cans onto the ground: 'What the hell is this shit?' Behind me, a Waffen-SS was noisily vomiting. I myself was ashen, the sight of the blood pudding made my stomach turn.
> (p. 127)

Häfner's execration of the rations as excrement, and Aue's description of their emetic function, reveals an unconscious fear of the introjection of human blood through its association with the body's waste products. The danger of transgressing a taboo, that of cannibalism, is the sign of another taboo, that of murder, which has been disavowed.

Conclusion

In Lanzmann's Einsatzgruppen fragments, the viewer is made to imagine the past of the 'Holocaust by bullets' and also left at a loss at how to do so. We hear traces of that past in the form of the stylized voices of trial transcripts and letters home, and also witness its ill-concealed living presence, not as trauma or involuntary reliving, as in the case of the survivors in *Shoah*, but in the form of surreptitious allegiance. Yet neither interview appears in the film's final version.

In the case of the Schubert footage, which was reported to the authorities by his family, this is partly for legal reasons. Lanzmann was forbidden by a German court from using any of the footage, having broken the law: not by secretly filming a former Einsatzgruppen trial defendant, as Frau Schubert's wish to summon the police suggests, but by illicitly using the airwaves (Lanzmann, 2009, p. 482). Lanzmann ascribes the omission also to aesthetic and structural factors, and this is something of a self-fulfilling absence: because he did not succeed in undertaking sufficient numbers of interviews with former Einsatzgruppen officers, the ones he did record do not have a place in his film.

Lanzmann was able to interview more death camp survivors than survivors of mass shootings, so in the latter case there is no possibility of the cross-cutting between perpetrators' words and those of witnesses that we see in *Shoah* with regard to the camps. The trope of trains is present throughout the film, in the dialogue, soundtrack and mise-en-scène, representing the experience of deportation as well as its administrative organization and the horrible prelude to arrival at a death camp. Ray Brandon and Wendy Lower (2008, p. 6) argue that the deportations by train to the camps are a crucial part of the resemblance of the Nazi genocide to the operation of a deathly factory. In *Shoah* footage of trains appears in different formats. It links different sequences: a tracking shot follows a locomotive towards Auschwitz, seen as if from the prisoners' viewpoint; the former locomotive driver, Henryk Gawkowski, travels along the same route in the present; Richard Glazar gives a sickening account of unloading people from cattle cars at Treblinka, the verbal 'reverse shot' of which is Suchomel's description of the unloading from a guard's perspective. The 'Holocaust by bullets' does not fit this historical or visual pattern. Likewise, the snippet of failed interview with the perpetrator Josef Oberhauser, lately of the death camp Bełżec, is included in *Shoah* although it is far more fleeting than that with either Schubert or Kretschmer. The shape of *Shoah* both constructs and demands its inclusion, coming as it does between Suchomel's description of the 'overflowing [burial] pits' at the camp and prosecutor Alfred Spiess's account of the Aktion Reinhard camps, of which Bełżec was one.

Lanzmann's Einsatzgruppen interviews have value, as I have explored them here, precisely as a supplement to *Shoah* that, as Jacques Derrida (1974) argues, is definitional for the whole. The reasons for their exclusion from the feature film itself are those that affect any representation of the Holocaust. The Holocaust in Ukraine, where the Einsatzgruppen massacres took place, has not been such a focus of attention from historians or writers as the more western locations of death camps, partly because of 'the Auschwitz syndrome', but also because of lack of access until 1991 to the regional archives of the former Soviet Union (Brandon & Lower, p. 6). Mass technologized death in the camps, with Auschwitz as its synecdoche, has come to stand, in terms of its literary and filmic representation, for the notion of 'modernity derailed' that is often seen to be horribly distinctive of the Holocaust (Brandon & Lower, p. 6).[27] Yet surviving the camps can afford recognizable narrative arcs, since subsistence, work, relationships and the effects of luck and coincidence can be represented in either testimony or fiction over a relatively sustained period. The experiences of the Einsatzgruppen victims were quite different in their sudden abruptness. It is not just paucity of material but the very unlikeliness of surviving an Einsatzgruppen massacre that accounts for the infrequency of such representations.

Notes

1. Translations throughout are my own. See also the English translation (Lanzmann, 2012).
2. The outtakes were created by Claude Lanzmann during the filming of *Shoah* and are used and cited by permission of the United States Holocaust Memorial Museum (USHMM) and Yad Vashem, the Holocaust Martyrs' and Heroes' Remembrance Authority, Jerusalem.
3. The exception to this 'ignored reality' is the mass murder of 33,771 Jews at Babi Yar, which took place near Kiev between 29 and 30 September 1941, the largest single massacre conducted by the Einsatzgruppen which is commemorated in Yevgeny Yevtushenko's eponymous poem of 1961, Dmitry Shostakovich's 1962 Symphony no. 13 based on the poem and novels by Anatoli Kuznetsov (*Babi Yar*, 1966), D.M. Thomas (*The White Hotel*, 1981) and Jonathan Littell (*The Kindly Ones*, 2008).
4. Such new work addresses both the 'Holocaust by bullets' (see, for instance, Desbois (2008)) and the history of the Holocaust in Ukraine (Brandon & Lower (2008); Rubenstein & Altman (2008)).
5. Despite his claim that the footage consists mostly of its subjects' legs and calves, the medium-shot of Schubert is relatively clear throughout the encounter.
6. In his autobiography Lanzmann describes the improvised nature of this set-up: the map was hastily pinned to the wall, while the pointer was in reality a fishing rod, constituting a mise-en-scène designed to give Suchomel the look of a death camp 'pedagogue' (2009, pp. 472, 464).
7. Kretschmer's Sonderkommando was responsible for a total of 59,018 deaths.
8. Imagery of this kind exists in both cases. Photographs of the Babi Yar massacre, perpetrated by Kretschmer's unit before he joined it, were taken by Johannes Hähle, a military photographer with the German Propaganda-Kompanie 637 of the 6th Army. There also exist photographs from Einsatzgruppe D's actions in Ukraine from 1941 and 1942, during which time Schubert was a member. In his *Night and Fog* (1955) Alain Resnais reproduces photographs of a December 1941 Einsatzgruppen massacre on a beach at Šķēde in Latvia, taken by SS Scharfuhrer Karl-Emil Strott. See also archive footage and interviews with survivors, witnesses and perpetrators in the film *Einsatzgruppen: Les Commandos de la Mort* (Dir. Michael Prazan, 2009).
9. See Astruc's 1948 essay 'Birth of a New Avant-garde: Le Camera-Stylo', reprinted in Corrigan (1999).
10. Thanks to Jennifer Cazenave for this reference.
11. All translations are my own, drawing on the German transcript and its French translation held at the USHMM.
12. Lanzmann paid Suchomel the equivalent of €2,000; he also paid Frau Michelson and Stier, and offered 2,000 Deutschmarks to Karl Kretschmer.

Although Schubert mentions men in his situation who have sold their stories, no such transaction takes place in his case.
13. See also Bruzzi's discussion of performativity in her *New Documentary* (2000). In the present case we witness what is perhaps a 'meta-performance', as it is Schubert's uncertainty about whether to grant an interview that constitutes it.
14. See Hilberg's comments on the 'psychological obstacles' which led to a 'blunted' awareness of impending disaster within much of the Soviet Jewish community (1967, p. 206) and on the lack of resistance among the victims (pp. 209, 249). Such a view is not shared by other historians: see Eck's rebuttal (1967) and accounts among the Einsatzgruppen Operational Reports of Jews attempting to escape, in Headland (1992).
15. *Nuernberg Trials*, Green Series, microfiche vol. 4, card 5, 1946–1949, p. 409. Thanks to Jenni Adams for her help in locating this source.
16. This is an ironic error, given Lanzmann's verdict on Marvin Chomsky's 1978 NBC miniseries *Holocaust* as 'a lie, a moral crime [which] assassinates memory' (2007b, p. 30), and in conversation with Kretschmer he emphatically denies any connection to it.
17. This is the Central Office of the State Justice Administration for the Investigation of National Socialist Crimes at Ludwigsburg.
18. All quotations from Kretschmer's letters are from Klee, Dressen and Riess (1991).
19. In the conversation with Lanzmann, Kretschmer refers to a two-year prison sentence for membership of the SS; an earlier sentence of eight years' hard labour had been suspended after a year due to Kretschmer's ill health (Langerbein, n. 35, p. 206).
20. This is mistranslated as a 'Persian rug' in Klee (p. 164).
21. See also Redles (2005, p. 174).
22. See also Rhodes' argument that the two months' span of Kretschmer's letters reveals a gradual process of 'incorporating the values' of the Sonderkommando (2002, pp. 219–221). In his article 'Ordinary Masculinity', Haynes argues that, 'Kretschmer indicates that preserving his identity as an honorable father and husband is essential to rationalizing his participation in Einsatzgruppe murders' (2002, p. 151): rather, it seems that the murders allowed him to remain a good father and husband, providing food and gifts for his family in wartime.
23. For instance, the following sentiment in Kretschmer's letter of 19 October shows just the over-determination of motive that Lanzmann is keen to reveal: 'it is a weakness not to be able to stand the sight of dead people; the best way of overcoming it is to do it more often' (Klee, p. 171). Langerbein observes that the antisemitism that allowed Kretschmer's actions is clear here, 'otherwise, he would not have classified his initial inability to shoot Jews as a weakness' (p. 123): the apparent registering of the vestige of a humane response actually reveals its extinction.
24. Lanzmann arranged the interview believing mistakenly that Kretschmer had been at Babi Yar (personal communication, 18.9.09). When he asks about 'Kulmhof' [Chełmno] –'did you see any gas vans?'– Lanzmann may be thinking of another Kretschmer, Erich, who was deputy in charge of the crematoria at that death camp, or simply baiting his interviewee.

25. It goes without saying that although these differences are borne out not only by Kretschmer's past record but also by his demeanour in the present, they did not prevent him becoming a mass murderer in 1942.
26. The phrase is Peter Bradshaw's, from his review of *Brüno* in *The Guardian* Film and Music supplement, Friday 10 July 2009.
27. See also Stone, 'Modernity and Violence' (1999) for a reconsideration of the usual dichotomy between technologized death in the camps and the chaotic cruelty of death meted out by the Einsatzgruppen squads. Stone argues that both are channels for the expression of the particular violence that characterizes modernity.

Works cited

Angrick, A. (2008) 'The Men of *Einsatzgruppe D*: An Inside View of a State-Sanctioned Killing Unit in the "Third Reich"', in O. Jensen & C. Szejnmann (eds.), *Ordinary People as Mass Murderers: Perpetrators in Comparative Perspective* (Basingstoke: Palgrave), pp. 78–97.

Astruc, A. (1999) [1948] 'Birth of a New Avant-garde: Le Camera-Stylo', in T. Corrigan (ed.), *Film and Literature: An Introduction and Reader* (Saddle River, NJ: Prentice Hall), pp. 158–162.

Beauviala, J-P. & Godard, J-L. (1985) 'Genesis of a Camera', *Camera Obscura* 5:13/14, 163–193.

Brandon, R. & Lower, W. (eds.) (2008) *The Shoah in Ukraine: History, Testimony, Memorialization* (Bloomington: Indiana University Press).

Bruzzi, S. (2000) *New Documentary: A Critical Introduction* (London: Routledge).

Chevrie, M. & Le Roux, H. (2007) 'Site and Speech: An Interview with Claude Lanzmann about *Shoah*', in S. Liebman (ed.), *Claude Lanzmann's 'Shoah': Key Essays* (New York: Oxford University Press), pp. 37–50.

Derrida, J. (1974) *Of Grammatology*. G. Spivak (trans.) (Baltimore: Johns Hopkins University Press).

Desbois, P. (2008) *The Holocaust by Bullets: A Priest's Journey to Uncover the Truth behind the Murder of 1.5 Million Jews* (Basingstoke: Palgrave).

Earl, H. (2010) *The Nuremberg SS-Einsatzgruppen Trial, 1945–1958: Atrocity, Law, and History* (Cambridge: Cambridge University Press).

Eck, N. (1967) 'Historical Research or Slander?', *Yad Vashem Studies* 6, 385–430.

Farr, R. (2005) 'Some Reflections on Claude Lanzmann's Approach to the Examination of the Holocaust', in T. Haggith & J. Newman (eds.) *Holocaust and the Moving Image: Representations in Film and Television Since 1933* (London: Wallflower), pp. 161–168.

Flitterman, S. (1981) 'Woman, Desire, and the Look: Feminism and the Enunciative Apparatus in Cinema', in J. Caughie (ed.), *Theories of Authorship* (London: British Film Institute), pp. 242–250.

Goldhagen, D. (1996) *Hitler's Willing Executioners: Ordinary Germans and the Holocaust* (New York: Little, Brown).

Haynes, S. (2002) 'Ordinary Masculinity: Gender Analysis and Holocaust Scholarship', *Journal of Men's Studies* 10, 143–163.

Headland, R. (1992) *Messages of Murder: A Study of the Reports of the Einsatzgruppen of the Security Police and Security Service, 1941–1943* (Madison, NJ: Fairleigh Dickinson University Press).

Hilberg, R. (1967) *The Destruction of the European Jews* (Chicago: Quadrangle).
Klee, E., Dressen, W. & Riess, V. (eds.) (1991) *'Those Were the Days': The Holocaust as Seen by the Perpetrators and Bystanders* (London: Hamish Hamilton).
Langerbein, H. (2003) *Hitler's Death Squads: The Logic of Mass Murder* (College Station, TX: Texas A&M Press).
Lanmann, C. (2007a) 'Entretien avec Claude Lanzmann: Le travail du cinéaste', in J.M. Frodon (ed.), *Le Cinéma et la Shoah: Un art à l'épreuve de la tragédie du 20e siècle* (Paris: Cahiers du Cinéma), pp. 111–130.
Lanzmann, C. (2007b) 'From the Holocaust to "Holocaust"', in S. Liebman (ed.), *Claude Lanzmann's 'Shoah': Key Essays* (New York: Oxford University Press), pp. 27–36.
Lanzmann, C. (2009) *Le Lièvre de Patagonie: Mémoires* (Paris: Gallimard).
Lanzmann, C. (2012) *The Patagonian Hare: A Memoir*, F. Wynne (trans.) (London: Atlantic Books).
Lanzmann, C., Larson, R. & Rodowick, D. (1991) 'Seminar with Claude Lanzmann: 11 April 1990', *Yale French Studies* (79), 82–99.
Littell, J. (2010) [2008] *The Kindly Ones*, C. Mandell (trans.) (London: Vintage).
Lower, W. (2005) *Nazi Empire-Building and the Holocaust in Ukraine* (Chapel Hill: University of North Carolina Press).
Musmanno, M. (1961) *The Eichmann Kommandos* (London: Peter Davies).
Redles, D. (2005) *Hitler's Millennial Reich* (New York: NY University Press).
Rhodes, R. (2002) *Masters of Death* (New York: Basic Books).
Rubenstein, J. & Altman, I. (eds.) (2008) *The Unknown Black Book: The Holocaust in the German-Occupied Soviet Territories* (Bloomington: Indiana University Press).
Saxton, L. (2008) *Haunted Images: Film, Ethics, Testimony and the Holocaust* (London: Wallflower).
Snyder, T. (2009) 'Holocaust: The Ignored Reality', *New York Review of Books* 56:12, 14–16.
Stone, D. (1999) 'Modernity and Violence: Theoretical Reflections on the Einsatzgruppen', *Journal of Genocide Research* 1:3, 367–378.

7
Reconciling History in Alain Resnais's *L'Année dernière à Marienbad* (1961)

Hannah Mowat with Emma Wilson

Context

In W. G. Sebald's novel *Austerlitz* there is brief mention of the spa town Marienbad, in the Karlovy Vary region of the Czech Republic. Marienbad, for Sebald's eponymous character, Austerlitz, is a peace-time destination, a location of memory, of serenity, before the madness to come. Austerlitz, who as a Jewish child will be sent away from Central Europe on a *Kindertransport* to England, losing his bearings, his parents, his history in this momentous journey, is, far after the war, brought to remember Marienbad. His memory of this summer retreat, and its loveliness, is already ghosted by his departure. He left for England from the same station from which the family departed, just the year before, for Marienbad. This coincidence is recalled for Austerlitz far in the future as he hears a narrative of his life from Vera, his former nursery maid:

> Towards evening, when I said goodbye to Vera, holding her weightless hands in mine, she suddenly remembered how, on the day of my departure from the Wilsonova station, Agáta had turned to her when the train disappeared from view, and said: We left from here for Marienbad only last summer. And now – where will we be going now?
>
> (2002, p. 289)

Vera's memory triggers that of Austerlitz himself who affirms, 'yes, in the summer of 1938 we all went to Marienbad together, Agáta, Maximilian, Vera herself and me. We had spent three wonderful, almost blissful weeks there' (p. 289). Marienbad becomes here an 'Island of the Blest' (p. 365), a Proustian childhood territory long blocked from memory. It is further transposed, too, perhaps, in its translation into the German from Austerlitz's childhood Czech, Mariánské Lázně. Austerlitz recounts: 'we took long walks in the country around Marienbad in the afternoons. I had retained no memory at all of that summer holiday when I was just four years old' (p. 290).

Yet 1938 also marks the year in which Marienbad, as part of the long-contested Sudetenland, was annexed by Nazi Germany. Idyllic as Austerlitz's childhood recall of the place may be, it is to be overshadowed by the events of October that same year. In Sebald's text, 'Marienbad' operates as an ambiguous signifier and might therefore carry less a memory of a subjective, lived past than an intimation of things to come; and this future emerges in a cinematic flicker, a shiver of recall of Resnais's icy summer idyll, *L'Année dernière à Marienbad*.[1] This connection seems further established by the hesitations of memory and forgetting with which this summer outing is associated, as if Austerlitz's memory is shaped from the mnemonic fabric, the layers of concerns with past, proof and resemblance which texture Resnais's film. Recall of the film's Germanic overtones, rather than of the Bohemian spa resort, a popular destination in the inter-war years, seems further implied as Austerlitz in his adulthood filters his experience of working in the Bibliothèque Nationale in Paris through both recall and anticipation of Resnais's *Toute la mémoire du monde* (1956).

The account runs as follows:

> Some years later, said Austerlitz, when I was watching a short black and white film about the Bibliothèque Nationale and saw messages racing by pneumatic post from the reading-rooms to the stacks, along what might be described as the library's nervous system, it struck me that the scholars, together with the whole apparatus of the library, formed an immensely complex and constantly evolving creature which had to be fed with myriads of words in its own turn. I think that this film, which I saw only once but which assumed ever more monstrous and fantastic dimensions in my imagination, was entitled *Toute la mémoire du monde* and was made by Alain Resnais. Even before then my mind often dwelt on the question of whether there in the reading-room of the library, which was full of a quiet humming, rustling and clearing of throats, I was on the Islands of the Blest or, on the contrary, in a penal colony.
>
> (2002, pp. 364–365)

In his 2010 *Souvenirs d'une année à Marienbad*,[2] pieced together from silent 8 mm footage by cast member Françoise Spira, Volker Schlöndorff – second assistant director on the shoot – explicitly links the inexorable travelling camera of *Marienbad* with its documentary predecessors: the gliding footage of the labyrinthine corridors of the Bibliothèque Nationale de France (BNF) in *Toute la mémoire du monde*, as well as of the perimeter fences of Auschwitz and Birkenau in *Nuit et brouillard*. The camera, he notes, is not merely an observer; it is an absorber, picking up and embedding the material traces of recent history in celluloid, 'always tracking remnants of the past, the silent monuments of remembrance'.

Steven Ungar, in a recent article 'Scenes in a Library: Alain Resnais and *Toute la mémoire du monde*', argues the case for *Toute la mémoire du monde* as 'a supplement to *Nuit et brouillard*, the 30-minute documentary on Nazi concentration and death camps that Resnais completed a year earlier' (2012, p. 58). He follows Edward Dimendberg's groundbreaking reading of *Le chant du styrène* (1959), a film that, on close reading, reveals 'a veritable return of repressed geopolitical relations' (Dimendberg, 2005, p. 65; Ungar, 2012, p. 58). In his analysis of Resnais's film about the National Library, Ungar asks what the film might tell us about 'the industrial, social, and political conditions in which it was made' (p. 59); what it discloses about 'aspects of daily life during a decade marked increasingly by silence surrounding Vichy and division concerning the French in Algeria' (p. 59); and finally what it questions about state 'assumptions concerning the concepts of library, archive, and memory' (p. 59). As its argument builds, through the amassing of detail, Ungar's article reveals, with coruscating effect, the links that the film establishes between the 'concentrationary universe' of the camps,[3] already denounced by Resnais in *Nuit et brouillard*, and the institutions of late Fourth-Republic Paris. Ungar writes:

> The film may end by invoking the prospect of universal memory as a safeguard against forgetting. But the still and moving images of concentration and death camps seen in *Nuit et brouillard* serve as visual cues extending to – and haunting – the depiction of the BN's daily operations evoked throughout *Toute la mémoire du monde*. And this to a point where the projections of instant access to and total recall of universal knowledge seem instead an alibi for the silence surrounding World War II and the Algerian War, which state censorship had blocked Resnais from engaging openly in 1955–56.
>
> (p. 75)

Ungar's reading of *Toute la mémoire du monde* also draws on Sebald's engagement with the Bibliothèque nationale or French National Library in *Austerlitz*. Looking at a later passage from the novel, where Austerlitz describes working in the new BNF and muses on the necessary coincidence between the perfection of a concept and its chronic malfunction, Ungar concludes: 'Sebald's words in 2001 state what Resnais had shown 45 years earlier – namely, that the idealized vision of rapid access to universal knowledge entailed control, surveillance, and exclusion that were best kept as much out of sight as possible' (p. 72).[4] Where Ungar shows the ways in which Sebald's text may be aligned with Resnais's documentary in its disclosure of the malign shadow behind state operations of surveillance and control of knowledge, he does not discuss the implications of Sebald's passing reference to that other location of resonance in Resnais's filmic world, the spa town of Marienbad.

The work of Dimendberg and Ungar has newly revealed the indirect critical interventions of Resnais's documentary-making. Their work has proceeded tellingly through attention to form and matter, through associative connectivity, revealing how Resnais uses the formal resources of cinema as art to adumbrate a political critique. In both arguments *Nuit et brouillard* serves as a point of reference and at moments a counterpoint. Neither critic entirely divides Resnais's documentary work from his later feature film-making. Dimendberg traces Resnais's tracking shots seamlessly from *Le chant du styrène* (1959) through *Marienbad* (p. 80). Ungar includes *Hiroshima mon amour* (1959) in his discussion, using it as evidence of Resnais's favouring of blurred distinctions between fiction and non-fiction films (pp. 60–62). But neither critic moves their direct focus on to Resnais's fiction features. Inspired by their new readings of the documentaries, we venture here an analysis of *Marienbad* as, to recall Dimendberg's title, more than an exercise in style, as a fiction film that is haunted by the political concerns Resnais has explored formally in his documentary work. As a fiction work, and as a film removed one further degree in historical terms from the aftermath of the war, edging as it does into a new decade, *Marienbad*'s methods are more indirect, more contested. An intimation of this, and its difficulties, inspires our treatment here.

In his introduction to Sigmund Freud's *An Outline of Psychoanalysis*, Malcolm Bowie warns of the dangers of over-interpreting locations with the benefit of hindsight. Marienbad, he notes, may have acquired a terrible resonance as an 'emblem of loss in its extreme form' (2003, p. x) through its wartime associations with the Nazi concentration camps, but prior to World War II, it was a lively Bohemian spa, popular with the upper classes and the venue of the 14th International Psychoanalytical Congress held in 1936. 'Marienbad is not empty but full, therefore, if we transport ourselves back' far enough, he concludes (p. xi). To take a film like *Marienbad*, from which overt reference to the Holocaust is arguably absent, is perhaps to run the risk of retrospective over-interpretation of precisely the type Bowie counsels against. We hope to tread carefully in what follows, mindful of the appeal of delusions of historical reference, of the fevered associations of which Marienbad is victim.

Indeed *Marienbad* is a film which, in its dialogues and its editing, works to confound a sense of historical reference and chronology. Gilles Deleuze, tracing the dismantling of flashback techniques in Resnais's filmography, notes: 'in *Last Year at Marienbad* we can no longer tell what is flashback and what is not' (1989, p. 118). He moves towards a reading of Resnais's cinema which emphasizes its formal display of layers of the past which are yet still to come; as he says: 'but it is possible for the work of art to succeed in inventing these paradoxical hypnotic and hallucinatory sheets whose property is to be at once a past and always to come' (p. 119). As we watch the film, there is no shared memory of 'last year' to sustain us and the present is left undated. Timeless eveningwear and refined rituals offer few clues in a Baroque setting itself dependent on historical analogy. We could conceivably be inhabiting any period between 1929 (a date cited in the film) and 1961, its year of release. If Resnais and Alain Robbe-Grillet were together reinventing cinema, confecting a perfect, timeless, self-reflecting arthouse object, what leverage do we have to respond to and name the film's historical resonances? Considering the temporal stretch of the film, the 30 or more years in which it might take place, we may be inclined to turn to an unspoken in-between, the history of its European locations.[5] It is tempting to fill the film's apparent void with the unspeakable: the horrors of a still-recent period of German history in which human matter and historical fact became subject to a process of everyday annihilation. Is the Holocaust in the recent past of Marienbad?

In Schlöndorff's *Souvenirs*, he narrates: 'One weekend we went to visit the nearby camp of Dachau'. He specifies that they went to the camp and then also visited the small Bavarian town next to it. There is no footage from Dachau here – 'the 8 mm camera did not roll inside the camp' – but there are images from the small town. Schlöndorff says: 'the little market, the fair, the beer garden, the auctioning and the Luna Park were fascinating to us for being so close to the camp'. The excursion, and its 8 mm record, illustrate a relation of proximity, of *voisinage*, that seems in some intuitive way explanatory for thinking about Resnais's *Marienbad*, located, or more properly floating, out of joint, in post-war Germany. Schlöndorff continues: 'when asked about this neighbourhood, the inhabitants weren't too interested to elaborate'. The silence around this proximity seems eerie; Schlöndorff reminds us that this little town was 'within earshot [of] the camp'. His voice-over points to a relation of unspoken spatial kinship where sound, sensory perception, defines the human, small-scale closeness of this quotidian world and the infernal camp. In speaking about Resnais's film-making, the signature travelling shots that track the remnants of the past in *Nuit et brouillard* and *Toute la mémoire du monde*, Schlöndorff in this gliding move associates Resnais's documentary work with his fiction feature *Marienbad*. He further gives an impression of Resnais as a filmmaker who instantiates connection, who finds in the mobility of his camerawork a means, arguably, of making *voisinage* explicit, of moving us in a single shot from one space to another and of reminding us of their closeness. As he attends to the silent monuments he films, Resnais's camerawork subtly articulates their history, their resonance.

Interviewed in a 2003 volume about what remains of the New Wave, Arnaud Desplechin argues that the first New Wave film, the film which floored the *Cahiers* cinephiles was historically *Nuit et brouillard* (Tassone, 2003, p. 111). To say that *Nuit et brouillard* was the first New Wave film, and thus to associate this documentary about the camps with a formally innovative field of feature and documentary film-making, instantiates a particularly emotive and visceral genealogy. It configures this new cinema as a mode of commerce with the dead. It locates this cinema of the present in relation to an uncertain history and to the distorting structures of a concentrationary universe. The primacy of *Nuit et brouillard* to reimagining cinema is reflected in Serge Daney's passionate acclamation of the film; he writes: 'And to understand that cinema (alone?) was capable of approaching the limits of a distorted humanity. [...] Was *Nuit et brouillard* a "beautiful" film? No, it was a *just* film' (2007, p. 20). He continues, '[t]he corpses in *Night and Fog* [...] are among those "things" that watched me more than I saw them' (p. 20). Sylvie Lindeperg writes that, for the orphans of the deportation, 'Alain Resnais's film functioned symbolically in revealing death and initiating a work of mourning' (2006, p. 241).[6] She discusses how the final sequences of the film mark out the end of a period of waiting, of a concerted desire for denial and the mad hope for restitution: now the orphan recognizes that his mother's hair, his father's bones are massed in the slaughterhouses Resnais represents.

The words of Daney and Lindeperg underscore what is effectively at stake in *Nuit et brouillard* as a generation seeks material evidence of its loved ones. The art of collaging and animating images of the dead has an extreme emotional undertow. *Nuit et Brouillard*'s play with images of the dead, its hesitation between life and death, in some way marks Resnais's later cinema, his formal innovation and his conjuring of story as well as history. In Desplechin's argument, *Nuit et brouillard* stands behind not only Resnais's later works, but the formally innovative works of a generation. But the recurrence of visual echoes of *Nuit et brouillard* in Resnais's later films, apparently removed from this specific, visceral, ghastly history, is no easy matter. One argument may suggest that Resnais continues to reflect on the way the present is touched by the past and the way the dead make themselves felt in the emotions and gestures of the living. His film-making, by this token, moves to explore the perpetuation of feeling and grief, the proximity, the *voisinage*, of the everyday and the concentrationary in post-war Europe. Yet in recognizing and naming the Holocaust images as palimpsests in the later films, there are also risks of appropriation, of delusions of reference. These issues can be seen to be particularly acute if we pursue links between *Nuit et brouillard* and *Marienbad*.

If the Holocaust is arguably absent, unreconciled, in *Marienbad*, visual echoes of its imaging in *Nuit et brouillard* still return. As Geneviève Sellier reminds us, in thinking about death in Marienbad, Georges Sadoul in *Les Lettres françaises* uses the title 'Eurydice à Marienbad', the lover of the film becoming a new Orpheus seeking to wrest his beloved from death (2005, p. 153).[7] A facet of this imaging of A as Eurydice is realized in the recall of body images from *Nuit et brouillard*; the latter film borrows the former's hesitation between stillness and movement, between stone and flesh. X describes her as if she were dead and at these moments of the sequence her staring eyes, half open mouth foster forth recollection of the petrified images of *Nuit et brouillard*. This is a moment of hesitation between life and death: 'It's not true', he says, 'You're still alive.' As he speaks of truth and untruth, her reflective, moving gestures, the breeze lifting the lace of her shawl, her almost imperceptible shudders show her gradually recoil from him as she will in sequences through the film. For long stretches the images of the camps seem forgotten only to return recalled in the bend of an arm, a self-protective gesture, the arcing of a body or widening of the eyes. The manipulation of body images through which the visceral force of *Nuit et brouillard* is felt leaves its imprint in the bodily and emotional contortions of *Marienbad*. This imprinting, this tracing of visual echoes, becomes part of the disturbance of viewing the film.

To find the imprint of *Nuit et brouillard* in the body images of *Marienbad* carries some emotive shock, and dislocation, for the viewer. Ginette Vincendeau speaks of the film as an expression of anxieties of the modern age, with its focus on figures apparently frozen in an eternal afterlife; she sees this as a film awash with emotion and reflective of the uncertainties of love.[8] The aesthetic of hesitation, of stasis and movement in *Marienbad* inherits, arguably repeats, the visceral hesitation between life and death of *Nuit et brouillard*. Catherine Russell (1995, p. 12) has suggested that 'narrative mortality is articulated through repetition and stasis, specifically through the incorporation of film stills, freeze-frames, and photographic images into the film's flow'. The techniques of edited sequences of still images in *Nuit et brouillard* look forward to the false match cuts of *Marienbad*. In recognizing this formally we may also be led to question the ways in which a certain visual economy and use of technology is associated with history and here its most infernal reaches.

Georges Didi-Huberman's volume *Images in Spite of All* has been particularly important in challenging the notion of the unimaginable.[9] For Resnais scholars his work has been the basis for a re-evaluation of the importance of *Nuit et brouillard*, a film which insistently uses archival footage, including the four surviving Sonderkommando images discussed by Didi-Huberman, in a manner marked out from the refusal of retrospective imaging espoused, for example, by Claude Lanzmann in *Shoah*. Didi-Huberman begins his defence of imaging and imagining with imperatives saying that we must conjure this world for ourselves, we must try to imagine it. For Didi-Huberman, the evidence, the props, which can allow this imagining are the fragments, words and images which resistant deportees tore from this hell. He writes: 'Those shreds are at the same time more precious and less comforting than all possible works of art, snatched as they were from a world bent on their impossibility' (2008, p. 3). His vocabulary is aptly emotive, visceral, in his choice to describe the precious evidence as 'shreds'. The French is *lambeaux*, a term used for fragments, paper scraps, material rags, yet which is also used, in more ghastly imagery, to evoke flaying and the shaving off of strips of flesh and skin. This fleshy, mortal relation to signification, this sense that the evidence produced is written with the lifeblood of the deportees, at the expense of their bodies, on fragments torn from their flesh, indelibly marks its relation to the future and imprints suffering into the very matter of the material messages. And so, aptly, Didi-Huberman conceives our relation to this evidence as one of debt. He speaks of our duty to imagine as 'a response that we must offer, as a debt to the words and images that certain prisoners snatched, for us, from the harrowing Real of their experience' (p. 3). He spells this out further saying: 'Thus, images *in spite of all*: in spite of the Hell of Auschwitz, in spite of the risks taken. In return, we must contemplate them, take them on, and try to comprehend them' (p. 3).

In *Nuit et brouillard*, Resnais already implicitly addresses questions of whether this contemplation and comprehension may encompass editing and new narrative organization. In allowing some echo of the Holocaust photographs to return in *Marienbad*, where gestures and forms are apparently recalled, without reference, index, or bodily matter, opens up these issues further, with no easy answers. We find in the film a hesitation about referentiality, about what we will discuss, below, as the 'reconciling' of history. Indeed in the diegesis of the film, as in its formal returns, mediated images are disturbingly open to manipulation.

To approach the question of *Marienbad* and recent history, Hannah Mowat offers a new close reading of the film tracing its uncertainties about control, surveillance, knowledge and temporality. She notes the ambivalence of visual and verbal landscapes in which the autonomy and traceability of matter – bodily and memorial – is relentlessly subjugated to the twin technologies of recording and translation, before moving on to focus attention on a sequence in which matter might escape mediation: one of the film's intertexts and points of reference, a poem by Rilke and a photograph of A. Drawing on Christine Buci-Glucksmann, she traces parallels between the allegorical *Trauerspiel* and the theatrical, dematerialized, mourning-laden environment of *Marienbad*. This is done in order to ask how the matter of memory, freed from the apparatus, might serve to reverse the 'baroque reason' that Buci-Glucksmann defines; a reason dependent on an unreconciled history, which, in its reversal, might open a way to engaging, implicitly yet meaningfully, with a recent past more explicitly revealed, as Ungar and others have suggested, in the traces of Resnais's documentary work.

Argument

Hannah Mowat

Marienbad is a film characterized by intrusive editing. The minutely choreographed gestures and poses of the protagonists and bit players are constantly in view. Stilted dances and slow, somnambulist perambulations propelled by limp arms swinging in tandem give way to long moments of stasis, the figures frozen mid-motion as the camera, travelling smoothly forwards, injects a purely technical animation into the stilled life around it. These are oddly insubstantial, wraith-like bodies; their alimentary rituals are catalogued in the trays of afternoon tea set before them, the beverages around them, but the trays are left untouched, glasses and bottles broken: only one sip of water is taken throughout the entire film. They are wrapped in a soundscape of uncertainty. The music of the opening credits, a pastiche of countless other sweeping film scores, swiftly gives way to a dissonant organ soundtrack that only rarely, and incongruously, cedes to the original music; an organ that is at times almost diegetic in its correlation with the rhythmic gestures on display, at others starkly at odds with our visual expectations as it superimposes itself on an image of a lively violin duet.

It is the off-screen that is in control here: the camera as the agent of motion in a landscape of statues of stone and flesh; the music, the insistently off-kilter phrases of which compete with those uttered by X, drowning out his dubious narrative of repetition and conquest. Black-and-white cinematography leaches the ornate interiors of their gilded glamour. In his *Souvenirs*, Schlöndorff tellingly recounts the primacy accorded to machinery, the personification of the camera, 'the beautiful old Mitchell', that is foregrounded over the actors embodying the faceless, nameless hotel guests. While the Mitchell, he observes, 'seemed to be at the core of the entire production', the actors spent most of their time in suspension, waiting for the camera to roll.[10] Like gesture and aural perception, therefore, visual acuity in *Marienbad* is deliberately determined by technology.

Two moments of overexposure remind us again that the play of light on celluloid that provides an image is always dependent on an adjustment of the mediating camera (Figure 7.1). As A hastens through the ground-floor lounge and steps out onto the exterior balcony, her arms momentarily moving alternately, the camera swiftly cuts ahead and spins around to show her, paralysed by natural light, pressing herself against the facade in a blur of white. Here, exposure leads to overexposure and the loss of the clear contours and spontaneous gestures of the body. On a second occasion, trapped in X's opulently Rococo fantasies as he weaves his narrative of rememorialization, a shimmeringly overexposed A is shown in her bedroom; the camera rushes towards her, cutting repeatedly back to the point of entry as, angel-like in her feathered negligee, her lips pulled back in an unnatural smile and her eyes glazed and averted, she opens her arms for a blind embrace that the

Figure 7.1 Stills from *L'Année dernière à Marienbad/Last Year in Marienbad*, Dir. A. Resnais (Optimum Home Entertainment, 2005 [1961]) [on DVD].

camera cuts leave repeatedly unconsummated. Here, the camera, by co-opting the motion integral to the human body and the sensitivity of the human eye, has once again dehumanized and frozen their materiality in a mediated moment of overexposure and aversion.

Forgoing the visual, we turn to the spoken soundscape for orientation and find ourselves led yet further astray. X's phrases, smooth and sinuous as the travelling camera that glides through the hotel passageways, offer an artificial calm as he enumerates a series of identical and interminable corridors and silent, empty rooms laden with Baroque ornamentation, which burdens them with the constructions 'of another century'. This is less dialogue than hypnosis, a monotonous monologue designed to imply, overwrite and impose. Situated uncomfortably between past and present, we cannot determine whether its insistent 'last years' and 'yesterdays' refer to the current setting or any one of its geographical precursors: Karlstadt, Marienbad, Baden-Salsa, Friedrichsbad. Referring to the hotel as a 'lieu de repos', it is never entirely certain whether this refers to a 'place of rest' where life might be restored or, indeed, a final 'resting place' where it might be relinquished. Paradoxically, X's interminable narrative of memory underscores time and again the verbal rifts that permeate the film – the lack of raised voices in the hotel environs, the multiple yet never-seen signs exhorting residents to 'Be quiet. Be quiet' and, above all, what X refers to as 'the same missing voices'. Increasingly, we perceive a mismatch between the spoken and observed as descriptions of gesture are repeatedly contradicted by on-screen actions. A's constant changes of apparel and backdrop, often within a single stretch of dialogue, defy continuity. Spoken language as an index of temporality and identity becomes tenuous; treacherous, even. If M is A's husband, we wonder, why does he call her 'vous'? If X has such absolute recall of the past, why does he so often intersperse his affirmations with the adverbs of mitigation, 'perhaps' and 'doubtless'? Meanwhile, the adverb of time 'already'– usually so suggestive of continuity – becomes embroiled in a present tense that leaves us poised between past and future. 'It is already too late,' says X to A, leaving the implied action unspoken; 'That's already not true any more,' replies M, as A assures him that she is by his side, pointing to a future that is left occluded while consigning truth and constancy to an unsubstantiated past.

Just as the camera and the organ soundtrack co-opt the spatial (visual and aural) autonomy and verifiability of on-screen bodies, so too does language undermine temporality to leave us with a present that can never be more than a void between time past and time to come. 'Je ne suis jamais restée aussi longtemps nulle part', A says to X, 'I've never stayed anywhere for so long' as the English subtitles would have it, sidestepping the ambiguity of 'nulle part' that would make 'I've never stayed nowhere for so long' just as valid a translation. Anywhere is nowhere is a somewhere poised in a historical setting between the past and present moment. Names are consistently denied importance – there is no need to name the statues in the garden, X insists. These seemingly solid pieces of crafted matter lose their monumental status when M further challenges their ability to 'speak' by describing them as a latter-day simulation of the ancient world, their antique apparel and allegorical overtones a 'pure convention'. Our attention is drawn to the incongruence of speech that is potentially always a translation, masking an original never heard. Similes abound, ushering matter towards the realm of the insubstantial, the living towards death: X is 'like a shadow', A says; A is 'as if dead', X counters. The film's geography is a composite, pieced together, Kuleshov-style, from a variety of Munich palaces and a Paris-based studio set. It is never accorded a precise location through language: instead, it is likened to other places by analogy, as we learn that it has a garden 'à la française'. X's Italian-accented narrative never cedes to his native language. There is always an origin beneath the surface that, all the while drawing attention to its absence, nevertheless refuses to reveal itself. We find ourselves – through the technical apparatus and through a language that positions itself in a zone of absence and translation between the present and a historically-inflected past – *in medias res*.

We are in the intermediate domain of what Buci-Glucksmann has called baroque reason, 'the reason of allegory and the Other, the reason of an unreconciled history' (1994, p. 89). Her work, drawing particularly on Walter Benjamin, offers a compelling perspective on allegory which, in its baroque manifestation rather than its Romantic re-imagining, acts both as a mask and a means of access to the present.[11] Her introduction, paraphrasing Francisco de Quevedo's *The World from Within*, introduces a 'traveller with no homeland and no source of rest' to a vision of the baroque city, a 'theatre', whose unmappable maze of streets and misleading beauty create a world at the intersection between reason and unreason, a 'multibody of the past and memory' (p. 39): a world curiously reminiscent of *Marienbad*'s grand hotel, its *trompe l'oeil* interiors and temporal palimpsests.

The homeless traveller meets an old man, 'Disillusion', who points to a radiantly beautiful woman – revealing, in one fell swoop, the decay that lurks beneath her expertly applied make-up and dyed hair. The illusion of beauty, its aesthetic appeal, Buci-Glucksmann concludes (citing Benjamin), cannot be separated from its decomposing interior, the corpse at the heart of the baroque *Trauerspiel* (literally the 'play' but also the 'game' of mourning):

> Dead bodies, ageing body, female body, corpse-body, martyr-body or ghost-bodies: life is never produced except when 'seen from the point of view of death'; as if 'the allegorization of the physus can only be carried through in all its vigour in respect of the corpse'
>
> (p. 71)

There are striking parallels to be drawn, too, between the ostentatious décor and transfixed bodies of *Marienbad* and the *Trauerspiel*'s play of alluring yet fragmentary surfaces, and corrupted interiors:

> the total or totalizing world of 'beautiful syntheses' breaks into fragments. It is the endless fragmentation of allegory into a frozen

portrait of horror, as enactment of an ultimate difference which displays a world of ruins and materially represents the dead and suffering body.

(p. 69)

We might root our philosophy of modernity, Buci-Glucksmann concludes, in the baroque and its tradition of indirect mourning 'outside the space of the subject, consciousness and intention', in which critical language 'seeks to construct that "excess" past with the present' (p. 69). Is there a way here, perhaps, to approach *Marienbad* as a reconstruction of excess past through a beautifully appointed here-and-now? Is there a connection to be found between the handsome yet transfixed bodies, the mediated matter, in the Baroque hotel and the *Trauerspiel*'s baroque allegories of mourning? And might seeking out the matter in *Marienbad* that *escapes* technology and translation, the material objects that *reverse* the logic of baroque reason – 'the reason of an unreconciled history'– enable us to reassemble our fragments; to reconstruct the present with excess past; to reanimate the dead and suffering; in brief, to reconcile history?

If matter in motion is rendered untraceable through technology, and the material resonance of the spoken language is diminished by a lack of origin that obfuscates continuity and temporality, where, we ask, might we find matter that is not subject to mediation? Turning away from the image in motion and the word in speech, we look instead for an image divorced from the apparatus of motion and a word free from the apparatus of translation. In brief, we seek matter undeviated by medium: an image without a camera, a word without a speaker – and we do so in an attempt to counter baroque reason, to reconcile history.

We seek and find these images and words in a pure moment of repose. A sits pensively in the lobby of the grand hotel, a small book clasped shut in her hand. Set against the sheer weight of the Baroque interiors, it stands out in its leather-bound simplicity. The camera glides towards her. A straightens her back and composedly, languidly, opens the book. As she starts to read, the camera travels in closer, turning to look over her shoulder. Between the leaves of the slim volume, we see what appears to be a bookmark, almost obscuring the text of the right-hand page. The camera cuts to a close-up, giving us an unobstructed view of the text. It hesitates for several seconds, seemingly unable to intervene so that, for once, we might join A in a moment of contemplation (Figure 7.2).

With a start, we realize that A is reading in German. For the first time, in an undeniably yet unverifiably Germanic setting, we have a

Figure 7.2 Still from *L'Année dernière à Marienbad/Last Year in Marienbad*, Dir. A. Resnais (Optimum Home Entertainment, 2005 [1961]) [on DVD].

material language that matches an environment otherwise interspersed with French-language theatrical posters and a glimpse of a downstairs English 'Tea Room'.[12] What is more, it is a textual source that can be traced and dated: she is absorbed in the fifth stanza of Rainer Maria Rilke's 'Aus einer Sturmnacht' ('From a Stormy Night'), part of his *Book of Images*, published in 1902:

> Nights like these, the unhealable know:
> we were...
> And among the ailing they take up
> some simple good thought
> again, there, where it broke off.
> Yet of the sons, whom they have left,
> perhaps the youngest walks down the loneliest streets;
> for such nights are to him
> as if for the first time he had thought:
> it has long covered him leadenly,
> but now everything will be unveiled –,
> and: so he will celebrate that,
> he feels...
>
> (1991, p. 225)[13]

Picking up on the curiously sanatorium-like qualities of the film's setting 'among the ailing', the stanza emits a unique, if tentative, glimmer of futurity. Incurable though the illnesses of confined souls may be, it suggests, future generations outside – 'the sons, whom they have left'– may yet shake off their shroud and find cause to celebrate.

Yet what future might the sons of 1902 look forward to in cautious, suspended celebration? We turn to the sixth stanza, shielded from view by the photographic bookmark:

> Nights like these, all the cities are the same,
> all decked with flags.
> And by the flags seized by the storm
> and as if by hair torn away
> into some country with uncertain
> contours and rivers.
> In all gardens then there's a pond,
> by every pond the same house,
> inside every house the same light;
> and all the people look alike
> and hold their hands in front of their faces.
>
> (Rilke, 1991, p. 227)

The narrative of sameness, the diffusely delimited zone with its identical ponds, houses, lights and people, chimes strangely with X's monotonous narrative of interminable corridors, endless rooms, countless thresholds passed in 'this unknown place' and his repeated account of past meetings with A 'behind every shrub, at the foot of every statue, by every fountain's edge'. Rilke's 1902 text, we find, not only predates X's account, which snippets of dialogue allow us, by deduction, to place in a period post-1929 – it prefigures it. There is a programmatic quality to this German text that reduces *Marienbad*'s spoken text to an echo. The sons' future, it seems, is already unavoidably set out in the images of this page. Rilke's poem, cited and obscured by Resnais, and pointing to a Germanic past defined by mortality, offers a memory of things to come.

And what of the photograph? The image of A, poised on a park bench and gazing laughingly out from the page towards us, overlies all but a few words of the sixth stanza. Our interest in the photograph is twofold: first, as physical matter whose originary camera is never seen and whose fixity thwarts the travelling camera's attempts to inject artificial motion into the bodies around it; second, as an indexical marker that is subject to progressive re-arrangement throughout the film.

The origins of the photograph initially appear as impenetrable as those of the other bodies of matter we encounter in *Marienbad*. It is summoned up from X's pocket as 'proof' of an encounter the previous year. Yet A resists it. It could have been taken in any given garden at any time in the past, she argues and the absence of the photographer casts doubt on its authorship. However, it is undeniably material, a physical and tangible leftover whose outline, like the Rilke, is repeatedly to be discerned throughout the film.

Significantly, too, it swiftly changes hands. A is relentlessly submitted to a predatory narrative of biographical appropriation that reconfigures her apparel time and again. Her flowing clothes change shape and hue at an almost dizzying speed, sometimes within a single sequence. Her nightdress shifts from elegant black to a feathered flurry of white as X redesigns her simple, Baroque bedroom as an opulent den of Rococo horrors. A memory of a shoe whose heel snaps as she walks through the garden is cited twice before the event itself is enacted. Her self-image is constantly subject to the imposition of accessories designed to serve as memory objects: objects that add pseudo-chronological layers to the body, retracing its contours and enveloping it in a misleading aura of temporality. The photograph, however, represents the one instance when A reclaims one of these memory objects for herself – one that, like the Rilke reminder/remainder, does not defer to a process of translation or to the technological manipulations of *Marienbad*'s authoritarian camera. She may not have access to the moment captured by the camera, but its trace offers a uniquely material testimony to her physical history in a film in which all other images are transitory plays of light and shadow, disturbingly open to manipulation.

We want to look at what A, once in possession of her material trace, chooses to *do* with it. First of all, she employs it as a marker by proxy: a placeholder that assumes the role of something else – of herself. Returning to the Rilke, we might argue that her image, superimposed over the sixth stanza, hides its meaning from view. On the other hand, however, by inserting a technologically unmediated stand-in for the material self on a text free from translation, A allies that trace with an originary voice. Hence, the marriage of poem and photograph allows the memory of the future to merge with the tangible matter of the recent past. It makes A traceable.

The photographic placeholder is also the only object of substance that resists reconfiguration in the threshold zone of A's bedroom. As the décor and apparel shift and mutate in tune with the film's volatile narrative and encroaching camera, the image of A stands out as a fragment of stable matter. It is seen on her dresser, still peeping out from between the pages of the Rilke. As the film progresses, the photograph – unlike A – is not diminished: instead, it multiplies strangely and in so doing, starts to invade areas otherwise reserved for the masculine machinations of X and M. A series of identical reproductions serves as a stand-in for the matchsticks, cards and dominos used to play Nim – the game whose aim is to finish empty-handed. The image is thus always on the verge of disappearance, of being taken away, yet its reproduction and proliferation also reassert its physicality. Furthermore, its physicality straddles the zones of reason and unreason: in proliferation, it is both geometrical and chaotic, part of a mathematically aligned arrangement of cards underscored by a chorus of off-screen voices explaining the game in terms of prime number and calculations, but at the same time the image is placed upside down, on its head. It gestures towards completeness, but is never quite 'all there'. Its final appearance speaks of utter randomness: A opens the drawer of her dresser only to find it stuffed haphazardly with copies of the photograph, identical but too numerous to count (Figure 7.3).

Thus, from its initial appearance as X's 'proof' of an absent memory, the image becomes decreasingly indexical; yet at the same time,

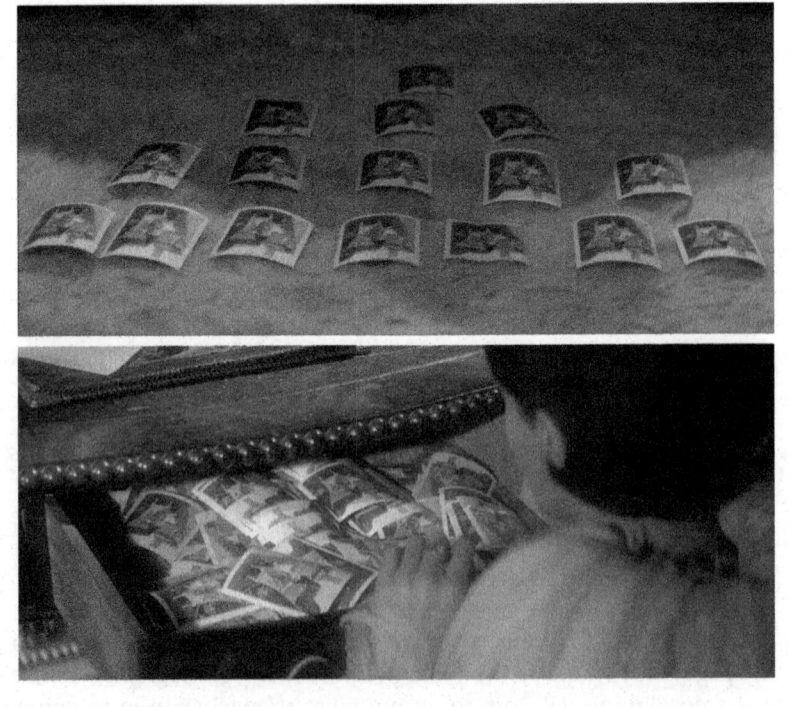

Figure 7.3 Stills from *L'Année dernière à Marienbad/Last Year in Marienbad*, Dir. A. Resnais (Optimum Home Entertainment, 2005 [1961]) [on DVD].

it swiftly changes hands to assume an increasingly omnipresent role as a material trace of A. Its alliance with a traceable, untranslated text, coupled with its endless physical reproduction offers the one anchor in the shifting substance of her tenuous present. There is a suggestion that, despite its own hazy origins, the photograph provides A with an opportunity to handle, manage and arrange her own material presence away from the interference of technology and translation. A, in appropriating her own trace, achieves an autonomy denied her elsewhere. The photograph is consequently a body that commemorates – and although its innate chemical fragility suggests that it is by no means immune to decay, its affinity with the untranslated and its reproducibility enable it to stand in for an infinitely more manipulable, more suggestible, human body.

Let us return for a moment to A, book in hand, in the lobby. An untranslated text offers a memory of things to come in a film without futurity; a photograph without a camera testifies to a recent past that *Marienbad* otherwise seeks to overwrite. Does this brief moment of repose offer material traces, freed from the intervening apparatus, that in some way respond to the spatial and temporal void at the heart of this film? Is this sequence the fulcrum around which the film's phantasmagoria – its shifting scenes and de-substantiated bodies – might pivot? Is it here that 'baroque reason' breaks down and we might go about filling the present with what Buci-Glucksmann calls 'excess', perhaps even excessive, past? Is it here that we might attempt to reconcile history – and call that history the Holocaust?

Conclusion

Hannah Mowat

> And yet they, who passed away long ago, still exist in us, as predisposition, as burden upon our fate, as murmuring blood, and as gesture that rises up from the depths of time. (Rainer Maria Rilke, in a letter to Franz Xaver Kappus dated 23 December, 1903)[14]

We have noted that there is little need to travel far back in time from the film's release date, 1961, to unearth a past that might be deemed 'excessive', a past that enduringly and terribly continues to inform the present. We have noted, too, the need for caution in reading that past as exclusively synonymous with the Holocaust. Yet we find a wealth of detail in *Marienbad* that resonates with compelling critical readings of his documentary feature *Nuit et brouillard* and *Toute la mémoire du monde*: the smooth, surveillant tracking shots that absorb the traces of past atrocities in the former and, through their recurrence, reinsert them into the latter. Here, too, we find a mobile camera; yet in *Marienbad*, it is more malignly subjective, more destructively active. Allied with a soundscape that is constantly prey to translation, it becomes an authoritarian figure, reducing the bodies around it to what Didi-Huberman calls *lambeaux*, scraps of matter that remain suspended, fragmented, ethereal, intangible.

We find striking parallels between the technologically-mediated, petrified bodies and Baroque backdrops of *Marienbad* and Buci-Glucksmann's concept of baroque reason: the reason of the *lambeau*, of the 'corpse-body', of an illusively beautiful present overwritten by palimpsests of elusive 'past and memory', of an 'unreconciled history'. We find, in *Marienbad*, all the ingredients of a *Trauerspiel*, a play, yet also a game, of grief. In short, we encounter an undercurrent of mourning, a death-in-motion in the spectral figures seemingly arranged and displaced by the totalitarian whim of the faceless yet omnipresent apparatus. Just as Ungar locates, in the 'daily operations' of the BNF a haunting reminder of the images of the camps and an 'alibi' for the policies of silence applied to atrocities past, we would like to suggest here that *Marienbad*, in privileging a technology that *co-opts and dematerializes* originary language and matter, is offering a political comment on authoritarian forms of surveillance and control that deliberately drain bodies of life and verbal apparatuses that stifle freedom of speech. Moreover, in positing the locus of (manipulated, silenced) memory in the recent past, 'l'année dernière', there seem valid grounds for seeking a point of reference embedded in the events and aftermath of World War II.

The question we have posed is whether *Marienbad* does not go one step further, in offering, perhaps, a glimpse of futurity. To test this, we have focused on details that might reverse the logic of baroque reason, restore the body's wholeness, transcend the compulsive play of grief and, in so doing, find some way to *reconcile* history. We have thus sought out the details of language and bodily trace that appear to defy the dictatorial grasp of technology. The Rilke poem – traceable, indelible, whole, Germanic – stops the camera in its tracks, while its text calls forth images of future generations both indebted to and burdened by their forefathers. It lays out a setting of endless repetition that echoes yet predates *Marienbad*'s (male) narrative voice. Rilke's poem emerges as an originary language, one that is not subject to mediation and which, in its stanzas, points both to the 'source' of the current setting and to a glimmer of a future – albeit tentative – that might be achieved if the 'sicknesses' of the past are overcome. The photographic bookmark of A between its leaves, meanwhile, offers a trace of the past whose authorship is uncertain, but whose physicality is allied with this originary voice and again remains technologically unmediated. As the film progresses, the image comes to represent the sole piece of A's bodily matter that she is able to reclaim and then consistently *rearrange* throughout. This material fragment is capable of reproduction; first as a stand-in for the pieces required to play the game of Nim – also arguably a game of loss, a strategic *Trauerspiel* – and later, in even greater proliferation, as an *uncontrollable* rearrangement of bodily traces in that epicentre of material uncertainty, A's bedroom.

What we would like to propose here is that *Marienbad* offers afterimages of authoritarianism in the strict surveillance and control of its camera, and 'afterechoes' of denial in the narratives and soundscape that seek, through translation and superposition, to overscore authentic memory. Yet at the same time, we suggest, it adds to a body of documentary films that bear the traces, explicit or implicit, of the Holocaust, in that it offers an *alternative* to the editing techniques that can reconfigure matter and memory retrospectively. In his film, Resnais presents us with matter that has been freed from the apparatus, too: a poem made up of memories to come and an image that can be reclaimed and rearranged. However, in both cases, what is needed – to enact the poem's latent futurity and to lay claim to the individual bodily trace – is a willingness to assume *responsibility* for the past and the way in which it will be remembered. Just as Didi-Huberman argues that our relation to the remainders of the Holocaust must be one of debt and that we must 'take them on, and try to comprehend them', so too does Resnais, in *Marienbad*, urge us to revisit the evidence of the past and seek ways of reconstituting its bodily traces and in so doing circumvent the apparatuses of control. To face past horrors, to 'reconcile history' and escape the deathly, repetitive, fragmentary play of the *Trauerspiel*, *Marienbad* suggests, what is needed is not controlled retrospection, but responsible introspection.

Notes

1. Abbreviated to *Marienbad* throughout.
2. Abbreviated to *Souvenirs* throughout.
3. See Griselda Pollock and Max Silverman's introduction to *Concentrationary Cinema* (2011, p. 24).
4. See Sebald (2002, pp. 392–393).
5. Resnais himself has connected the film to the political present of its moment of production, noting the film's unspoken relation to censorship and the Algerian War (Wilson, 2006, pp. 84–85).

6. This is my translation (EW).
7. See Wilson, *Love, Mortality and the Moving Image* (2012, pp. 135–136) for discussion of Eurydice in *Nuit et brouillard*, through Griselda Pollock's evocation of Bracha Ettinger's Eurydice series.
8. These comments are drawn from Ginette Vincendeau's 'Introduction' to the Optimum Releasing DVD of *Marienbad*.
9. See Chare's *Auschwitz and Afterimages* (2011) for an important evaluation of Didi-Huberman's work on photography and matter.
10. We learn, too, from Schlöndorff that the nameless throngs drafted in to people the scenes shot in the Hall of Mirrors at Amalienburg were positioned primarily to ensure that the camera was flanked at all times, thereby obscuring its reflection in a scene that required a 360-degree range of camera motion.
11. In later chapters, Buci-Glucksmann has much to say about the position of the female body within this baroque configuration of reason. For the purposes of this piece, however, we choose to remain with her Benjaminian appropriation of baroque allegory in the *Trauerspiel*, inflected by displays of mourning and theatricality.
12. Poster and sign both feature in the studio set meticulously constructed in the Photosonar Studios in Courbevoie, Paris to capture the corridors that Resnais was unable to find in his Munich locations (Schlöndorff, 2010); we can conclude, therefore, that their inclusion here is entirely deliberate.
13. If this Rilke poem is literally in *Marienbad*, it may also be illuminating to recall his many references to the dead and their untouchability, as memorably, in 'Orpheus. Eurydice. Hermes' from *New Poems*. (1907, 1908)
14. Accessed online at http://articles.poetryx.com/16/ on 20 March 2012.

Works cited

Bowie, M (2003) 'Introduction', in S. Freud, *An Outline of Psychoanalysis*, H. Ragg-Kirkby (trans.) (London: Penguin), pp. vii–xxi.

Buci-Glucksmann, C. (1994) *Baroque Reason: The Aesthetics of Modernity*, P. Camiller (trans.) (London: Sage Publications).

Chare, N. (2011) *Auschwitz and Afterimages: Abjection, Witnessing and Representation* (London: I. B. Tauris).

Daney, S. (2007) *Postcards from the Cinema*, P. Grant (trans.) (Oxford: Berg).

Deleuze, G. (1989) *Cinema 2: The Time-Image*, H. Tomlinson & R. Galeta (trans.) (London and New York: Continuum).

Didi-Huberman, G. (2008) *Images in Spite of All: Four Photographs from Auschwitz*, S. Lillis (trans.) (Chicago: University of Chicago Press).

Dimendberg, E. (2005) '"These Are not Exercises in Style": *Le chant du styrène*', October 112, 65–88.

Lindeperg, S. (2007)'*Nuit et brouillard*': *un film dans l'histoire* (Paris: Odile Jacob).

Pollock, G. & Silverman, M. (eds.) (2011) *Concentrationary Cinema: Aesthetics as Political Resistance in Alain Resnais's Night and Fog* (London: Berghahn Books).

Resnais, A. (1961) 'Interview with Alain Resnais', *Premier Plan* 18, 36–89.

Rilke, R. M. (1991) 'From a Stormy Night: Eight Leaves with a Title Leaf', in *The Book of Images*, E. Snow (trans.) (San Francisco: North Point Press), pp. 215–231.

Russell, C. (1994) *Narrative Mortality: Death, Closure and New Wave Cinemas*. (Minneapolis: University of Minnesota Press).
Sebald, W. (2002) *Austerlitz* (London: Penguin Books).
Sellier, G. (2005) *La Nouvelle Vague: Un cinéma au masculin singulier* (Paris: CNRS).
Tassone, A. (ed.) (2003) *Que reste-t-il de la Nouvelle Vague?* (Paris: Stock).
Ungar, S. (2012) 'Scenes in a Library: Alain Resnais and *Toute la mémoire du monde*', *SubStance* 128, 41:2, 58–78.
Vincendeau, G. (2005) 'Introduction' on the Optimum Home Entertainment DVD edition of *Marienbad* (see filmography, below).
Wilson, E. (2006) *Alain Resnais* (Manchester: Manchester University Press).
Wilson, E. (2012) *Love, Mortality and the Moving Image* (Basingstoke: Palgrave Macmillan).

Filmography

L'Année dernière à Marienbad/Last Year in Marienbad, Dir. A. Resnais (Optimum Home Entertainment, 2005 [1961]) [on DVD]

Hiroshima mon amour, Dir. A. Resnais (Arte Vidéo/Argos Films, 2004 [1959]) [on DVD]

Souvenirs d'une année à Marienbad, (ed.) V. Schlöndorff from original footage by F. Spira (2010), accessed online on 15 July 2012 at laregledujeu.org/2010/07/23/2445/last-year-at-marienbad-making-of/

Le chant du styrène/The Song of Styrene, Dir. A. Resnais (Arte Vidéo/Argos Films, 2004 [1959] as an extra on the DVD of *Muriel ou le temps d'un retour*) [on DVD]

Muriel ou Le temps d'un retour/Muriel or The Time of Return, Dir. A. Resnais (Arte Vidéo/Argos Films, 2004 [1963]) [on DVD]

Toute la mémoire du monde/All the Memory in the World, Dir. A. Resnais (Arte Vidéo/Argos Films, 2004[1956]) [on DVD]

8
Gender and Sexuality in Women Survivors' Personal Narratives

Cathy S. Gelbin

Over the past four decades, gender-specific differences in personal narratives from the Holocaust have been the subject of heated academic debate and there is a growing body of research on manifestations of gender and sexuality in personal camp narratives. While Lawrence Langer, a leading scholar in the study of Holocaust testimonies, sought to counter nascent feminist research in the field by asserting the 'severely diminished role that gendered behaviour played during those crucial years' (1998, p. 13), his position has in turn been rejected in recent studies by Hutton (2005), Waxman (2006) and in the co-edited volume by Hedgepeth and Saidel (2010), who variously argue for women's distinct experiences in the camps or distinct narrative patterns derived from female socialization.

The issue of sexuality, which is closely linked to representations of gender, occupies an even more controversial position within Holocaust scholarship and has been sidelined by most scholarship to date. The present chapter, however, will propose that, when considering personal survivor narratives by women in particular, accounts of sexuality may galvanize the gender-specific aspects of survivor narratives and that ignoring or marginalizing these accounts thus severely limits our understanding of the social fabric of the camps. As I will argue in the first part of this chapter, this is particularly the case when we look at written memoirs. I will then turn to the *Archive of Memory*, an audiovisual survivor project carried out in Germany in the 1990s, to examine the additional complexities that the genre of audiovisual narratives may introduce to the study of gender and sexuality during the Holocaust.

Gender and sexuality in written camp narratives

By the early 1990s, the seminal studies by Heinemann (1986) and Ringelheim (1992) had already drawn attention to the fact that Jewish women arriving at Auschwitz were immediately selected for killing if discovered with children or found to be pregnant. Women who fell pregnant while in the camp were also immediately sent to their deaths. Furthermore, as Heinemann asserted, personal narratives by women are more likely to focus on emotional and physical contact among inmates, including maternity, pregnancy, sexual assault, as well as close friendships (Heinemann, p. 33). While acknowledging certain aspects of female-specific experience in the camps, chiefly childbirth and maternity, Heinemann rejects the notion that men and women in the camps may have experienced friendships and sexual relationships in fundamentally different ways. She concludes that gender differences in camp survivor narratives instead result from the stronger emphasis on the personal and interpersonal in female upbringing, and are therefore more readily reflected in women's personal narratives.

Echoing Heineman, Waxman (p. 128) has more recently emphasized gender differences in narrative structures rather than gender-specific ways of coping with the actual camp experience. Hutton, however, takes a more forthright stance, declaring that the argument for gender-neutral camp experiences is 'quite simply ill-considered' (2005, p. 104). Pointing to factors already observed by Heinemann and Ringelheim, such as the immediately lethal consequences of pregnancy and maternity, Hutton argues that 'it seems blindingly obvious that men and women had different experiences in the camps and experienced similar events differently' (p. 104). Indeed, a comparison with male survivor testimonies not only confirms the arguments of the proponents of experiential and narrative differences alike, but also shows that accepting the case for the former does not necessarily entail the adoption of an essentialist position.

As Hutton points out (p. 140), a non-gendered study of the camp experience would risk obliterating large portions of evidence. The same, I would like to argue here, can be said about the treatment of sexuality more specifically, which forms an important facet of the gendered aspects of Holocaust memoirs. Sexuality, as Amesberger and Halbmayr (2008, p. 180) point out, was of heightened importance to National Socialist ideology, whose racist goals demanded the control of female sexuality in particular. It is beyond doubt that pregnancy and maternity led to higher mortality rates among women in the first instance, even though the intended aim of the Nazis' extermination policies was the death of all Jews, female and male. It also seems plausible that the stronger focus on social relations in women's upbringing produced a different emphasis on social networks within the camp itself. However, the exact nature of these differences is hard to ascertain, given that all inmates depended on close relationships for their survival and given also that we must rely on narrative alone for evidence of how these relationships functioned. What is immediately noticeable is that memoirs by male survivors focus far less on emotional and physical intimacy. Sexual exploitation, such as the frequenting of camp brothels by 'privileged' male inmates or the abuse of young boys by male kapos and SS, is reported by only a few male autobiographers including Wiesel (1958) and Levi (1986), as well as in some fictionalized accounts by writers such as Ka-Tzetnik (1961), Borowski (1992) and Kertész (2006). This, however, should not lead us to assume that interned men were unaffected by sexual exploitation and violence. Again, social factors, in particular the misogynistic coding of women as sexual objects, may have reinforced actual conditions in the camp and resulted in more widespread sexual exploitation of female camp inmates. However, according to the male writers cited above, young boys too, in particular, were sexually exploited by kapos and also, according to Ka-Tzetnik, by the SS. It seems that both female and male internees were subjected to, and in some cases themselves also enacted, sexualized power relations in the camp. However, it can be assumed that due to the reasons outlined above these factors played a greater role in camp life for female inmates and that they are therefore also more strongly manifest in women's survivor narratives.

Yet the study of sexual acts in camp narratives remains both a contested and as yet under-examined field. This may be because male survivor narratives, such as those of Primo Levi or Elie Wiesel, have been more readily canonized, but also because any such investigation risks the charge of sexualizing and thus trivializing the Holocaust. A major scholar in the field of Holocaust literature, Alvin Rosenfeld, for example, asserted that 'one of the characteristics of Holocaust writings at their most authentic is that they are peculiarly and predominantly sexless' (1988, p. 164). While it is indeed true that first-person narrations of sex and desire are notably absent from Holocaust memoirs, women's narratives in particular make ample reference to sexual acts occurring among other inmates and sometimes between inmates and their guards. Rosenfeld's claim thus exemplifies how an important body of material can be relegated to oblivion by the rejection of a gender-specific approach to Holocaust narratives.

What I propose is required instead is a complex and nuanced analysis of the inextricably entwined roles of gender, sexuality and power in the camps. In particular, while necessarily framed by the camps' dehumanizing conditions, any examination of sexual acts in the camps should resist the blanket condemnation of them as coercive or exploitative that is commonly found in memoirs and most scholarly works to date. This is especially true in the case of same-sex relations. While narrations of sexual acts in the camps attribute lesbianism with a particularly negative status, the budding feminist historiography on the Holocaust has surprisingly skirted any in-depth investigation of this theme (such as Baumel, 1998; Laska, 1983; Ofer & Weitzmann, 1998). Even more recent studies within this body of scholarly work, which do account for the issue of sexuality, have paid comparatively little attention to the issue of sexual acts among women in Holocaust memoirs. In her article on sexual violence and gender identity in the camps, Monika Flaschka (2010), rather surprisingly, devotes entire sections to heterosexual and male–male rape, while eliding a matching discussion of sexual coercion among women. At the same time, those works which do examine same-sex relations as part of wider scenarios of sexual violence in the camps, such as Waxman's study, pose serious conceptual problems and inadvertently replicate the anti-lesbianism found in many of the memoirs themselves. Hutton's study, in contrast, offers a rare example of the subject of sexual acts among women being treated with some complexity, albeit with respect only to French women's memoirs.

The German historian Claudia Schoppmann's seminal study (1991) remains the only scholarly monograph to date that does any justice to the study of lesbianism under Nazi rule. However, this work has not enjoyed the broad international reception it deserves.[1] Schoppmann (pp. 236–247), and more recently Hutton (pp. 104–119), detect a double standard in survivor memoirs, seeing a tendency in these writings to associate innate homosexuality with the 'asocial' women marked with the black triangle, while depicting sexual relationships among Jewish women or politicals as contingent. The French-Jewish *chanson* singer Fania Fénelon, who survived as the singer of the women's camp orchestra, provides a rare example of a camp romance in her depiction of the tender relationship between two members of the female camp orchestra, 'Marta' and 'Little Irene', although she does not elaborate on the exact physical nature of their bond (1977, p. 145). In her own memoir, however, the cellist Anita Lasker-Wallfisch, on whom 'Marta' is clearly modelled, does not corroborate the suggested erotic nature of her friendship with 'Irene', nor with any other members of the camp orchestra. Whether these discrepancies arise from the sensationalist streak apparent in Fénelon's work or were deemed too sensitive to figure in Lasker-Wallfisch's memoir, will have to remain the subject of speculation.

However, Fénelon's positive portrayal of this relationship remains an exception, even within her own memoir. Elsewhere in her work, Fénelon reports sexual acts involving 'Black Triangles' in an unequivocally scathing tone. Schoppmann convincingly argues that through the negative portrayals of predatory 'Black Triangles', memoirists sought to distance their own close bonds with other interned women, bonds on which they depended for emotional and physical survival, from the homophobic stereotype of the lesbian. Intent on rescuing the image of the lesbian from historical silencing on the one hand and homophobic stereotyping on the other, Schoppmann herself, however, somewhat downplays the sexualized power relations between women in the camp.

In contrast, I propose here that a more complex view of gender aspects in the camp requires a careful analysis of enactments of sex and power among female inmates themselves, as well as between female camp guards[2] and internees. Waxman's (pp. 128–129) assertion that the 1970s women's movement inspired a stronger focus on female-specific themes in survivor memoirs, including the topic of sexuality, rings only partially true, since sexual acts and sexualized enactments of power play a surprisingly important role in the writings by female camp survivors from the immediate post-war period. A number of these writings contained graphic reports of homo- and heterosexual acts during internment that are sometimes romantically transfigured, but more often appear as forms of sexualized violence and prostitution. Although the separation of inmates according to gender displayed the camp regime's intentions to curb heterosexual romance – sexual relations among inmates, and especially occurrences of lesbianism, being severely punished by the guards – women's memoirs convey a sexualized regime of power as an integral part of female camp life in particular. The sexualized control of women's lives and bodies in the camps was intended to routinely humiliate the inmates and strip them of their dignity and humanity.

Autobiographers such as the Hungarian-Jewish doctor Gisella Perl describe how female internees were subjected to sexualized power from the moment of their initiation into Auschwitz-Birkenau, as lewd SS men observed the naked women being shaved and tattooed (1948, pp. 43–45). The exercise of sexualized power over female inmates by the guards was part and parcel of the constant selections in the camp, which continually reduced the inmate population and routinely required women to strip naked before the male SS. Fénelon describes how on at least one such occasion, SS Rapportführer Tauber sent those women whose breasts were no longer firm to the gas chamber (p. 15).

As a gynaecologist, Perl was keenly aware of the physical and sexual state of women in the camp. Initially selected to assist the SS camp doctor Josef Mengele with his abortion experiments, Perl, observing the death sentence meted out to pregnant women, unilaterally performed or induced abortions on women on the floors of the barracks, thus saving countless lives. Perl also carried out frequent breast surgery on women to repair injuries from the habitual breast whippings that were part of the punishment ritual in the women's camp. Perl reports that the overseer Irma Grese, whom many memoirs reference for her surpassing beauty and cruelty, had a special proclivity for breast whippings and would invariably arrive at the camp infirmary to observe the excruciating operations performed on her victims' breasts with apparent sexual excitement. Grese's sexualized violence against female internees is also reported by other autobiographers (Dribben, 1970, pp. 205–207; Fénelon, 1977, p. 83; Leitner, 1994, pp. 52–56).

According to Olga Lengyel, who like Perl survived as a medical worker in the camp, Grese had sexual relations with both female and male inmates. Lengyel (1980, p. 193) reports that according to her friend, who was Grese's camp maid, Grese 'frequently had homosexual relationships with inmates and then ordered the victims to the crematory'. While Lengyel's assertion that the SS at Auschwitz 'were noted for their aberrations' (ibid.) invokes the problematic association of the Nazis' moral evil with sexual deviance, a stereotype that I have critically examined elsewhere (Gelbin, 2007), none other than Auschwitz camp commander Rudolf Hoess claims in his memoirs that

> Like homosexuality among the men, an epidemic of lesbianism was rampant in the women's camp. [...] Time and again, I received reports of intercourse of this sort between supervisors and female prisoners.
> (Hoess, 1961, p. 130)

Hoess's report conveys the full cynicism of the camp leadership with regard to perceived sexual deviance. On the one hand, Auschwitz saw one of the largest cohorts of interned gay men in the German camp system, with the professed goal of identifying 'innate' and contingent gay men through heterosexual intercourse with female inmates. Men who failed to consummate heterosexual intercourse were condemned to death. In the women's camp, lesbian acts among inmates were severely punished through internment in the punishment block, where up to 30 inmates per day, belonging to all interned groups, may have died at Grese's hand alone (Brown, 2004, p. 43). On the other hand, Hoess reports that the SS leadership deliberately set female kapos variously marked with the black or green triangle to oversee Jewish women. These kapos were 'Germans by blood' whom the SS leadership believed to be particularly suited to this task. Previously interned at Ravensbrück as 'prostitutes', a category of perceived sexual deviance that the SS used synonymously with lesbianism, they were transferred to Auschwitz in 1942 for the sole purpose of overseeing Jewish women.

As Schoppmann and Grau have shown in their respective works, there was no wholesale extermination plan for homosexuals and, in contrast to the persecution of gay men, it has been virtually impossible to substantiate lesbianism as a direct cause for deportation and camp internment. German kapos were also exempt from the systematic selections for death to which Jewish prisoners were subjected, as well as enjoying more favourable labour details and better food rations. These 'privileges' enabled them to trade food for sex with deprived Jewish inmates or force sex upon them, a situation which fuelled the intense outbursts of hatred against 'Black Triangles' in the memoirs by Fénelon and others. Krystyna Żywulska (1988), who was able to hide her Jewish origins and survive as a functionary inmate in the dead persons' goods depot, the 'Canada' outfit at Birkenau, relates how a female kapo marked with the black triangle lured a young girl into the washroom with the promise of giving her hot potatoes. The girl did not initially understand the sexual implications of this offer; however, when she did, she attempted to escape, with the kapo pouncing on her. Żywulska's closing phrase 'they were lost in the dark' (p. 252) suggests the possible rape of the girl.

Perl reports that SS guards were amused at heterosexual transactions in the latrines (p. 79) and it seems that the same double standards – both formal prohibition and selective toleration of sexual acts among inmates – were applied to homosexuality. Perceived sexual debasement, it seems, was part and parcel of the SS scheme to divide and rule among inmates and destroy even their dignity. Due to the total absence of privacy, sexual acts in the camp necessarily took place in close proximity to other inmates and often right before their eyes. Autobiographical writers relate such incidences to highlight the traumatic nature of camp internment with its radical assault on the bourgeois sense of normality.

Although most memoirists condemn sexual exchanges for food, Lengyel (p. 90) and Żywulska (p. 328) acknowledge that some women may have drawn a certain degree of physical and emotional sustenance from such heterosexual encounters and we can assume that the same may have been true for certain same-sex relations.

Narration in the audiovisual genre

As we have seen above, written memoirs by women authors frequently engage with the issue of sexual acts in the camps. Male memoirists tend to downplay these themes or omit them completely, and the most explicit depictions are found in Ka-Tzetnik's fictional writings rather than in memoirs. A different picture again emerges when we turn our attention to audiovisual survivor narratives, which emerged into public view with Yale's Fortunoff Video Archive for Holocaust Testimonies, a project which started in the late 1970s and now constitutes the largest body of personal narratives on the Holocaust. Yet recent historiography on gender and the Holocaust continues to focus on written memoirs and has made only scant reference to this rich resource.

Between 1995 and 1998, I had the unique opportunity to coordinate and study the *Archive of Memory*, the first collection of audiovisual survivor narratives in Germany. Over two years, the *Archive* recorded interviews with 79 women and men whom the Nazis had persecuted on the grounds of 'Jewish race'. The project was conducted at the Moses Mendelssohn Centre for European-Jewish Studies at Universität Potsdam in collaboration with the Fortunoff Video Archive for Holocaust Testimonies, whose co-founders, Geoffrey Hartman and Dori Laub, closely advised on the academic and psychological aspects of the undertaking (see Diekmann et al., 1998; Gelbin, 1998; Gelbin et al., 1998; Miltenberger, 1998a, 1998b).

The project took its central aesthetic cues from the Fortunoff Video Archive, which relies on a sparse aesthetic that consciously abstains from visual elements that could distract from the interviewees and their narrations. Interviews are taken in a specially created studio, where interviewees sit on a chair before a monochrome studio background. They are filmed at eye level in medium close-up shot with the camera occasionally zooming in to reveal details in facial expression, gestures or the display of personal objects such as photos, or zooming out slightly for a broader appreciation of body language.

In his foundational study on Holocaust testimonies, Lawrence Langer expands on the powerful impact of this plain aesthetic that aims to limit artifice, seeking instead to emphasize the veracity and authenticity that he attaches to the audiovisual genre:

> Nothing [...] distracts us from the immediacy and the intimacy of conducting interviews with former victims (which I have done) or watching them on a screen. [...] I often found myself naked before their nakedness, vulnerable in the presence of their vulnerability.
> (1991, p. xiii)

As Weisman observes, the crucial aspect of mediation seems notably absent from Langer's vision of 'testimony' as the direct expression of memory free of any form of narrative mediation, be it the interview itself, the spoken word or the visual medium (2004, p. 105). This problem derives at least partially from the term 'testimony', whose legalistic origins conflate narrative and factual truth, potentially obliterating the very essence of narrative as (self-)construction. For this reason, in my discussion here, I will use the more permeable concept of the audiovisual survivor narrative, which opens itself up more readily to the analytical practices of literary and film studies, as well as the sociological field of biography studies, which in Germany has gained some prominence through the work of scholars such as Fritz Schütze, Ulrich Oevermann and Gabriele Rosenthal.

On the levels of both spoken narrative and visual image, audiovisual survivor narratives are no less constructed and mediated than any other form of narrative. I would like to point here to the distinct aesthetic of the Fortunoff video testimony which, in its very invocation of authenticity, is an important visual clue to its highly constructed and mediated nature. What separates the audiovisual genre from written memoir is, after all, its visual nature, with the screen both mediating between and physically separating the viewer from the interviewee.

It may well be that the particular power of the video recording arises specifically from its mediated, as opposed to immediate, nature. In his *Theory of Film*, the early film critic Siegfried Kracauer argued that film was particularly suited to mediating the shocks of atrocity. For Kracauer, Georges Franju's 1949 documentary on a Paris abattoir in Paris evoked 'the litter of tortured human bodies' seen in footage from the liberated Nazi concentration camps. Such scenes, he maintained, might be too difficult to behold in material reality (Kracauer, 1965, p. 306). The filmic screen, however, akin to Athena's shield in ancient Greek myth, both reflected and deflected material reality, enabling the viewers to take in something of the horrors from which they might otherwise have turned away.

In addition to employing Dori Laub's 'non-directive' interviewing method, which draws on conversation techniques derived from psychoanalytic therapy, the project also took inspiration from the German school of biographical narrative (qualitative) interviews developed by Schütze and Oevermann. Both methods converge in that they place the interviewee's narrative at the centre of the interview. However, while interviews according to Laub focus primarily on the period of persecution in order to capture traumatic aspects of the narrative, the Schütze-Oevermann approach records entire life-history narrations in order to detect 'the interplay between historical circumstance and the particular biographical context of that experience' (Rosenthal, 1987, p. 1). In keeping with this method, the *Archive of Memory* recorded life-history interviews lasting several hours, sometimes taken during several day-sessions over a number of months.

By drawing on notions of narratology, the concerted study of such narratives within the German school of biography studies shares essential traits with literary analysis rather than traditional historiography, which tends to mistrust 'oral history' documents as subjective and factually unreliable. It can be said that for this very reason, personal narratives can afford us far richer perspectives on the past and present, although, as I will argue, the medium of narration may condition the emergence of different types of gendered narratives.

In the course of our study of the interviews, a conspicuous gender pattern emerged. Whereas there was overall gender parity among the recorded narratives, only three out of seventeen camp survivors – approximately one sixth – were women. In comparison, Berlin's Memorial to the Murdered Jews of Europe also holds considerably fewer interviews with female camp survivors, whereas the collection of our cooperation partner, the Fortunoff Video Archive for Holocaust Testimonies, displays near gender parity.[3] It may be a coincidence that the *Archive of Memory* was less successful in recording the narratives of female camp survivors; however, it is tempting to speculate about the possible reasons for this.

As has been mentioned above, female survivors more readily discussed in their written memoirs issues of sexuality and sexual violation that are normally deemed inappropriate and relegated from the realm of public interaction. These authors did so through the private act of writing, where certain boundaries of privacy are seemingly retained, albeit with a public audience in mind. In contrast, the audiovisual medium radically breaks down the imagined separation between public and private. It may well be that the embodied setting of the video interview, coupled with the physical location of the intended public collection in Germany, the land of the former perpetrators, impeded not only the emergence of narrative strands relating to sexual acts in the camps, but also the participation of more female camp survivors more generally.

What separates the audiovisual genre from written memoir most strikingly is, after all, the awareness of an embodied speech act in motion, delivered before an audience. The very process of interviewing for the *Archive of Memory* was a public act, with two interviewers present at each recording session, as well as a cinematographer and a volunteer assistant taking notes during the recording to act as a back-up source in case of technical breakdown (which fortunately never occurred). Added to that were the aforementioned public goals of the *Archive of Memory*, which began its recordings at a crucial historical and discursive juncture in German history: 50 years after the end of the Holocaust, when the generation of survivors was beginning to rapidly pass away, but also less than five years after German unification, when public discourses about the German present and past saw a decisive shift.

The heightened public and political implications of the *Archive of Memory* may well have hampered the emergence of narratives about the radical invasion of the private sphere and the body, which had affected female internees in particularly radical ways. Such stories may surface more readily when the act of narration occurs in a more intimate setting, a space maintaining some separation between public and private, such as the private act of writing or, in the case of dialogic encounter, a setting with fewer public or even therapeutic implications. It is no coincidence that this corresponds to Dori Laub's vision of the video interview. Laub, himself a child survivor and psychoanalyst whose theoretical and practical approach to video-recorded survivor narratives springs from his clinical practice, argues that it is the dialogic, and necessarily intimate, interaction between the survivor and a listener that makes for the particular quality of the 'testimony', for it is in this encounter that trauma can emerge for the first time or in a new way. While historical records and cultural artefacts about the event causing the trauma may indeed exist, the trauma itself

> has not been truly witnessed yet, not been taken cognizance of. The emergence of the narrative which is being listened to – and heard – is, therefore, the process and the place wherein the cognizance, the

'knowing' of the event is given birth to. The listener, therefore, is a party to the creation of knowledge *de novo* [...], the blank screen on which the event comes to be inscribed for the first time.

(1992, p. 57)

The spontaneous and dialogic nature of the video interview thus has the potential to generate new stories or certainly new detail in stories that may have been told previously in other contexts. Like Langer, Laub sees in this testimony an unmediated essence – trauma – that seems exempt from the influence of social conditioning. And yet the interviews taken in the *Archive of Memory* suggest that the forms of this traumatic narrative do not follow a universal schema. These narratives respond not only to the parameters of the interview set by the interviewers and their capacity to listen to and engage with the narrative empathetically, a point Laub indeed concedes, but also to the norms of social and political acceptability within which this narrative emerges. As Gabriele Rosenthal (1998, p. 14) argues,

Personal life stories must be understood both in terms of events that occurred in actuality and that are interpreted subjectively. They are past experiences that are subjectively altered in the process of remembering.

This was nowhere more apparent than in the interviews given by survivors who had lived in the East German republic after 1945, where political resisters, especially communists, had received public recognition, whereas Jews were treated as second-class victims because they were seen to have failed to resist collectively.

During the post-war decades, a number of our East German participants had spoken on numerous occasions – often to school classes – about their experience of Auschwitz, without however mentioning that they had been held there as Jews. Instead, these survivors deliberately nurtured the perception that they had been interned as resisters. Some, such as Kurt G., had indeed been detained in prisons or other camps as communists or for other acts of resistance before their deportation; but all – except for Irmgard K., who successfully hid her Jewish descent throughout her time at Birkenau – were sent to Auschwitz solely because they had been defined as Jews. Six years after unification, the decision of these survivors to speak for the *Archive of Memory* publically asserted the Jewish dimension of their stories of persecution.

Yet their narratives themselves remained largely within the old pattern, focussing on their own acts of resistance, setting themselves apart from the mass of seemingly passive Jewish inmates and tending to omit stories of extreme fear, powerlessness or physical violation. Occasionally, the video interview was able to break through this pattern, such as in the case of Willi F., who related how he had witnessed the public whipping of a fellow inmate at Birkenau. During the following weeks, new memories began to surface in Mr F. He now recalled that he himself had been the inmate who had received, rather than witnessed the whipping, and he returned to the studio several weeks later to record this memory that had been repressed for six long decades.

Interview with Irmgard K.

In this section, I will discuss one representative interview from the *Archive of Memory* in order to make some tentative suggestions about the ways in which the audiovisual medium may impact on gender-specific patterns of narration. The interview with Irmgard K., which I will explore in greater depth, alongside those of two other female camp survivors, displayed the gender-specific narrative patterns observed in written memoirs only to a certain degree, insofar as this interview revealed a similarly heightened focus on the emotional as well as the social.[4] Themes relating to maternity, another facet traditionally linked to femininity, also played an important role in Ms K.'s interview in particular. Almost entirely missing, however, were the narrative strands of sexuality with which we are familiar from many written survivor accounts. As already indicated above, this absence may be linked to the problems of enunciating such themes in the context of the heightened public associations of audiovisual narrative, especially given the temporal, geographical and political setting of the *Archive of Memory*.

Irmgard K. belonged to the group of survivors who settled in East Germany after liberation. Born in Breslau in 1915 to a Jewish father and a non-Jewish mother, she joined the socialist workers' movement as a youngster. After 1933, Ms K. was incarcerated several times on the grounds of her political activity and she had also been ordered to wear the yellow star in 1941.[5] Following another arrest in 1942, Ms K. was deported as a political from Breslau jail to Auschwitz. 'Knowing what Auschwitz implied', she removed the star from her garments while on transport and, realizing that her papers had not travelled with her from Breslau, did not report when Jews were called up upon arrival at Auschwitz. She was therefore marked as a German political and ultimately became a functionary inmate in the Birkenau women's camp.

In 1943, however, Ms K. voluntarily signed up for a transport of *Mischlinge* to Ravensbrück, believing that conditions there would be more favourable. This was true to a certain degree, given that Ravensbrück did not have mass extermination facilities; however, large numbers of inmates did not survive the camp due to its murderous slave labour regime for Siemens, as well as other forms of maltreatment, starvation and disease. After liberation, Ms K. briefly lived in France before moving to East Berlin, where she died in 2003.

Irmgard K.'s interview stood out among the *Archive of Memory* collection for its heightened emotional quality, but also because it had to be recorded in two sessions over nearly two years. During the first interview in August 1995, Ms K. told her life story from the years of her youth in Breslau until her deportation from Auschwitz 1943. It was only in May 1997, after a period of illness and other delaying circumstances, that Ms K. was able to return to the studio to record the second part of her life history, from Ravensbrück to the present. Throughout both recordings, Ms K. spoke with intense emotional affect about her female companions and the important friendships she had formed in both camps, and particularly in Auschwitz, which had helped her survive the cruelty of camp life.

Whereas male interviewees among the politicals tended to avoid stories of victimization and weakness, instead focussing on acts of resistance and courage (Miltenberger, 1998), Irmgard K. presented thematic strands of agency together with those relating fear, pain or exasperation. Having emerged from the so-called sauna, into which the SS had chased the naked new arrivals, Ms K. successfully persuaded the inmate sewing on the camp badges to affix only her number to the uniform. To prove that this is true, she holds up the photograph taken after her induction into the camp:

> Look very closely and you will see that Irmgard does not even wear a star, no red [laughs, then chuckles] triangle, nothing. I was probably the only one walking among the thousands at Auschwitz without anything [laughs].

Such acts of resilience and solidarity form important clues for Ms K. in preserving shreds of the inmates' individuality and humanity that the SS sought to erase. Ms K.'s vivid descriptions of the lack of opportunities for maintaining personal hygiene and the restricted access to the latrines, interspersed with moments of silence and her faltering voice, highlight the radical assault that camp life made against the inmate on the most basic physical level. The food bowls and spoons that the inmate received at her induction into the camp were essential for survival; without these items, her life was under threat. After a few days in the camp, however, Ms K. realized that these bowls had come from the quarantine block where new arrivals, having been pent up for days without access to the latrines, had used the bowls instead.

The inability to wash formed another source of despair for 'after the sauna, there was no more washing [long pause] or brushing teeth [...] The sauna was the first and last time most [inmates] felt water on their bodies.' Even when, after eight weeks in the camp, Ms K. finally found some opportunities for rudimentary washing, this act of self-preservation and dignity appears marred by the debasing filth in the camp:

> Another piece of Auschwitz [pauses]: the Germans [long pause] from Block 10 [long pause] had a place for nature's call and that was a kind of stables [...] with a pit at the back [...], and I saw pipes running along there and water dripping from the pipes. And I [pauses] went there in the evenings after roll call with my food bowl and gathered water running along the pipes and cleaned my face and washed down a little.

Throughout the interview, Ms K. emphasizes that solidarity among inmates was essential for survival, both emotional and physical. Indeed, she suggests that emotional resilience may have had an impact on physical survival and, in her view, 'most were destroyed in spirit, unless they died of typhoid, malaria or other diseases'. According to the interviewee, the help of numerous female inmates repeatedly saved her life. Among them is her camp mate Manzi, who told Irmgard, when the latter was sick with typhoid, that she had 'a good heart'. The double meaning of the 'good heart', as both physically strong and morally sound, helped the narrator retain the will to live. It is particularly the politicals who help Irmgard K. to survive by placing her on better work details and ultimately persuading her to enlist for Ravensbrück.

In contrast to many written memoirs, Irmgard K. refers only sparingly to violence by SS guards and kapos, as well as refraining from denunciatory portrayals of women marked with the black triangle. The story of Klara provides one example of this narrative strategy. Placed as the new block elder in the sick barracks for typhoid cases and pregnant women, Ms K. unwittingly oversees the killing of a newborn Jewish child:

> I had never seen a newborn, no baby until then [pauses]. And the child was born [pauses], the midwife Klara [pauses] carries it into the Block Office, takes a bucket and drowns the child [pauses] while I'm standing by [long pause].

Once a midwife in civilian life, Klara had been convicted for killing babies. Here in Auschwitz, she performs the same gruesome deed, now in keeping with the camp rules that all Jewish babies must be killed. One senses in Ms K.'s repeated pauses in this excerpt her profound sense of shock and guilt over this act, for which she as block elder seemingly held some responsibility. This moral conflict is tempered in another section of the narrative, in which Ms K. recounts Klara's corruption on the one hand, with her theft of food from patients to conduct illegal camp deals and, on the other, Ms K.'s own bold rescue of a pregnant Dutch woman from Block 25, where those selected for death awaited transport to the gas chamber.

In contrast to her description of Klara, who stole food from patients to improve her own situation in the camp, Irmgard K. relates how her role as block elder enabled her to redistribute the food rations of deceased women on her block to the quarantine block, which many new arrivals did not survive because of its atrocious conditions. Such acts of help enabled the narrator to preserve a sense of her own humanity in the face of extreme moral conflict and adversity, and motivated her to survive:

> I felt that I could help and achieve something, and later as Block Elder I probably also had a different standing, sure, than those who [...] were merely exposed to death and did not have the strength to develop friendships. [...] Many of course wandered about on their own. I met women from the Warsaw Ghetto who had arrived by themselves [...] and also didn't make contact with anyone, who were left to themselves.

Irmgard K.'s omission of condemnatory remarks about other inmates is particularly evident in her references to the camp elder Klara Pförtsch, known in Auschwitz as Leo. Ms K. had witnessed Leo aiding Rapportführer Tauber's deadly selections for Block 25:

> That time I got out the young Dutch woman, [...] I witnessed her during selections, when she made sure that [pauses] those who were sent to the left did not get back to the right.

Figure 8.1 Still from interview with Irmgard K. for the *Archive of Memory*, Moses Mendelssohn Zentrum für europäisch-jüdische Studien (Universität Potsdam). Courtesy of the interviewee's family.

Ms K.'s sober description of Leo contrasts starkly with the depiction of the camp elder in some written memoirs as a masculine figure conducting sexual relationships with other women (Dribben, 1970, pp. 185, 190). In a calm, factual manner, Ms K. relates Leo's metamorphosis from a communist textile worker dedicated to the anti-Nazi struggle to a ruthless killer of Jewish women in Auschwitz. 'Her character probably transformed [...] in Ravensbrück [...] and in Auschwitz', Ms. K. concludes, asserting elsewhere in the interview that Auschwitz brought about a change in personality: one could fall very low in the camp and become vicious, or transcend oneself with the help of one's friendships.[6] This seemingly idealistic narrative of self-control is modified elsewhere in the interview when Irmgard K. touches on the total disempowerment of Jewish inmates who arrived at the camp without a sense of community or access to 'privileged' labour details (Figure 8.1).

Conclusion

Whereas acts of sexual assault and sexually 'improper' behaviour serve in most written memoirs by women survivors to epitomize the degrading nature of camp life, the silence on this subject of the female camp survivors interviewed for the *Archive of Memory* suggests that the audiovisual genre may present us with a more limited view of the particular experiences of women in the camps. To verify these suggestions, it will be necessary in the future to conduct further extended research not only on the German interviews, but on the whole body of videotaped survivor narratives that has been collected across Europe, Israel and the United States over the last 40 years. What Irmgard K.'s interview does attest to, however, is the potential of the spoken word, allied with the emphatic act of listening, to recuperate at least partially the humanity and dignity of those who went through the camps.

Notes

1. An excerpt from this study appeared in English in Grau and Schoppmann, 1995.
2. These are often incorrectly referred to as SS guards. The SS, however, was an exclusively male organization, and women serving as camp guards were formally SS 'auxiliaries' rather than members.
3. Between 2009 and 2012 Berlin's Memorial to the Murdered Jews of Europe recorded a total of 51 interviews, 22 of these with women and 29 with men. However, only one third of the interviewed 35 camp survivors were women (12 women and 23 men). I thank Daniel Baranowski, Head of the Memorial's Audiovisual Department, for sharing this information with me in his email of 24 September 2012. In contrast, out of the more than 4,400 audiovisual interviews with witnesses and survivors of the Holocaust recorded by Yale between 1979 and today, 1,039 interviews are with female camp survivors and 1294 with their male counterparts. I thank Joanne Rudof, Archivist of the Fortunoff Video Archive, for relating this information to me in her email of 7 September 2012.
4. Cathy Gelbin and Angela Reinhard, *Interview with Irmgard K.* Archiv der Erinnerung, Moses Mendelssohn Zentrum Potsdam, 1995.
5. The Nazis' racial laws had exempted those classed as Jewish *Mischlinge* ('mixed-race Jews of the first-degree'), that is, those with two Jewish grandparents while not themselves affiliated with the Jewish religion, from wearing the yellow star as well as from routine deportation. However, the *Archive of Memory* recorded several cases where local Nazi authorities had forced former *Mischlinge* to wear the star, each time with the consequence of deportation. Whereas historians of the Holocaust previously relied heavily on Nazi legislation to assess the plight of former *Mischlinge*, judging this as 'comparatively slight' (Hilberg, 1985), our findings suggested personal narratives as an essential supplementary resource for any study of this group.
6. Pride in her own agency shines through when Ms K. relates how she helped bring Pförtsch to justice after the war. In 1948, just after Ms K.'s own daughter Monika was born, Pförtsch turned up at the Ravensbrück survivors' association, confident that no witnesses to her cruelty had survived. Ms K., however, recognized her immediately and reported her to the East German authorities,

who subsequently arrested Pförtsch. Pförtsch was then extradited to Rastatt in West Germany, where the French sentenced her to death. In 1950, however, her conviction was commuted to a life sentence and she was granted early release from jail in 1957. See Leo, 2006, p. 517, n. 19.

Works cited

Amesberger, H. & Halbmayr, B. (2008) 'Nazi Differentiations Mattered: Ideological Intersections of Sexualized Violence During National Socialist Persecution', in E. Hertzog (ed.) *Life, Death and Sacrifice: Women and Family in the Holocaust* (Jerusalem: Gefen), pp. 181–196.

Baumel, J. (1998) *Double Jeopardy: Gender and the Holocaust* (London: Vallentine Mitchell).

Borowski, T. (1992) *This Way for the Gas, Ladies and Gentlemen* (London: Penguin).

Brown, D. (2004) *The Beautiful Beast: The Life & Crimes of SS-Aufseherin Irma Grese* (Ventura, CA: Golden West Historical Publications).

Diekmann, I., et al. (eds.) (1988) *Archiv der Erinnerung: Interviews mit Überlebenden der Shoah. Video-Edition mit pädagogischem Begleitheft* (Potsdam: Medienpädagogisches Zentrum Land Brandenburg).

Dribben, J. (1970) *A Girl Called Judith Strick* (New York: Cowles).

Felman, S. & Laub, D. (1992) *Testimony: Crises of Witnessing in Literature, Psychoanalysis, and History* (New York: Routledge).

Fénelon, F. (1977) *Playing for Time*, Judith Landry (trans.) (New York: Atheneum).

Flaschka, M. (2010) '"Only Pretty Women Were Raped": The Effect of Sexual Violence on Gender Identities in Concentration Camps,' in S. Hedgepeth & R. Saidel (eds.) *Sexual Violence against Jewish Women during the Holocaust* (Waltham, MA: Brandeis University Press), pp. 77–93.

Gelbin, C. (1998) 'Die NS-"Vergangenheitsbewältigung" in der DDR und ihre Widerspiegelung im narrativen Prozeß', in K. Grözinger et al. (eds.) *Menorah. Jahrbuch für deutsch-jüdische Geschichte* (Bodenheim: Philo), pp. 224–244.

Gelbin, C. (2007) 'Double Visions: Queer Femininity and Holocaust Film from Ostatni Etap to Aimée & Jaguar', *Women in German Yearbook* 23, 179–204.

Gelbin, C. & Lezzi, E. *Interview with Willi F.* Potsdam: Archiv der Erinnerung, 2 October 1995 and 28 March 1996.

Gelbin, C., et al. (eds.) (1998) *Archiv der Erinnerung: Interviews mit Überlebenden der Shoah. Videographierte Lebenserzählungen und ihre Interpretationen* (Potsdam: Verlag für Berlin-Brandenburg).

Grau, G. & Schoppmann, C. (eds.) (1995) *Hidden Holocaust? Gay and Lesbian Persecution in Germany 1933–1945* (London: Cassell).

Hedgepeth, S. & Saidel, R. (2010) *Sexual Violence against Jewish Women during the Holocaust* (Waltham, MA: Brandeis University Press).

Heinemann, M. (1986) *Gender and Destiny: Women Writers and the Holocaust* (New York: Greenwood Press).

Hilberg, R. (1985) *The Destruction of the European Jews* (New York: Holmes & Meier).

Hoess, R. (1965) *Commandant of Auschwitz* (New York: Popular Library).

Hutton, M.-A. (2005) *Testimony from the Nazi Camps: French Women's Voices* (London: Routledge).

Ka-Tzetnik 35633. (1961) *Piepel*, M. Kohn (trans.) (London: Anthony Blond).
Kertész, I. (2006) *Fateless*, T. Wilkinson (trans.) (London: Vintage).
Kracauer, S. (1965) *Theory of Film: The Redemption of Physical Reality* (New York: Oxford University Press).
Langer, L. (1991) *Holocaust Testimonies: The Ruins of Memory* (New Haven & London: Yale University Press).
Langer, L. (1998) *Preempting the Holocaust* (New Haven & London: Yale University Press).
Laska, V. (1983) *Women in the Resistance and in the Holocaust: The Voices of Eyewitnesses* (Westport, CN: Greenwood Press).
Lasker-Wallfisch, A. (1996) *Inherit the Truth 1939–1945* (London: Giles de la Mare).
Leitner, I. (1994) *Isabella: From Auschwitz to Freedom* (New York: Anchor).
Lengyel, O. (1980) *Five Chimneys* (London: Granada).
Leo, A. (2006) 'Ravensbrück-Stammlager', in W. Benz & B. Distel (eds.) *Der Ort des Terrors. Geschichte der nationalsozialistischen Konzentrationslager* (München: C.H. Beck), pp. 473–520.
Levi, P. (1986) *Survival in Auschwitz*, S. Woolf (trans.) (New York: Collier Books).
Miltenberger, S. (ed.) (1998a) *Archiv der Erinnerung: Interviews mit Überlebenden der Shoah. Kommentierter Katalog* (Potsdam: Verlag für Berlin-Brandenburg).
Miltenberger, S. (1998b) 'Kommunist – Deutscher – Jude: Eine politische Biographie', in C. Gelbin et al. (eds.) *Archiv der Erinnerung: Interviews mit Überlebenden der Shoah. Videographierte Lebenserzählungen und ihre Interpretationen* (Potsdam: Verlag für Berlin-Brandenburg), pp. 231–264.
Ofer, D. & Weitzman, L. (eds.) (1998) *Women in the Holocaust* (New Haven: Yale University Press).
Perl, G. (2006) *I Was a Doctor in Auschwitz* (North Stratford, NH: Ayer).
Ringelheim, J. (2003) 'The Unethical and the Unspeakable: Women and the Holocaust', in N. Levi & M. Rothberg (eds.) *The Holocaust. Theoretical Readings* (Edinburgh: Edinburgh University Press), pp. 169–177.
Rosenfeld, A. (1998) *A Double Dying: Reflections on Holocaust Literature* (Bloomington: Indiana University Press).
Rosenthal, G. (1987) *'...Wenn alles in Scherben fällt...' Von Leben und Sinn der Kriegsgeneration. Typen biographischer Wandlungen* (Opladen: Leske + Budrich).
Rosenthal, G. (1995) *Erlebte und erzählte Lebensgeschichte. Gestalt und Struktur biographischer Selbstbeschreibungen* (Frankfurt a.M.: Campus).
Schoppmann, C. (1991) *Nationalsozialistische Sexualpolitik und weibliche Homosexualität* (Pfaffenweiler: Centaurus-Verlagsgesellschaft).
Waxman, Z. (2006) *Writing the Holocaust: Identity, Testimony, Representation* (Oxford: Oxford University Press).
Weisman, G. (2004) *Fantasies of Witnessing: Postwar Efforts to Experience the Holocaust* (Ithaca, NY: Cornell University Press).
Wiesel, E. (1981) *Night*, S. Rodway. (trans.) (London: Penguin).
Żywulska, K. (1988) *Tanz, Mädchen... Vom Warschauer Getto nach Auschwitz. Ein Überlebensbericht* (München: dtv).

9
Art as Transport-Station of Trauma? Haunting Objects in the Works of Bracha Ettinger, Sarah Kofman and Chantal Akerman

Griselda Pollock

The notion of art as a 'transport-station of trauma' was created by artist and feminist philosopher of psychoanalysis Bracha Ettinger (2000, p. 91). Ettinger explores the processes by which an aesthetic encounter – what she names 'aesthetic wit(h)nessing' – can become a site of transformation of the traces of trauma that inhabit an individual or a culture in post-catastrophic histories. In this chapter, I want to consider the aesthetic and the psychic economies involved in enabling such a transformation when using objects that remain as material indices of persons or worlds destroyed by racially-targeted genocide.[1] The philosopher Sarah Kofman wrote about, and wrote because of, the pen of her rabbi father murdered in Auschwitz. Chantal Akerman made a film, finally, about her grandmother's diary, the only trace of a life destroyed at Auschwitz. Bracha Ettinger made an installation in Sigmund Freud's home in exile using her father's ghetto diary and a spoon surviving from his maternal family.[2] What is the significance of the object and these varied positionings within the process of aesthetic wit(h)nessing that Ettinger has theorized on the basis of her own practice between memory, the archive and transformation through artworking?

Invisible strings of time: The paternal diary, the maternal spoon and the daughter's notebook

I had asked the artist to complete the installation of certain objects and photographs she had promised as part of an exhibition in the Freud Museum in London in June 2009. As curator I was responsible for the completion of the 'hang' in a two-day window. When the artist had finished her new work in the consulting room of 20 Maresfield Gardens, the home in exile of Sigmund Freud after 1938, an unanticipated encounter-event had occurred through the creation of a virtual network of invisible strings that the artist had spun across the iconic space full of its freighted objects: Freud's desk and the psychoanalyst's spectacles, his specially designed chair, his collection of antiquities, the couch, pictures, books, family photographs. On the desk the curators at the Freud Museum have laid a facsimile of Freud's laconic, one-line-a-day diary, kept between 1929 and 1939, the original being in the Library of Congress. The diary is hardly discursive. For me, the cryptic daily entries serve one purpose: to affirm that death had not come this day. Beside this facsimile of a Freud autograph the artist placed a trio of her own documents (Figure 9.1).

One is a finely written document, in Polish, with dates 1942, 1944, 1945, suggesting a diary or a memoir of dark times. It was written by Uziel Lichtenberg of Łódź, Poland, the artist's father. It is a reconstructed

Figure 9.1 Freud's desk with the diary of Uziel Lichtenberg and the notebooks of Bracha (Lichtenberg) Ettinger. Bracha L. Ettinger, *Father you see?* (series n° 2), installation view at *Resonance/Overlay/Interweave*, Sigmund Freud study room, Freud Museum, London, 2 June–29 July 2009, curated by Griselda Pollock. Photograph © Bracha L Ettinger 2009. Courtesy of the artist.

account of his years in the Łódź Ghetto, created there when the Germans invaded and conquered Poland, and the years of his escape to fight with partisans, and imprisonment in Hungary, his reunification with his now wife and the melancholy pregnancies of the creation of their future family. There was a handwritten text of a lullaby, also in Polish, its notations suggesting its musical rhythms, sung by the artist's mother in a language her daughter never knew, being herself born in Israel shortly after the state's foundation to her parentless survivor parents. There was another, smaller artefact, handwritten but also bearing colour and graphic additions suggestive of drawing, on handmade paper, bearing references to Freud's famous analysand, known as 'Dora'. This latter, a 'draw-notebook', as the artist names one of her constant artistic activities between writing and drawing, registers her own analytical-aesthetic reading of a classic Freudian text on female hysteria and deranged Oedipal relations.

Father diary, mother lullaby, daughter text. Something of the classic Oedipal triangle seems reproduced and at the same time analysed by papers bearing, however, histories of traumatic loss and dislocation, and the inheritance by the daughter of the traumas of the singing mother and writing father, mediated by a language she does not speak.[3]

Freud's working space was, as we know, filled with the objects he collected. Many – those on his desk particularly – were classical sculptured forms from China, Egypt or Rome. But Freud also collected objects that were not figurative and have more archaic connotations through their basic, perhaps gendered, forms. Lying on a table behind Freud's sculpture-laden desk, amidst a collection of nourishing pottery bowls and deadly iron arrowheads, Ettinger placed a glinting silver spoon (Figure 9.2). The spoon's evocation of feeding will set up its own relation to Freud's poignant diary of his years suffering oral cancer. It links to Uziel Lichtenberg's diary as it recaptures his terrifying experiences in the Łódź Ghetto in 1940 and beyond when he escaped its liquidation and fought with the partisans, later retrieving his wife who had also escaped the ghetto and survived in hiding as a farmworker in Slovakia. When Uziel Lichtenberg's new but destitute family finally moved into their own quarters in Israel, his surviving sister gave the family one silver spoon with which to feed themselves.

The spoon was a precious relic from their grandmother passed down the female line. It was to be his new family's only eating implement. When their second child, the later artist, Bracha Lichtenberg Ettinger, was born anorexic – having internalized prenatally her mother-to-be's own traumatic anguish, mourning and prolonged starvation – the

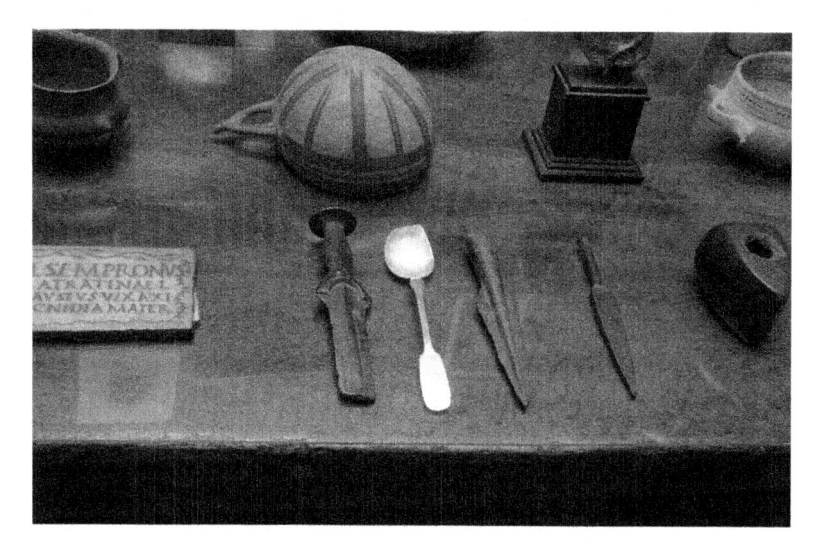

Figure 9.2 Freud's table with mother's spoon. Bracha L. Ettinger, *Father you see?* (series n° 2), installation view at *Resonance/Overlay/Interweave*, Sigmund Freud study room, Freud Museum, London, 2 June–29 July 2009, curated by Griselda Pollock. Photograph © Bracha L Ettinger 2009. Courtesy of the artist.

mother bent the spoon to try and force life-sustaining nourishment between her starving infant's lips. This beautiful piece of now-deformed silver functions as a link to a pre-war European Jewish heritage that became an instrument of attempted nourishment as child and mother mirrored each other in the uncannily transgenerational transcryptum of transmitted trauma stretched between orality, silence, song and now woven strings of compassionate connection.

Psychoanalytically, the spoon *is* 'mother' in several registers. Ettinger's simple gesture of placing the spoon thus, iconically beautiful yet bearing its meaningful deformation, engendered a virtual thread across the Freudian space back to the father-desk with the two paternal diaries to unsettle the classic psychoanalytical failure to think femininity. This string disturbs the self-blinding emphasis in Freudian theory on the paternal-filial-masculine, the father and Oedipus complex as the only logic in the formation of subjectivity and sexual difference. Ettinger's most radical theoretical gesture from her aesthetic research on the field of trauma and history is to decipher a subjective, non-gendered sexual difference 'from the feminine' donated by the psychic borderspace, generated late in prenatality from shared experiences between the becoming mother and the becoming child co-emerging in a primordial subjectivizing severality. This other string between prematernal subject and subject-to-be touches both sons and daughters but becomes particularly significant in reshaping our understanding of femininity as a difference not from the masculine other, but from the m/Other and later postnatally the Mother.

Most notably in the infamous 'Dora' case study of 1905, evoked by Ettinger's placing her own analytical-aesthetical notebook on the case in this space just beyond the two fathers' diaries, the mother was foreclosed in Freud's speculations on psychic life. So how does the daughter negotiate her place in history notably when what she has inherited from such primordial severality may include traces of a historical trauma? By means of a psychically and historically freighted object, by virtue of the spoon's glinting presence, its intense luminosity, its nurturing yet blunted shape, the 'mother' calls out for recognition from the paternal men of a shared and shattered Jewish European world represented by Freud and Uziel Lichtenberg's different registers of continued daily life – Freud under threat of morbid cancer, Lichtenberg from genocidal racism. The spoon also, however, forges a visible link to the starving daughter who grew up to become both an artist and an analyst, and a mother too, to ponder on and paint about traces of trauma in the space of aesthetics, and to create the theoretical moves that enable me to ask questions about the role of the object in the economies of the transformation of trauma, or the failure of its passage that could become deadly. Let me now quote the full passage from which the title of this chapter comes:

> The place of art is for me the transport-station of trauma; a transport station that, more than a place, is rather a space that allows for certain occasions of occurrence and encounter, which will become the realization of what I call *borderlinking* and *borderspacing* in a *matrixial trans-subjective space* by way of experiencing with an object or process of creation.
>
> (Ettinger, 2000, p. 91 [original italics])

In positing a theory of a supplementary dimension of subjectivity she names the matrixial in order to grasp subjectivity as an archaic encounter with a co-emerging, intimate but unknown otherness that carries a sexual difference of the feminine unmarked by a phallic opposition to the masculine, Bracha Ettinger therefore proposes a different way of understanding the aesthetic encounter with traumatic residues embodied or materialized in objects that persist across the gap that marks the catastrophic rupture (Ettinger, 1992a, 2007). The word 'gap' suggests the opened space of a void or an abyss that lies between the world in which Freud lived and died, and in which her parents grew to modernizing hope, post-World War I Europe with its potentialities for Jewish life as part of modern states. But time flows over the gap, relentlessly, and the daughter is born into a world on the other side of the abyss to which she is none the less linked. Coming afterwards, she is also bound to look back towards it. She is both the product of that history and the one who, in looking back, but with a matrixial, rather than an Orphic (hence a deadly) gaze, must catch up its grains and threads into spaces, not just narratives, for an encounter that receives the transmissions and may transform them.

Ettinger's distinctive contribution lies in her final sentence. There she suggests the effect occurs affectively in 'experiencing with [...] an object or a process of creation'. It is not the experience *of* the object or the artworking, but rather an event-encounter that activates subjective processing in a co-eventing *with* the affectively coloured and historically freighted object, or *with* the time-encoded process by which the artist has made a work of art that invites a virtual participation in its prolonged attention, what the artist theorizes as a different kind of gazing, 'fascinance'.

Fascinance is a counter-force of 'fascinum', which was theorized by Lacan as the missed encounter with death that is hidden within the visual encounter with the world or with the gaze of the world. Medusa would be its figure, the evil eye its cultural fantasy. Fascinance counters this notion that at the end of vision is the void of our subjective nothingness, death. Fascinance is a site of a temporally-prolonged aesthetic, affective working through *with* a scene that has deep subjectivizing resonances:

> Fascinance is an aesthetic effect that operates in the prolongation and delaying of the time of the encounter-event and it allows for the working through of matrixial-differentiating-in-jointness and co-poeisis. Fascinance can only take place if borderlinking within a real, traumatic and phantasmatic encounter-event meets compassionate hospitality. Fascinance might turn into *fascinum* when castration, separation, weaning or splitting abruptly intervenes.
>
> (Ettinger, 2006, p. 61)

Ettinger makes clear that different logics – the phallic and the matrixial – sustain different if supplementary dimensions of subjectivity and each has a different outcome in regard to an aesthetic encounter. What she calls 'compassionate hospitality' is a condition of transformation of the traces of trauma. Without it, the encounter with the past may open onto deadliness, fixating us in fascinum. This is my wager in this chapter, considering two further examples of art works that hinge upon objects that become momentary transport-stations of trauma. But each produces a different outcome.

The unwritable trauma of Sarah Kofman's father's pen

On 24 March 1994, a slim memoir was published by French philosopher Sarah Kofman which became the last book of a voluble and prolific writing career. On 16 October 1994, Kofman took her own life. Could the return in writing to a scene of trauma be deadly? Titled *Rue Ordener, Rue Labat*, the memoir is an account of the author's childhood between eight and eighteen, passed as a Polish-Jewish immigrant's child born in France forced into hiding by the German occupation of France in 1940, during which her life as a Jewish child was constantly under threat of capture, deportation and immediate death. The main elements of the story the book will replot are as follows.

Foreign-born Jewish citizens of France were initially targeted by the occupying German forces with the collaboration of the French authorities. On 16–17 July 1942 a mass arrest was carried out, taking 13,152 seized men, women and children to a bicycle racing stadium known as the Vélodrome d'Hiver (the Vél d'Hiv for short) or to a holding camp in a U-shaped modern apartment block in the suburb of Drancy before being deported to Auschwitz-Birkenau, which had just started operating as a death factory a few months earlier. Under French law there had been no census on religious affiliation. But a German ordinance of 21 September 1940 required all Jewish people in occupied France to register with the police. These files were handed to the Gestapo where they were colour-coded and classified by nationality (there was a large Polish-Jewish immigrant population), by region, by profession, by street. It revealed 150,000 Jewish residents in the Paris area. By 1944, 76,000 Jewish people had been deported from France under the Nazi Occupation. Only 811 returned.

Sarah Kofman's father, Berek Kofman, was the rabbi of a small Polish-Jewish community in Paris. He spent the days preceding the leaked round-up in July 1942 warning his congregation to flee or to go into hiding. He could not himself do so for fear that they or his family would bear the retribution for his escape. He was, therefore, taken on 16 July, leaving his wife and their six children without visible means of support and themselves at risk from subsequent actions. Madame Kofman renamed her elder children and hid them out of Paris. But little Sarah would not be separated. In her noisy grief and refusal to eat non-Kosher food, she risked exposure. Thus her mother brought her back to live at peril in Paris. One night in February 1943, Madame Kofman was warned that their names were on the list for arrest that night. Leaving their meagre meal on the table, mother and vomiting daughter Sarah fled to the home of a Christian woman who had helped them hide before. Hidden in her house until June 1944, Madame Kofman was powerless to prevent the Christian woman, known in Kofman's memoir only as 'mémé', from taking over her child. Renamed Suzanne and almost converted to Christianity by baptism (the child ran away instead), Sarah was made to eat horsemeat in broth and steak *sanglant* while being taught that the family's Orthodox Judaism was intellectually archaic, physically unhealthy and culturally backward. According to the memoir, Sarah-Suzanne became enthralled by this luminous and sexual woman who also introduced her to philosophy, her later profession, telling her of secular Jewish philosophers such as Spinoza and Bergson. The bond with her anxious mother was broken forever. When the war ended, Madame Kofman reclaimed her children from hiding including Sarah. The Christian lady, however, sued in court to adopt her. She lost. Sarah's life had been nonetheless altered irrevocably. Fighting her mother with her recurring anorexia and relentless study in lieu of earning money, Sarah remained attached to the Christian lady during her student years. But then she broke off this relation too. The memoir ends with mémé's funeral. Sarah Kofman writes that she could not attend.

The text is thus testimony to a historical event – the rescue and preservation of a hidden Jewish child during the German occupation and genocidal persecution of Jewish Europeans. But it also registers the destruction of a family in the wake of the arrest and disappearance of the author's father, a rabbi.

The opening line of her memoir has haunted many of its readers.

> *De lui il me reste seulement le stylo* (Kofman, 1993, p. 9).
> [Of him all that remains to me is the pen.]

What could be more poignant? All that remains of a man's entire life is a single object. But this is not true of a man who is a father. What relation does the pen hold for the daughter? The object is highly symbolic, the pen, the instrument of writing, the emblem of the writer, the necessary tool in a pre-digital age. But this writer to whom the pen belonged was a rabbi, a learned man, a teacher, a scholar in a culture which had, for centuries, engendered writing. In pre-modern times all Jewish men were literate, schooled to read and write from the age of three. Writing men swings us back to the diary-text of Sigmund Freud, composed between 1929 and 1939, and to the diary of Uziel Lichtenberg, recording his survival from 1940 to 1948. But here we have the daughter as the final recipient of a pen, the sign of writing and the missing father. Where does she come in such a culturally specific genealogy?

'Of him all that remains to me is the stylo, the fountain pen'. *'De lui*/Of him' as if a possession, *'de lui*/ from him' as if a bequest, *'de lui'*, a remnant as if part of him, the pen remains, but it remains alone and to *me*. This claiming of this lonely writing implement forges linguistically a link between *'lui'*, 'him' and 'me'. The usual French grammatical formulation would be *De lui il ne me reste que le stylo*. Kofman avoids the use of the standard negative in order to stress the solitary condition of the pen and the desolation of the 'me' who only has this one remnant of/from him. Now we see that it was not the only relic but one which remains 'only to me'. The text continues:

> I took it one day from my mother's handbag where she had kept it with other souvenirs of my father. It is the kind of pen that is no longer made, the kind one has to fill with ink. I used it through my school days and studies. It 'failed' me before I was ready to let it go. Yet I have it with me still, patched up with scotch tape, it lies before me on my desk and it constrains me to write, to write.
> (Kofman, 1993, p. 9; 1996, p. 3)

Stolen from his wife, the writer's mother, the pen is already seen as an anachronism, hence a carrier of the past, not the present. Moreover, it is in effect a dead pen, for it has failed this writer before she was ready to 'let it go'. It had been a companion throughout her own entry into education and scholarship. Vicariously, its use reforged a link with the missing owner, the scholar-writer-father. It had indeed been her instrument, allowing her to enter into his place and space by this rather obviously Freudian association between pen and masculinity. Yet this wounded, defunct, patched-up pen that is so closely identified with him, the father, cannot be abandoned. Even in its failure, it is preserved, where he cannot be. Where? Not in a handbag, the maternal space, but on the desk, the space of writing and of men who write. Again I return to Freud's emblematic desk where the great psychoanalyst who was to be one of Kofman's most investigated authors sat confronted not by writing instruments, but by sculptures, images from other times and other cultures, icons of their negotiated fears of love, life, death and even thought.

Kofman's terse passage also creates a scenario. The writer begins to write a book. Before her, on her desk, is the wounded and bandaged pen that is [of] her father. It is endowed with power. It constrains her to write. It does not inspire her. It does not quite command. It is experienced as both an obligation and a restricting, directing force. The Latin root *constringere* means to bind together, tie tightly, fetter, shackle, chain but also to draw together. There is pain in this word, a forced bonding. There is also a kind of binding back. An even more powerful sentence then comes which we must first read in the original:

Mes nombreuses livres ont peut-être été des voies de traverse obligés pour parvenir à raconter 'ça'.

(Kofman, 1993, p. 9)

My numerous books have perhaps been the necessary detours to bring me to write about 'that'.

(Kofman, 1996, p. 3)

In the end, therefore, this book, this writing is different from the others she had profusely undertaken – 30 books published in her prolific career as an academic philosopher. This writing arrives only after many detours of other writings at a destination: telling 'ça' it, this, 'that'. Did telling 'ça' /'that', however, lead to a catastrophe that writing as an encounter with its hidden, unspeakable trauma engendered?

A change had occurred in Kofman's professional writing already in 1987, when the philosopher first interjected an autobiographical reference to her father's deportation and death in Auschwitz into a more personally scripted text titled tellingly *Paroles suffoquées / Smothered Words*, which was an intended homage to Maurice Blanchot and to Robert Antelme, author of *L'espèce humaine*, for writing about Auschwitz. So it cannot be in acknowledging the facts of her father's death that 'ça' was spoken.

In her astute thesis on Kofman's last years, Ashlee Mae Cummings plots a web of connections between the final projects of Kofman: on *The Portrait of Dorian Gray*, on Nietzsche's anti-Semitism and an essay on Rembrandt's painting *The Anatomy Lesson* which was posthumously published from the notes. These texts are linked across the space between *Paroles suffoquées* (1987) and *Rue Ordener, Rue Labat* (1993). Cummings also states:

> In the introduction to their co-edited book, *Enigmas: Essays on Sarah Kofman*, Penelope Deutscher and Kelly Oliver offer their analysis of this sentence. 'Kofman opens her autobiography with the suggestion that her works of philosophy have been a way of recounting "ça"'. On the contrary, I would have to argue that Kofman is saying the exact opposite of what Deutscher and Oliver claim in this statement. Her works of philosophy have not been a way of recounting this ambiguous *ça*. Rather her earlier works had carved out a circuitous path which Kofman was *obliged* to follow in order to reach this moment. It is only upon reaching this moment that she is therefore able to recount the story of *ça*. Her previous writings and *ça* are not at all one in the same and they are certainly not interchangeable. One could even go so far as to say that every work that Kofman wrote before *Rue Ordener, rue Labat*, served the purpose of evading her own personal traumatic story and I would argue that *not* writing about *ça* in those earlier works was the only way that she could arrive at the moment of writing about *it* later.
>
> (2009, p. 13 [original italics])[4]

Kofman's professional academic career was a necessary detour from, and not a means of ultimately arriving at, the point of writing 'ça'. After having written so much, being so published, and thinking through the big fathers of philosophy and psychoanalysis, a space opened up to make a place in writing for what came before them. The traumatic past had set out her destiny, to write, and the pen is its symbol. Yet some kind of settlement of accounts with the past had *now* to be written, demanded by the dead pen. In finally ceasing to evade 'ça/it', the unprocessed past, of which she was the effect, flashed into the present as her own becoming. But 'ça' remains an enigmatic signifier of that becoming and its moment in writing in 1993. It is the enigma Kofman bequeathed to her readers. Thus the question, for all the analysts of this little book, is not what is the referent for the tantalizing 'ça' but what remains encrypted in the word:

> Maybe all my numerous books have been the pathways required for me to reach the point of telling 'that'.
>
> (Kofman, 1996, p. 3)

This is my inelegant retranslation replacing detours with pathways. *'Voies de traverse'* have Lacanian psychoanalytical overtones that echo, but differ from, Ettinger's transport-station of trauma. *'Voies de traverse'* are the difficult and complex routes of our psychological movement from the frozen, repressed, disavowed, repetitions of our arrested neurotic or traumatized condition into a certain kind of fluid or fluent self-knowledge. It is the movement, not the destination, which psychoanalysis attempts to facilitate as a transformation from petrified blockage locked into symptoms into the possibility of a mobile economy of *life*, engagements with the world and others. Kofman is playing here with the notion of a *voie*: the railway track in French, along which the transports to Auschwitz rumbled and the Lacanian psychological passage, a transfer and a journey. Kofman has undertaken an academic journey, but precisely not to arrive here.

Ça is the least descriptive, least referential indicator of something. Perhaps it is akin to *das Ding, la Chose*, the Thing in Freudian-Lacanian psychoanalytical vocabulary, where it stands for a substance-less void before and beyond representation, the latter, in the form of the object, invisibly determined by this element of the unsignified Real.[5] It is also, of course, the French term for Freud's *id*, the repressed remnant of the most intractable and infantile of psychic organizations and impulses. Kofman's memoir will register her body's hysterical imprisonment in anorexia, vomiting and digestive pain.

Ça is also a signifier for what has none: trauma. Rather akin to the dark navel Freud postulates in his analysis of the dream of Irma in *Interpretation of Dreams*, that marks the limits of his interpretation of dreamwork, trauma confounds the interpretative enterprise as much as the representational one. It is, however, the structuring void that shapes the words curling around it. In his essay on 'Traumatic Knowledge' via literature *qua* literature, Geoffrey Hartman (1995, p. 537) writes:

> Traumatic knowledge would seem to be a contradiction in terms. It is as close to nescience [unknowing] as to knowledge. Any description or modelling of trauma, therefore, risks being figurative itself, to the point of mythic fantasmagoria.

He explains that trauma belongs to the Real (in the Lacanian sense) – but

> the real is not the real, in the sense of specific, identifiable thing or cause;[...] the encounter with the real takes place, on the part of both

analyst and analysand, with a world of death-feelings, lost objects, and drives. It might be described, in fact, as a 'missing encounter' (the *troumatique*, Lacan puns) or an unmediated shock.

(p. 539)

Elaborating the psychoanalytical concept of trauma in the field of cultural analysis for literature (and art), Hartman, therefore, argues that that which he names 'literary knowledge' 'finds the "real", identifies with it'. He continues:

> This leads towards literary theory, because the distinction between experiencing (phenomenal or empirical) and understanding (thoughtful naming, in which words replace things, or their images) is what figurative language expresses and explores. The literary construction of memory is obviously not a literal retrieval but a statement of a different sort. It relates to the negative moment in experience, to what in experience has not been, or cannot be, adequately experienced. That moment is now expressed, or made known *in its negativity;* the artistic representation modifies the part of our desire for knowledge (epistemophilia [desire for knowledge]) which is driven by images (scopophilia [desire to see]). Trauma theory throws light on figurative or poetic language, and perhaps symbolic process in general, as something other than an enhanced imaging or vicarious repetition of a prior (non)experience.
>
> (p. 540)[6]

The traumatic event or its affects are not represented; yet through art or literature that can aesthetically affect, that is perform more than representation, something of trauma's radical otherness may be intimated and hence encountered aesthetically and affectively almost across the gaps between letters and words or in forms that wander around it. *Something* is the key word here. Not everything, but some aspects may be allusively *encountered*, but neither mastered nor fully seen. The original, creative gesture of art becomes an originary site for an encounter with the affective ripples around the non-experienced, hence, absent traumatic pool, so that we know about trauma rather than reducing it to a representation it cannot but evade. Hartman continues:

> Periphrasis, for example, as it moves toward the riddle [...] indicates a real whose indeterminacy creates a tension between signified (solution to the riddle) and signifier (the riddle form). Since every object

can be riddled this way [...] This tension is constitutive rather than provisional and opens a creative play-space, the possibility of singing 'in the face of the object'.

(Wallace Stevens, p. 540)[7]

When aesthetic or literary activity creates its forms, these are not a repetition of that which already exists as a memory or a known event in the subject or in culture. There cannot be repetition because that to which art or literature is giving a form, *and is doing so for the first time*, creating a form by means of which to know it affectively, is, in fact, a negative moment in experience. Art/literature creates what has neither yet nor ever entered into experience, that being the definition of trauma. Art can be, however, periphrastic rather than constative, moving around, evoking, seeking to touch the elusive 'something'– ça – that structures subjectivity and yet is impossible to know while being affecting and making its own kind of sense. Trauma is the exceptional non-experience that, nonetheless, certain kinds of aesthetic practices may access through creating new modes for encounter with its traces, remnants or scenes.

The structure of Kofman's text riddles the trauma that the writing, called for by the pen, compelled her to undertake. The book operates by means of a rhyme between two deaths – both of which she missed: her father's unseen over there, *'là-bas'*, that of *la dame* from Rue Labat unwitnessed. Kofman's book, titled by street names, plots out the spaces across which her subjectivity was formed in its critical moment in 1943–1944. One was a Jewish space, the other a Christian one. In the passage from the one world to another the child was both hystericized and, in a Laplanchian rather than a literal sense, 'seduced' into a new identity as the condition of survival both actual and emotional. The missing deaths of the father and the saviour, and the two scenarios, one paternal and the other maternal that is a new paternal, reconfigures an Oedipal triangle in which the Christian French woman, by virtue of those empowering identities takes over the place of the disappeared Father, determining the law of what enters into the child, to re-organize the Oedipal triangle, stringing the vulnerable child between two mothers, one Jewish, disempowered, abjected and hated, the other French-Christian, empowered, loved and fascinating.

In her re-reading of the 'Dora' case, in which 'Dora' perplexingly spends several hours before a Raphael painting of the Christian Madonna, Bracha Ettinger introduced her concept of fascinance to restore to psychoanalysis a means of understanding the formations of femininity, precisely in terms which might explain the seduction and its consequences in the text of Kofman. Ettinger explains:

> If Oedipal difference is the key to feminine sexual difference, the question *'what does a woman want?'* quickly turned into the question *what does a woman want from a man?*
>
> (2006, p. 62 [original italics])

Ettinger will shift Freud's blocked question:

> It is not sustained long enough at the level of *what does a woman want from a woman?* Dora's case is one of Freud's most glorious failures. Freud corrected himself *a postieri*, claiming that Dora was not in love with a man but with a woman – with Frau K. After such a courageous correction, it is easy to proclaim that, again, Freud did not grasp what Dora wanted. Yet such is the case.
>
> (p. 62 [original italics])

Ettinger now introduces her concept of *fascinance* as a mechanism for a different process of sexual subjectivization of the girl/daughter:

> Dora's fascination with Frau K., like Dora's admiration of the Madonna were not an expression of homosexual desire. Dora did not desire Frau K. sexually. She desired to be caught in a move of fascination that *belongs to femininity,* a move composed of a girl toward a woman-figure, who is fascinated too by the daughter-girl and who allows her sufficient proximity to sustain the illusion of inclusion in her mature elusive maturity – a femininity which is not directed at the girl but outside and away from her. Yet the girl desires to be included inside it for instants of eternity whereby she participates in advance, and by proxy, in a world not yet fit for her own immature sexuality.
>
> (p. 62 [original italics])

Instead of the utterly negative theories of classical psychoanalysis in which the feminine subject is created through her reactive hatred of the mother for offering her no phallus, Ettinger argues that we have plenty of evidence from art and literature that the becoming feminine subject, the girl-beneath-the-woman, desires to know from what Ettinger names the 'ffam' (*femme-fatale-autre-mère*), the desired and desiring adult sexual woman, what it is she might become. This is a prolonged kind of gazing: a relationship of fascinance that involves hospitality to this longing and endowing the girl with sense of being desirable. Ettinger theorizes this as a matrixial encounter when a certain fragilization of the borders between distinct subjects occurs to allow mutual yet assymetrical affects: it can occur with aesthetic objects, with images as with others.

Many scholars read the story of Kofman's childhood recounted in *Rue Ordener, Rue Labat* as a painful struggle between the two mothers, the hated Jewish rebbetzin, Madame Kofman, and the lovely Christian saviour. There is no doubt that Kofman's relation with her own mother did not survive her childhood. We do not know if it could have otherwise. In one of two curious deviations from her own story, Kofman inserts a chapter about Leonardo da Vinci's cartoon of *The Virgin Mary, St Anne, the Christ-child and John the Baptist.* The drawing is the topic of Freud's first psychoanalytic study of the visual arts. A print hangs in the Freud Museum. Da Vinci had two mothers, his peasant birth mother and the adoptive aristocratic mother, childless wife of his seigneurial father. So there is suggestive evidence for Kofman's identification with da Vinci and this model of a child with two mothers. But behind the second lies the veiled face of the beloved primary mother – is that Kofman's story? No.

The conflict of her life was not, in my opinion, a tug of war between two maternal subjects for one child. The historical conflict in which Sarah Kofman found herself was hugely over-determined by long-standing religious contestations between Judaism and Christianity, aggravated by the conditions under which a Christian woman 'saved' a Jewish child in the presence of another woman, castrating as it were the child's own mother ethnically, a woman bereaved terribly by the terrifying arrest and deportation of her husband, without any money, powerlessly responsible for the survival of her scattered hidden children, herself living in daily fear of being discovered and deported to her death. She was then forced helplessly to witness a systematic attempt to appropriate the child and alienate its affections from its own mother and to remake the child's subjectivity within an alien, and hence, self-hating system. Whereas Kofman could as an adult decide to abandon Orthodox or any religious practice, what she experienced as a child fell below the threshold of theological or philosophical decision. It concerned being alienated from what had hitherto constituted being *tout court*, a world without an outside.

Plotting the *conte* out with Freud and against Freud, the Christian woman who 'saved' the child effectively took over the place of the father who had been deported. It was she who now determined what was eaten and how, disempowering the Jewish mother, and in so doing abjecting Judaism itself. She controlled the input and output of the little girl's guts, already twisted with anxiety, hysterically closing against forced ingestion of forbidden foods, already symptomatically responding to oral seduction. Red meat, that is meat with blood, is mentioned for more than factual reasons. The bloodiness is deeply symbolic of the depth and resonance of what was being perpetrated on the body of the child phantasmatically, now registered in the author's refined Nietzschean-Freudian prose.

I am suggesting that the topographical distance between the two apartments signalled by the two addresses in the title of the memoir dramatize the overlay between the structural formation of subjectivity in the Freudian Oedipal triangulation by the historical and ethnically specific conditions by which it was exploded. That traumatic reconfiguration, like the Oedipus complex itself was written, symbolically and literally, on the child's body. The f(n)ormative structure was shattered by the departure/deportation of her father. It was rewritten by the insertion, into his space of authority over the child's body and being, of a woman. This Christian woman was not empowered by the phallus but ethnically by her Christian Frenchness. That was, however, embodied in another kind of femininity that, in effect, seduced the child, not sexually, but emotionally. This submission was the passport to survival. Yet acceding to survival on these grounds, enacted upon the child a trauma of deracination that was in effect a desubjectivization that humbled all things Jewish (father-identified), turning what was innermost in her identity and its intergenerational connections into what was most to be abjected.

Within this larger structure of the two topographies and the bookends of two deaths lies a series of vividly described scenes, which are in effect primal scenes. One is clearly of the seduction, which I cannot discuss in this chapter. I shall focus on those concerning the father, the *lui* of whom all that remains to the child-daughter is the pen.

A scene, 16 July 1942: Having warned his congregants to hide, the rabbi returns to await the Gestapo in his study. When the police come, the mother tells them her husband is not there. Afraid that they will take her and the children instead, the father comes forward. Knowing some of the rumoured conditions for escaping arrest, the mother lies about her youngest child's age and she pretends she is pregnant. Thus she bargains for their lives. The writer, a watching, witnessing child, is shamed at her mother's mendacity, worries about the news of a forthcoming child and tries to make sense of her father's unresisting sacrifice. But the wife must go to the police in her last ditch attempt to convince them of the two conditions that might save him (her son being under two – he was in fact over two, born 14 July 1940, and her fake pregnancy). So we have the first primal scene of the traumatic past: six orphaned children standing in the Parisian street weeping like a Greek chorus: *o fate* which comes out in French as *o papa*, rather than *o popoi* (Kofman, 1993, p. 14; 1996, p. 7). The invocation of the Greeks, Kofman knew well in her philosophical capacity, here allows a truly frightful moment of violent fear, grief, confusion, total abandonment and loss of all safety to be secured into a ritualized evocation of 'fate'. Deflection is at work, but for the reader tuning in to the condition of six children under ten, alone in a foreign land – they speak Yiddish and Polish and only learn French at school – watching those who are meant to guard them being taken brutally by the French police, this is a truly traumatizing scene. Nothing can be the same again when parents are thus officially 'castrated' by alien authorities.

The blank in the page pauses the narrative but Chapter III begins: 'As it turned out, never again did we see my father' (Kofman, 1993, p. 15; 1996, p. 8). Removed for ever, the story must now be told again– it was first averred in the text in 1987, *Paroles suffoquées*. At the age of 42, Rabbi Kofman had been selected on the ramp for slave labour, probably in Auschwitz-Monowitz, and was not sent for immediate gassing. Yet he was killed. This is the bookend writing of his death. After the bleak death certificate, an Auschwitz survivor who apparently witnessed that death gives the family a report. Refusing to work one day and wanting to pray on a Sabbath for all who were there, Rabbi Berek Kofman was beaten with a pickaxe by a French-Jewish butcher-turned-kapo and then buried alive.

The full and horrific import of the title of the first book to dare to speak of her father's death, *Paroles suffoquées / Smothered Words*, now hits us. That text transferred the horrible dying onto the very words that had been written to speak of the entire trauma that culminated in something worse than ordinary death, in Auschwitz. Chapter II of this text begins:

> Since Auschwitz all men, Jews and non-Jews die differently: they do not really die; they survive death because what took place – back there – without taking place, death in Auschwitz was worse than death: 'Humanity as a whole had to die through the trial of some of its members (those who incarnate life itself, almost an entire people, a people that had been promised an eternal presence). This death

still endures. And from this comes the obligation never again to die only once, without however allowing repetition to injure us to the always essential ending'.

(Kofman, 1987, p. 15; 1998, p. 9)

Framed philosophically with a paraphrase of Theodor W. Adorno's final meditations on metaphysics 'after Auschwitz' (1966), the passage also cites Maurice Blanchot's afterword to *Vicious Circles* (1989) before returning to the brutal statement:

> Because he was a Jew, my father died in Auschwitz: How can it not be said? And how can it be said? How can one speak of that before which all possibility of speech ceases? Of this event, my absolute, which communicates with the absolute of history, and which is of interest only for this reason. To speak: it is necessary – *without (the) power*: without allowing language, too powerful, sovereign to master the most aporetic situation, absolute powerlessness and very distress, to enclose it in clarity and happiness of daylight. And how can one not speak of it, when the wish of all who returned – and he did not return – has been to tell, to tell endlessly, as if only an infinite conversation could match the infinite privation.
>
> (Kofman, 1987, pp. 15–16; 1998, pp. 9–10 [original italics])

To tell endlessly, because such endless telling alone matches the infinite privation recalls the *telling* to which the author was eventually constrained by the pen itself, all that remained because he did not return, and he did not return since he died '*because* he was a Jew'. Not *as* a Jew under Nazi racial laws. But he died being a Jew, speaking to his God, 'beseeching God for all of them, victims and murderers alike' (pp. 10, 16). *This* has to be spoken, voiced, enunciated by a language that threatens to betray those 'smothered words' by its own illuminating power to master every experience, to cover over the void, the aporia that it must remain.

Calling upon Jean-François Lyotard, Adorno, Blanchot and Antelme, honouring them for writing and speaking, *Smothered Words* is a wilfully painful journey through other writers' words to the impossible place where the father, the rabbi, the Jew, died a death worse than death, as part of a historical catastrophe that afflicts all humanity (according to Blanchot) through what happened to two peoples, the Jewish people in particular, *back there, là-bas*, in the event collectively remembered after Adorno as 'Auschwitz' which, however, for many, like Rabbi Kofman, was the actual site. Berek Kofman did not die in the special industrially manufactured killing machinery of that place, Auschwitz-Birkenau, where as a Jewish man he would have been starved, overworked and eventually gassed or worse, left to die the death of internal disintegration they called becoming a *muselmann*. He was buried alive after suffering a brutal beating by a fellow Jew for daring to carry out an act of religious fidelity, senseless in a place where all such human aspiration and ambition for grace or hope had been systemically abolished.

It is of this man, suffocated to death so he would not say such words, that all that remains, as the writer of these texts writes, is a patched-up, unusable fountain pen that constrains the daughter to write this now. That object is the material index, the affective icon and the intellectual symbol as well as the link in an affective chain between child and father, a chain severed by what Blanchot named an absolute, both personal and historical, while being maintained precisely by the power of the object to 'speak' a command: write, write. Yet, all the books the author did write were to avoid coming to tell 'that'. 'That' cannot be simply what she had already written in *Smothered Words* about the nature of the killing/dying of her father. The 'that' cannot just be the story of the contestation over her identity and affections that forms the narrative of *Rue Ordener, Rue Labat*.

I suggest that the 'that' that must be finally written is her irrevocable dislocation from the act from which her father died. The act of saying words, words that got him smothered, words that signify a relation to a non-relational, radical alterity which sustains the humanity of the utterer by means of a formal religious performance.

> In this unnameable 'place', he continued to observe Jewish monotheism, if by this, with Blanchot, we understand *the revelation of the word as the place in which men maintain a relation to that which excludes all relation: the infinitely Distant, the absolutely Foreign*. A relation with the infinite, which no form of power, including that of the executioners of the camps, had been able to master, other than by denying it, burying it in a pit with a shovel, without ever having encountered it.
>
> (p. 42, pp. 34–35)[8]

I do not think that Sarah Kofman was longing to return to the faith of her father. She remained Jewish, but was never religiously so. Via Blanchot, she can nevertheless understand the symbolic or even philosophical function of her father's *gesture*: speaking words that defied the horror of a concentrationary universe in which the refusal of an alterity beyond humanity had allowed humanity itself to become utterly vulnerable to what Hannah Arendt (1951) would later name total domination of man and hence humanity's ultimate superfluousness. The concept of a divinity as radical alterity is *philosophically* the projection by human thought of its own aspirations beyond mere utility. The concentrationary and genocidal system was a total assault on the human reducing those it designated as Others to total exploitation and ultimate uselessness. Berek Kofman defied the political terror with the only resource he had left with which to resist dehumanization: uttering words of human aspiration and, most crucially, total compassion that embraced the humanity of inhuman torturers.

Thus the pen also constrains the daughter to write of what happened in the chain of events following the round-up on 16 July 1942 that arrives at the Rabbi's fidelity as words uttered 'in that place', *là-bas*. All that remains from *là-bas/Labat* is a pen. The pen was the rabbi's pen, the sign of all the writing, speaking and practices in faithful observance of which he was murdered in the most ghastly way imaginable. His death did not occur as part of the process of annihilation of the Jewish population under racial laws. It happened in a confrontation over the very religious identity and philosophical possibility Sarah Kofman had been seduced into abjuring as a vulnerable child searching for a means to become a woman, in an extreme historical situation, and as the condition of physical and emotional survival.

For me, the deep unsaid of Kofman's text lies smothered, buried, here. The father's pen links writing to daring to confess what I can only overdramatically name a forced but unknowing apostasy – a radical alienation from her father and all his life and thought offered to her – while plotting out the conditions of psychological/ emotional/historical complexity that had made it a necessity and a pleasure. That is what she confesses obliquely in writing about what happened in Rue Labat. About Auschwitz and after Auschwitz, no story – *récit* – is possible she says, if by a story one means to tell a story of events which makes sense. So the pen incites a memoir that is not a story that makes sense. It is the writing of its senselessness that is contained in the presence of the pen, instead of the father, and in the life of writing of the daughter who now has to write her way back through not only unbearable grief but also an unspeakable shame that is not generalizable, but hers as she rediscovers her own past. She cannot hide behind other men-writers-thinkers, the topics of her many philosophical studies, as the means to undertake this journey into the traumatic fissure in the historical formation of her self.

The trauma remains in senselessness – the unnegotatiable, irrecoverable trauma of the daughter, who, having broken the covenant in fidelity to which her father outrageously suffered an exceptional and unthinkable living death, and in her having loved and been loved for it, touches the unspeakable shame at the process of her survival – *seduction* into apostasy – covered over by her later, secular, academic compensatory but transgressive identification with the masculine scholar.

On 15 October 1994, a year after completing the book that begins 'Of him all that remains is the pen', six months after its publication, Sarah Kofman took her own life. We are left to wonder if the writing of this text, the final utterance of words that never directly spoke of '*ça*' but tracked their way to a realization of what had not before been recognized as the encrypted trauma, function, therefore, catastrophically? Rather than being a transport-station of trauma, the pen of the father called forth an encounter with the affect at the core of her trauma that gave no relief. Her writing's revelations smothered her as if the surrogate identification with the writing man-pen fractured to leave a breach between father and daughter that could not find a link or a string to transport the trauma to anywhere but nothing: death was where no more writing would come.

A gesture, some tears and a flow of words

In 2004, Belgian filmmaker Chantal Akerman created an art installation about a diary, a bought *Tagebuch*, partially inscribed by a Polish-Jewish teenager in the early 1920s, that came into her possession during the 1980s. This object would have two incarnations in 2004. One occurred in a fiction film made by Akerman about the relation of a widowed mother and her writer-daughter, commissioned to complete an erotic novel in the chaos following her mother's moving in with her, *Tomorrow We Move*. The other was in a digitally filmed encounter between the filmmaker and her own mother, Nelly Akerman, in the latter's home in Brussels. This filming was at once 'research' for the movie and the raw footage that would be remade as a double-screening projection for the installation *Marcher à côté de mes lacets dans une frigidaire vide / To Walk Next to One's Shoelaces in an Empty Fridge*, first installed at the Marion Goodman Gallery in New York.

The diary in question belonged to Sidonie Ehrenberg, the filmmaker's grandmother, the mother of Nelly Akerman, who survived the genocide in which Sidonie Ehrenberg was murdered. Somehow, she does not recall how, this fragile diary was returned to Nelly Akerman. She had written a tender message to her missing mother on its pages. Lost in the house, the diary was rediscovered by Chantal Akerman when she was about 11 years old. Reading her mother's inscription, she also added a tender message to her mother, as did her sister Sylviane. Watching the video installation, the viewer knows nothing of this relay of words that connect three generations. What we witness is Nelly Akerman being asked by Chantal Akerman to decipher the Polish handwriting in a diary. Only slowly does Nelly Akerman realize she is reading the anguished confessions of her own mother, an Orthodox Jewish woman with aspirations beyond the confined world of her birth as a woman in that society. Writing becomes the space for an imagined companion and confidant for her forbidden longings. This opens onto a discussion between mother and daughter about dates and the age of Sidonie at her death in 1943. Then Nelly Akerman falls silent, as she reads without translating. Then, with tears seeping gently from her eyes, she turns and caressing the cheek of her daughter, kisses her.

Later, I came to know that this gesture of intense affection was her response to reading the three passages appended to Sidonie Ehrenberg's writing. The filmmaker took it over and into her fiction film, showing the raw footage to Aurore Clément who would play the mother character. Nelly Akerman was invited to watch the filming of the recreated scene of the two women reading the diary together. Akerman writes:

> Suddenly I saw tears in her eyes. She tried to hold them back. But she could not. They were little tears, very discreet. The next day I telephoned and she said, you know I was a little overwhelmed yesterday, but I finally feel better.
>
> All these films have finally brought me to that. She finally feels better. She finally shed a tear. Thirty-three years of work with so many turns and detours, and she finally feels better. Is this what I was looking for?
>
> I have no idea.
> Maybe
> I'd like to believe it.
> But honestly not just that.

Akerman here acknowledges that her career as a filmmaker had been both a series of detours and an indirect journey to something that had now occurred not in a single film, but in a process around two filmings. Had her work always been an unconscious search for a form to create a transport-station, not of her own trauma, but of her mother's, that had, by transgenerational transmission, become hers to work through by means of making film after film? To make mother feel better, sounds at once slight and monumental. Akerman's films as *voies de traverse* did seem, however, to have for once become a transport-station. The final phrase, however, deserves close attention. We might be tempted to close the case, finding the single cause of Akerman's cinematic trajectory. 'Not just that' allows this traumatic thread to be plaited into the contingent, personal, cultural and historical factors shaping a rich range of cinematic projects that nonetheless are linked by one thread that runs through the many films she has made. That string had the force not quite of Kofman's constraining pen, but it was a knotted string, forcing repetition. Akerman writes of her discovery when making *D'Est / From the East* (1993–1995):

> I have to face facts. It is far behind and always in front of all images barely covered by other luminous or even radiant ones. All images of evacuation, of walking in the snow with packages toward an unknown place, of faces and bodies placed next to one another […]And it was always like that. Yesterday, today and tomorrow, there were, there will be, there are at this very moment people whom history (which no longer has a capital H) whom history has struck down. People who were waiting there, packed together, to be killed, beaten or starved or who walk without knowing where they are going, in groups or alone. There is nothing to do. It is obsessive and I am obsessed. Despite the cello, despite cinema. Once the film is finished I said to myself, 'so, that's what it was; that again'.
>
> (Lebow, 2008, p. 7)[9]

That again is the mark of traumatically induced repetition. The formal signature of the installation *Marcher* was, however a flowing spiral across which streamed words as fluid as the tears seeping twice from Nelly Akerman's affected eyes. This labyrinth had to be traversed by the viewer in order to enter the room in which the diary and a portrait that formed its frontispiece were screened on a scrim beyond which was the double-screened projection of Nelly reading the diary in Brussels one Sunday afternoon. After the moment when Nelly

Akerman turns to kiss her daughter, the video records the flow of words. Mother and daughter speak openly, for the first time, about the past, Nelly Akerman's survival, her loss, her life after. Akerman records the silence in her family about the past. This generated her imaginative work.

> Memory is always reinvented but with a story full of holes it's as if there is no story left. What to do then? Try to fill the holes – and I would say even this hole– with an imagination fed on everything one can find, the left and the right and in the middle of the hole. One attempts to create one's own imaginary truth.[10]

In her own notebooks, Bracha Ettinger (1992b, p. 85) wrote:

> My parents are proud of their silence. It is their way of sparing others and their children from suffering. But in this silence, all is transmitted except the narrative. In silence, nothing can be changed in the narrative which hides itself.

Thus, I suggest, the moment of re-encounter with the object-diary, the obliviated trace of a vanished mother and grandmother, but also a cross-inscribed register of feminine compassion traversing the bereaved past and the new generation, becomes an occasion for '*borderlinking* and *borderspacing* in a *matrixial trans-subjective space* by way of experiencing with an object or process of creation' (Ettinger, 2000, p. 91). The transformative effect occurs across the durational aesthetic staging of fascinance that 'can only take place if borderlinking within a real, traumatic and phantasmatic encounter-event meets compassionate hospitality' (Ettinger, 2006, p. 61).

Akerman's filming for the installation and its restaging for her own mother as a piece of cinematic rescripting, performatively created a transport-station for the unspoken traumatic freight of her mother's bereaved past that it could be said was the shaping void around which the daughter-filmmaker's creative career had been unconsciously wrought. It was the repressed that returned, unknown, until Akerman, carrier of this object-diary, this register of the voice of a disappeared woman, found a form through which to risk an encounter with it, with her mother's trauma, and with cinema.

In one reading, the work of Akerman belatedly revealed in 2004 its deeply traumatic structuration to which her own comments bear regular witness. In a matrixial reading, however, her fidelity reveals more than obsession or repetition compulsion. Fidelity witnesses fascinance: a prolonged and necessary aesthetic contemplation of a certain enigma lying between mother and daughter precisely in those zones that are also mother as daughter with her missing mother.

Walking/Marcher is not the final key. It is the scene that independent cinema, bleeding into contemporary installation time-based art, made possible. The matrixial trauma of the lost mother/grandmother-matrixial severality could be re-approached and transported through occasioning and being able to witness the matrixial compassionate gesture of the daughter to her orphaned mother so that she could become the mother the daughter herself needed. Something happened that Sunday in Brussels that had waited long to occur in the intertwining lives of both women. In Nelly Akerman's silent return to the site of her own inscription to her mother and the discovery of her daughter's compassionate embrace of her and her loss, she makes a gesture, accompanied by the soft seep of tears, to reach out, touch, stroke and kiss her daughter. It is in experiencing with – aesthetic wit(h)nessing – both the object and the process of the creation of the installation and the fiction film that a transport occurred, a movement, a passage and a relief for the historically affected participants in this singular narrative of Auschwitz and for this viewer.

Three works, three women-artists-writers, three objects, weave a net of possible relations between the catastrophic signified by the place and the word 'Auschwitz', the traumatic residue of its transcrypted transmission across generations to daughters who inherit and must fashion art forms to encounter such residues that line their own being, and a theory, Ettinger's aesthetically derived proposition of a matrixal dimension in subjectivity, that identifies the psychic-aesthetic processes and conditions for creating transport-stations of trauma as opposed to blocked and deadly *voies de traverse*. The tragedy of Sarah Kofman's self-inflicted death is not alleviated by the knowledge of other possibilities. But I hope that in our scholarly explorations of the encounter with the catastrophic past we remain aware of the risks involved, for objects are such *voies de traverse* leading back into darkness that we must face and mourn. They can, however, also be transport-stations when we are prepared to carry and transport, process and transform, the affective burden with which these objects are still so charged. That requires us to retheorize the nature of our glance towards the past and our capacity to share in the affective opening and transmission of its human burden.

Notes

1. In my book, *After-affect/After-image: Trauma and Aesthetic Transformation* (2013), I offer extended theoretical reflection on, and substantive studies of, these three cases presented here.
2. Independently I became fascinated by these objects. But any research on such materials must defer to the foundational work of Marianne Hirsch and Leo Spitzer (2006). My orientation is less towards the testimonial value of the objects than their function in transmitting and transforming trauma.
3. See Pollock (2009) and De Zegher & Pollock (2011).
4. The reference to Deutscher and Oliver is from p. 7 of their introduction to *Enigmas* (1999).
5. For an elaboration of Freud's concept of the Thing, see Lacan (1992).
6. My additions.
7. Hartman references Winnicott's *Playing and Reality* (1971) in relation to playspace.
8. My emphasis.
9. Transcript from the film cited in Lebow (2008, p. 7).
10. I am deeply grateful to Chantal Akerman and to Marion Goodman for providing me with English translations of the artist's statements.

Works cited

Adorno, T. (1966) *Negative Dialektik* (Frankfurt: Suhrkamp), trans. as *Negative Dialectics*, E. B. Ashton (trans.) (New York: Seabury Press, 1973).

Antelme, R. (1947) *L'espèce humaine* (Paris: Gallimard).

Antelme, R. (1999) *The Human Race*, Annie Mahler & Jeffrey Haight (trans.) (Evanston: Northwestern Press).

Arendt, H. (1951) *The Origins of Totalitarianism* (New York: Harcourt, Brace and Co.).

Blanchot, M. (1989) *Vicious Circles*, Paul Auster (trans.) (Barrytown, NY: Station Hill Press).

Cummings, A.M. (2009) *The Shelter of Philosophy: Repression and Confrontation of the Traumatic Experience in the Work of Sarah Kofman*. [online] MA Thesis. Miami University. Available at: <http://etd.ohiolink.edu/view.cgi?acc_num=miami1248976254>.

De Zegher, C. & Pollock, G. (eds.) (2011) *Bracha L. Ettinger: Art as Compassion* (Brussels: ASP Publishers).

Deutscher, P. & Oliver, K. (eds.) (1999) *Enigmas: Essays by Sarah Kofman* (Ithaca: Cornell University Press).

Ettinger, B. (1992a) 'Matrix and Metramorphosis', *Differences: A Journal of Feminist Cultural Studies* 4:3, 176–208.

Ettinger, B. (1992b) *Matrix Halal(a) Lapsus: Notes on Painting* (Oxford: Museum of Modern Art).

Ettinger, B. (2000) 'Art as the Transport-Station of Trauma' in *Bracha Lichtenberg Ettinger: Artworking 1985–1999* (Gent: Ludion), pp. 91–115.

Ettinger, B. (2006) 'Fascinance and the Girl-to-m/Other Matrixial Feminine Difference' in G. Pollock (ed.) *Psychoanalysis and the Image: Transdisciplinary Perspectives* (Boston and Oxford: Blackwells), pp. 60–93.

Ettinger, B. (2007) *The Matrixial Borderspace* (Minneapolis: University of Minnesota Press).

Hartman, G. (1995) 'On Traumatic Knowledge and Literary Studies', *New Literary History* 26:3, 537–563.

Hirsch, M. & Spitzer, L. (2006) 'Testimonial Objects', *Thamyris/Intersecting* 13, 137–164.

Kofman, S. (1986) *Paroles Suffoqués* (Paris: Galilée);

Kofman, S. (1994) *Rue Ordener, Rue Labat* (Paris: Galilée).

Kofman, S. (1996) *Rue Ordener, Rue Labat*, A. Smock (trans.) (Lincoln and London: University of Nebraska Press).

Kofman, S. (1998) *Smothered Words*, M. Dobie (trans.) (Evanston: Northwestern University Press).

Lacan, J. (1992) *The Ethics of Psychoanalysis Book VII 1959–1960*, D. Potter (trans.) (London: Routledge).

Lebow, A.S. (2008) *First Person Jewish* (Minneapolis: University of Minnesota Press).

Pollock, G. (2009) *Resonance, Overlay, Interweave: Bracha L Ettinger in the Freudian Space of Memory and Migration* (Leeds: CentreCATH Documents)

Pollock, G. (2013) *After-affect/After-image: Trauma and Aesthetic Transformation in the Virtual Feminist Museum* (Manchester: Manchester University Press).

Winnicott, D. (1971) *Playing and Reality* (London: Tavistock).

10
Coda: Reading Witness Discourse

Hayden White

I open the second volume of the highly acclaimed book of Saul Friedländer, *Nazi Germany and the Jews, 1933–1945: The Years of Extermination, 1939–1945* (2008), expecting to find something like the statement which opens the second volume of Richard J. Evans's similarly acclaimed *The Third Reich in Power, 1933–1939* (2006). Evans's book begins: 'This is the story of the Third Reich, [...] from the moment when it completed its seizure of power in the summer of 1933 to [...] the beginning of September 1939' (p. xv). But I do not find this kind of opening in Friedländer's book; I do not even find any statement about this being a 'history' of Nazi Germany and the Jews. Instead, I find – just after the title and the dedication – on a single page by itself, the following words presented in the following format:

> The struggle to save myself is hopeless.... But that's not important. Because I am able to bring my account to its end and trust that it will see the light of day when the time is right...And people will know what happened...And they will ask, is this the truth? I reply in advance: No, this is not the truth, this is only a small part, a tiny fraction of the truth.... Even the mightiest pen could not depict the whole, real, essential *truth*.
>
> Stefan Ernest, 'The Warsaw Ghetto,'
>
> written in hiding 1943 on the 'Aryan' side of Warsaw.
>
> (p. viii)

I still do not know or have not been told whether this is a 'history' and whether, if it is a history, it is organized as a 'story' or as some other variety of narrative. Turning to the next page, I find it entitled 'Contents' and after that a page and a third of 'Acknowledgements'. And only after *that* do I find a page entitled 'Introduction'. But this page begins with the following statement:

> David Moffie was awarded his degree in medicine at the University of Amsterdam on September 18, 1942. In a photograph taken at the event, Professor C. U. Ariens Kappers, Moffie's supervisor, and Professor H. T. Deelman stand on the right of the new MD, and assistant D. Granaat stands on the left.
>
> (p. xiii)

Then follows a full enough description of the contents of the photograph and an account of the 'historical' significance of what it records: an 'act of defiance' on the part of the university officials in granting a degree to a Jew on the very eve of the day that the German occupiers' prohibition of Jews' attending university in the Netherlands was to go into effect. In addition to this account of the historical significance of this photograph, the author provides us with another account of its significance. He notes the presence on David Moffie's tuxedo of the Davidic star with the word 'Jood' embroidered on it, that all Jews coming under German jurisdiction were required to wear. Friedländer points out that this star not only identifies its wearer as a Jew, it also indicates that the wearer has been marked out to be murdered. Indeed, the star is interpreted as a 'portent' of that programme of extermination of everything Jewish which is one of the most important if not the most important aspect of the German Nazi 'final solution' to 'the Jewish Question' (p. xxvi).

Here, then, in the account of this seemingly minor event which occurred on the periphery of the Third Reich and which by chance happened to have been photographed, the author claims to have provided his readers with 'the quintessence' of that 'situation' which he will wish to name as 'extermination'. Only after this prefatory anecdote does Friedländer finally state the nature of the text he has placed before us.

> The 'history of the Holocaust,' he writes, 'cannot be limited only to a recounting of German policies, decisions, and measures that led to this most systematic and most sustained of genocides; it must include the reactions [...] of the surrounding world and the attitudes of the victims, for the fundamental reason that the events we call the Holocaust, represent a totality defined by this very convergence of distinct

elements. [...] Thus the history of the Holocaust should be both an integrative and an integrated history.

(p. xv)

There then appear three asterisks (* * *) followed by the statement: 'No single conceptual framework can encompass the diverse and converging strands of such a history' (p. xvi).

Now, I have nit-picked my way through the opening pages of Friedländer's great book (praised for its impeccable scholarship, citation of secondary scholarship and its literary qualities) in order to identify features of it that are generically *literary* rather than specifically historiographical in kind. And I have taken this tack because I wish to deal in this essay with the differences in kind among the variety of testimonial writings (witness discourse). Friedländer is himself a survivor of the programme of extermination about which he writes. Does his 'history of the Holocaust' qualify as a kind of 'witness' writing? Does witness writing manifest features or attributes that other kinds of writing do not? Survivors of the Holocaust typically 'bear witness' to that event, or complex of events, by telling of their experiences of it. Moreover, they do so in different situations or contexts, religious, journalistic, archivalist, legal, literary, theatrical, political and so on. These situations and contexts set limits on what can be said and what cannot be said or is not allowed to be said. And they determine what will count as a historical account of an event and what will count as a fictional account thereof.

We can gain insight into how to read the written or recorded testimony of witnesses to the Holocaust by looking at how witnesses who are literary artists write about it. This recommendation presupposes an important qualitative difference among kinds of testimony related by survivors, victims, onlookers, perpetrators and others. I am not speaking about such differences as those between oral and written testimony, legal depositions, confessions, autobiographical reflections or novelizations of experiences, etc. I refer to the difference between the kind of testimony given in interviews or reports of experiences, on the one hand, and crafted or artistic productions, on the other. The differences might be likened to those thought to exist between a canon and the apocrypha of a body of writing held to be sacred or at least deemed worthy of special care and tactful handling by interested communities of readers. Canonical works not only contain important information about events and personages believed to be foundational of a community's identity, they also provide paradigms of what will be permitted to count as a proper presentation of the kinds of events and personages deemed to be foundational for the identity of the group. Canonical works or works considered to be canonical prominently feature the poetic and metalinguistic function over the affective and expressive functions of the speech event. This is to say that canonical works feature an explicitly identifiable 'set' (*Einstellung*, or mental orientation) towards the message of the text and a concentration on the use of the principal of equivalence to transform *series* of events into *sequences*. The poetic function distributes meaning between surface and depth of the text, the metalinguistic function distributes it along a horizontal axis between beginning and end.

In prose discourse, it is the rule that the Preface will provide instructions on how to get into a text. Thus, a prominent historian of Germany introduces his three-volume work on the Third Reich with the overt instruction to read the entire work from beginning to end consecutively in order to understand its overall argument. To be sure, there are differences between the 'raw' oral testimony of witnesses and the more self-consciously crafted presentations of writers and other kinds of artists. The important point might be, however, that, except for testimony offered in courts of law, the witness is less interested in adding to the database or contributing new information about the Holocaust than *expressing* the hurt suffered by the experience of it. Put in discursive terms, the raw witness operates on the expressive level in his or her testimony and the legal witness on the referential level primarily. The literary artist puts other levels in play, specifically the poetic, in which the discourse patterns the message for presentification, emphasis and internal modulation, and the metalinguistic, which highlights the various codes used in semantification. A writer like Primo Levi, even in his first forays into witnessing, was especially interested in speaking for or on behalf of his fellow prisoners in Auschwitz, in order to provide a sense of what it felt like to have been there, but he fashions his account of camp life and death in order to produce a specific range of affects and emotions in his projected audience.

On the referential level, where the aim is to provide truths of a factual kind in the mode of correspondence Levi is as meticulously literal-minded as he can be. But his principal aim seems to be to evoke the daily life in the camp in such a way as to lay a burden of guilt or shared responsibility on his readers both for the prisoners' travails and whatever possibilities for survival they could imagine.

It is important to remember that when it comes to an important historical event like the Holocaust, there is no 'original' structure of happenings to which any given account can be likened or considered to be a contribution. Friedländer is famous for having advocated the construction of a 'stable normative narrative' by comparison to which any given account of a part or the whole of the Holocaust could be compared for evidence of its appropriateness, its adequacy to some agreed-upon 'substance' of the Holocaust (*Shoah* or 'Final Solution'). That a programme for the extermination of the Jews of Europe had been undertaken by Nazi Germany during World War II was undeniable (except to those who denied that such a programme had ever existed), but what exactly to call this programme, its execution and its effects was as unclear as the criteria needed to determine the nature of its historicity (when it began, how it developed, its consequences and, indeed, its legacy).

Works cited

Evans, R. (2006) *The Third Reich in Power, 1933–1939: How the Nazis Won Over the Hearts and Minds of a Nation* (New York: Penguin).

Friedländer, S. (2008) *Nazi Germany and the Jews, 1933–1945: The Years of Extermination, 1939–1945* (New York: Harper Collins).

Index

Note: Letter 'n' followed by locators refers to notes.

Adorno, Theodor, 7, 23, 27n.10, 59, 61, 63, 212
aesthetic, 8, 46–8, 59, 62, 67–8, 74–5, 78–9, 117, 121, 124n.4, 130, 135, 145, 158, 163, 181–2, 194, 196–200, 206–9, 218–19, 220n.1
affect, 85–8, 99–100, 117, 119, 126n.10, 146, 176, 184, 187, 199, 206–9, 213, 215–17, 219, 220n.1, 225
Agamben, Giorgio, 26n.1, 92
Ahrendt, Karl, 93
Akerman, Chantal, 8, 194, 215–19
Akerman, Nelly, 215–19
Aktion Reinhard, 12–13, 131, 146
Alterity, 213–14
Amesberger, Helga, 175
Amis, Martin, 90
Ancel, Jean, 12
Angrick, Andrej, 130–1
Anidjar, Gil, 21
Antelme, Robert, 203, 212
antisemitism, 143, 148n.23
aporia, 121, 212
Arad, Yitzhak, 12
archive, 4, 12, 21, 25, 34–5, 100, 133, 135, 143, 146, 147n.8, 153, 174, 181, 183–91, 191n.3, 191n.5, 194
Arendt, Hannah, 7, 11, 99, 122, 125, 214
art, 6, 8, 14, 62, 68, 75, 154–5, 157–8, 194–6, 198–200, 206–9, 215, 219, 224–5
Aubuoy, Bernard, 132, 142
audiovisual, 174, 181–6, 191, 191n.3
Auerbach, Rachel, 4, 6, 81n.4, 92n.8
Auschwitz, 1–9, 11–12, 14, 22–6, 27n.2, 27n.8, 27n.9, 33–5, 37–8, 42–4, 50, 56, 58–60, 63, 65, 68, 70, 78–80, 81n.4, 81n.5, 85, 89, 94, 97, 100, 127n.13, 131, 134, 136–7, 146, 153, 159, 172n.9, 175, 178–80, 185–90, 194, 200, 203, 205, 211–14, 219, 225
Auschwitz-Birkenau, 2, 4, 6, 14–15, 22–4, 33–4, 39, 44–5, 49–51, 53, 55–6, 63, 68, 85, 90, 95, 153, 178, 180, 185–7, 200, 213
Auschwitz-Monowitz, 211
autobiography, 130, 147n.6, 204
Avant-garde, 7, 62, 80, 147n.9

Babel, Isaac, 99
Babi Yar, 144–5, 147n.3, 147n.8, 148n.24
Ball, Karyn, 20
barbarism, 11, 23, 26, 33, 55–6, 59
Baron Cohen, Sacha, 144
baroque, 155, 159, 161, 163–5, 167, 169, 170, 172n.11
barter, 114–16, 118–19, 126
Baudrillard, Jean, 94, 122
beauty, 163, 179
Belarus, 12
Bellour, Raymond, 136
Belsen, 136
Berg, Mary, 4
Birkenau, see Auschwitz-Birkenau
Benjamin, Walter, 33, 56, 104, 122–3, 127n.15, 128n.16, 163, 172n.11
Bielas, Max, 66–7
Bielsko, 114
Blanchot, Maurice, 203, 212–13
Bomba, Abraham, 134, 137
Borderlinking, 198–9, 218
Borowski, Tadeusz, 176
Bowie, Malcolm, 154–5
Breslau, 186–7
Bronfen, Elisabeth, 48
Browning, Christopher, 11, 18–19, 21, 115–16, 124n.2
Buber, Martin, 62

Buchenwald, 1, 78–9
Buci-Glucksmann, Christine, 159, 163–4, 169–70, 172n.11
Butler, Judith, 8, 20

Çà, 203–7, 215
Caméra-stylo, 136, 147n.9
Caruth, Cathy, 19
Celan, Paul, 59, 62
Chare, Nicholas, 7, 22–3, 27n.2, 81n.5, 85, 89, 97, 172n.9
Chełmno, 4–6, 131, 144, 148n.24
Christian, 70, 201, 207, 209–10
cinematography, 8, 160
civilization, 23, 33, 56
collaboration, 55, 181, 200
conservation, 35, 55, 121, 127n.13
coping, 175
Coulmas, Corinna, 132–4, 136, 139–40
crematoria, 2, 4, 14, 33, 36, 44, 47, 60, 72, 80, 85, 89, 97, 148n.24
Crownshaw, Richard, 19
Cummings, Ashlee Mae, 203–4
currency, 116, 118

Dachau, 155
Daney, Serge, 156–7
Dantón, Helena, 6
Dawidowicz, Lucy, 15, 17
Deleuze, Gilles, 155
Derrida, Jacques, 54–5, 146
Des Pres, Terence, 65, 81n.4
desire, 9, 36, 45–7, 49, 63, 67, 74, 116, 156, 176, 206, 208
diary, 4–5, 24, 27n.7, 60, 76, 194–6, 202, 215–18
Didi-Huberman, Georges, 1, 6, 16, 36–40, 42–4, 49–53, 56, 158–9, 170–1, 172n.9
Dimendberg, Edward, 153–4
Dora, 196, 198, 207–8
Dragon, Shlomo, 22
Drancy, 200
drawings, 78, 94
dream, 54, 64, 67, 71–3, 100, 205
dreamwork, 205
Dubnow, Simon, 91
Dwork, Debórah, 2, 16

Ehrenberg, Sidonie, 215–16
Einsatzgruppen, 7–8, 13, 95, 130–47, 147n.3, 147n.8, 148n.14, 149n.27
empathy, 7, 33, 36–40, 48–50, 52–6, 56n.3, 73, 137
Ephrussi, Charles, 93, 99
epistemology, 21
erotic, 52, 177, 215
Ettinger, Bracha, 1, 8, 172n.7, 194–9, 205, 207–9, 218–19
Evans, Richard J., 222
Ezrahi, Sidra DeKoven, 66–7

facts, 5, 8, 20, 23, 25, 61, 72, 97, 144, 203, 217
factum, 120
Farr, Raymond, 135, 137
fascinance, 199, 207–9, 218–19
Fassin, Didier, 19
Felman, Shoshana, 7, 19, 21, 40, 43, 59, 61
Fénelon, Fania, 177–80
femininity, 48, 133, 186, 197–8, 208, 210
film, 7–8, 39–45, 52–3, 69, 71, 89, 130–7, 139–40, 145–6, 147n.2, 147n.8, 149n.26, 152–60, 162, 165–7, 169, 171, 171n.5, 181–2, 194, 215–19, 220n.9
Final Solution, 4, 11, 15, 25–6, 223, 226
Finchelstein, Federico, 87, 97
Flaschka, Monika, 177
foodstuffs, 113, 115–16, 118
Fortunoff Video Archive, 181–3, 191n.3
Foucault, Michel, 96
Fraleigh, Sondra, 74
France, 154, 187, 200
Franju, Georges, 182
Frank, Anne, 96, 98
Friedländer, Saul, 8, 12, 16–18, 27n.4, 98, 222–4, 226
Freud, Sigmund, 87, 89, 96, 98, 154, 194–9, 202–3, 205, 208–10, 220n.5
Freud Museum, 194–5

gaps, 24, 33, 35, 50, 52–3, 56, 206
Garbarini, Alexandra, 18, 22
Gawkowski, Henryk, 134, 137, 146
gaze, 47, 122–4, 133, 199
Gelbin, Cathy, 8, 67
gender, 7–8, 11, 17, 174–8, 181, 183, 186, 196–7, 202
genocide, 14–15, 20, 34, 48, 67, 92, 104, 131, 134, 146, 194, 215, 223
German occupation, 24, 200–1
Gestapo, 200, 210
gesture, 8, 37–8, 40–1, 44, 53, 70, 74, 94, 133, 157, 159–62, 168–9, 181, 197, 206, 213, 215–16, 219
Ghetto, 2–5, 11–12, 14, 16, 24–6, 27n.7, 27n.8, 36, 51, 60, 65, 76, 119, 130, 134, 144, 189, 194, 196, 222
Gilbert, Martin, 4, 15–17, 27n.3
Glazar, Richard, 146
Godard, Jean-Luc, 135–6
Gold, Artur, 67
Goldberg, Amos, 17–18
Goldhagen, Daniel, 20, 94–5, 143
Gradowski, Zalman, 7, 16, 22–4, 26, 27n.2, 27n.4, 27n.10, 33–4, 44–54, 56n.4, 58, 60–1, 68–71, 77, 80
Grau, Gunter, 180, 191n.1
Greenspan, Henry, 18
Greif, Gideon, 27n.10, 46, 56n.4, 81
Grese, Irma, 179–80
Grey Zone, 2, 44, 97
Grojanowski, Jakob, 4, 6
Grubrich-Simitis, Ilse, 86

Halbmayr, Brigitte, 175
Hartman, Geoffrey, 181, 205–6, 220n.7
Hedgepeth, Sonja M., 8, 174
Heinemann, Marlene E., 175
Herman, Chaim, 27n.7, 44, 47
heterosexuality, 48, 177–81
Hijikata, Tatsumi, 62, 68, 73–5, 79, 81n.4, 82n.9
Hilberg, Raul, 15, 17–18, 91, 135, 140, 142, 148n.14, 191n.5
Hirsch, Joshua, 39, 41–2
Hirsch, Marianne, 88, 220n.2

historian, 5, 7, 11–21, 24–6, 43, 47, 58, 65, 67, 86–8, 91, 97–100, 119–20, 131, 146, 148n.14, 177, 191n.5, 225
historiography, 7, 11, 13, 15–16, 18–21, 58, 86, 120–1, 123, 177, 181, 183
history, 2, 11–14, 17, 19–25, 28, 37, 56n.3, 62, 75, 86–8, 90, 94, 99, 117, 120–1, 123–4, 126n.10, 142, 147n.4, 151–9, 163–4, 167, 169–71, 183–4, 187, 197–9, 212, 217, 222–4
Hoess, Rudolf, 179–80
Hoffman, Eva, 4
Holocaust, 1–3, 6–8, 11–22, 26, 27n.6, 36, 39–40, 43–4, 52, 58–63, 67, 74, 79, 85–100, 127n.14, 130–1, 133, 135–6, 141–2, 145–6, 147n.2, 147n.4, 148n.16, 155, 157, 159, 169, 171, 174–7, 181, 183–4, 191, 223–6
Holocaust (Miniseries), 142, 148n.16
homosexuality, 75, 177, 179–80
Horkheimer, Max, 23, 27n.10
Hornblow, Michael, 75
Hungary, 11, 12, 114, 196
Hutton, Margaret-Anne, 174–5, 177

icon, 19, 36, 195, 197, 203, 213
ideology, 23, 87, 175
IKL, 12
index, 34, 53, 55, 93, 159, 162, 166, 168, 213
Iser, Wolfgang, 50
Israel, 16, 132, 191, 196

Josipovici, Gabriel, 98–9
Judaism, 201, 209–10
Judenräte, 11

K, Irmgard, 185–91, 191n.4
Kansteiner, Wulf, 19
Kaplan, Chaim, 4
Kapo, 48, 114, 176, 180, 188, 211
Karski, Jan, 134
Ka-Tzetnik, 176, 181
Katznelson, Yitskhok, 4
Kertész, Imre, 176

Kindertransport, 151
Klein, Melanie, 19, 98–9
Kofman, Berek, 211–12, 214
Kofman, Sarah, 8, 194, 200–9, 211–15, 217, 219
Kopytoff, Igor, 120, 127n.12
Kracauer, Siegfried, 182
Kretschmer, Karl, 130, 132–7, 142–6, 147n.7, 147n.8, 148n.16, 148n.18–19, 148n.22–5
Krzepicki, Abraham, 4, 6, 65, 80, 81n.4, 82n.7
Kuntzel, Thierry, 136
Kushner, Tony, 17

Lacan, Jacques, 199, 206, 220n.5
Lacanian, 205
LaCapra, Dominick, 17, 39, 85, 87, 89–92, 94–5, 98
Lang, Berel, 59, 62
Langer, Lawrence, 96, 174, 181–2, 185
Langerbein, Helmut, 143, 148n.19, 148n.23
Langfuss, Leib, 4–5, 15, 22, 24, 27n.2–3, 34–5, 51, 54–5, 56n.5–6, 58, 68–9, 71–3, 75, 77, 80–1, 97
Lanzmann, Claude, 7–8, 43, 89–91, 94–5, 130–46, 147n.1–2, 147n.6, 147n.12, 147n.16, 148n.19, 148n.23–4, 158
Lasker-Wallfisch, Anita, 177–8
Latvia, 39, 147n.8
Laub, Dori, 3, 7, 22–3, 40, 43–4, 87, 97, 181, 183–5
Lautréamont, Comte de, 62
Lengyel, Olga, 179, 181
lesbian, 177–80
Levi, Primo, 2–3, 16, 21, 44, 59–62, 91, 94, 97, 115, 117, 124n.1, 126n.8, 176, 225
Levin, Nora, 15
Libido, 47
Lichtenberg, Uriel, 195–6, 198, 202
Liepāja, 7, 40–1
Lindeperg, Sylvie, 156–7
literary, 18, 20–3, 58–62, 65–71, 77, 80–1, 85, 97, 104, 130, 146, 182–3, 206–7, 224–5
Littell, Jonathan, 144, 147n.3

Łódź, 4, 25–6, 27n.7–8, 76, 196
Loewenthal, Zalman, 4–5, 7, 16, 22, 24–6, 27n.3, 27n.7–8, 35, 53, 58, 68, 76–7, 80
Longerich, Peter, 11
Lower, Wendy, 12, 143, 146, 147n.4
Lubtchansky, William, 137
Lyotard, Jean-François, 212

Maier, Charles, 85
Maków Mazowiecki, 51
Mark, Ber, 4, 24, 27n.2–3, 68, 81n.5
Mark, Esther, 24, 68, 81n.5
Marrus, Michael, 13, 91
Masculinity, 148n.22, 202
materiality, 85, 97, 161
matrixial, 198–9, 209, 218–19
Mauss, Marcel, 119
McCloy, John, 139
Memoirs, 17, 174–81, 183, 186, 188, 190
memory, 5, 8, 11, 18, 21, 45, 60, 63, 85, 87, 89, 91–2, 94, 96–8, 101n.3, 122–3, 125n.4, 127n.13–14, 137, 148n.16, 151–3, 155, 159, 162–3, 166–71, 174, 181–7, 191, 191n.5, 194, 206–7, 218
Mengele, Josef, 179
metaphor, 1, 9, 20, 44–6, 62, 68–9, 97
metonymy, 55, 123
Milner, Marion, 52
mise-en-scène, 133–6, 140, 146, 147n.6
Miyabi, Ichikawa, 75
'MM', 6
Moffie, David, 223
Moore, Michael, 144
mourning, 60, 72, 86, 98–9, 156, 159, 163–4, 170, 172n.11, 196
Mowat, Hannah, 8, 159
muselmann, 213
Museum, Auschwitz, 34–5, 60, 81n.5, 127n.13
Musmanno, Michael, 138

Nadjary, Marcel, 27n.7, 35
Nakamura, Tamah, 74
narrative, 8, 12–15, 23, 34–5, 44, 47–8, 50, 58, 60, 70–2, 89, 95–7, 136,

146, 151, 158–60, 162–3, 166–7, 170–1, 174–6, 181–6, 188–91, 191n.5, 199, 211, 213, 218–19, 222, 226
Nazi policy, 131
Nazism, 13, 89, 91, 93, 212
Neumann, Franz, 14, 118–19
Nichanian, Marc, 20–1
Nietzsche, Friedrich, 203, 210
Novick, Peter, 17
Nuremberg, 15, 131, 138–9, 141
Nyiszli, Miklós, 44

Oberhauser, Josef, 146
Oedipal, 196, 207–8, 210
Oedipus complex, 197, 210
Oevermann, Ulrich, 182–3
Ohlendorf, Otto, 138–40
Olson, Charles, 62, 78–80, 81n.4
Operation Barbarossa, 131, 140
organizing, 62, 82, 114, 115, 116, 119
Orth, Karin, 12
Oyneg Shabes, 4

Pankiewicz, Tadeusz, 134
paper, 35, 55–6, 56n.5, 81, 127n.10, 158, 186, 196
pathology, 88, 99
Pelt, Robert van, 2, 16
pen, 49, 81, 194, 200–4, 207, 210, 212, 213, 214–17, 222
Perl, Gisella, 178–80
Pförtsch, Klara, 189, 191n.6
Phallic, 198–9
phenomenology, 36–9, 42
photograph, 1–2, 6–7, 16, 22, 35–45, 48–53, 147n.8, 158–9, 166–9, 171, 172n.9, 187, 194–5, 223
photography, 172n.9
Płaszów, 90, 127n.11
poetic, 20, 45, 62, 64, 79, 206, 225
poetry, 4, 20, 58–9, 62–3, 74, 77–80, 172n.14
Pohl, Dieter, 12
Poland, 12–13, 24, 62–3, 70, 76, 90, 105, 195–6
Poliakov, Léon, 15
Pollock, Griselda, 1–2, 8, 48, 55, 93, 171n.3, 172n.7

Pontecorvo, Gillo, 48
postmemory, 88–9
Prabhu, Allama, 68, 81n.4
Prose, Francine, 98
Proust, Marcel, 123, 152
psychiatrist, 93–4
psychoanalysis, 7, 87, 99, 154, 194, 204–5, 207–8
quarantine block, 188

Quevedo, Francisco de, 163

Rabbi, 24, 194, 200–2, 210–212, 214
rape, 177, 180
Ravensbrück, 180, 187–8, 190, 191n.6
Rechtman, Richard, 19
Reitlinger, Gerald, 15
remains, material, 11, 33, 109, 120
remembrance, 8, 34, 92, 122, 124, 147n.2, 153
Resnais, Alain, 8, 48, 147n.8, 151–66, 171, 171n.5, 172n.12
representation, 6, 25–6, 38, 55, 71, 78, 95, 101n.3, 130, 135, 146–7, 174, 205–6
restoration, 35–6, 55, 97
Rilke, Rainer Maria, 159, 165–7, 169–70, 172n.13
Ringelheim. Joan, 175
Robbe-Grillet, Alain, 155
Rococo, 160, 167
Romania, 12, 114
Rose, Jacqueline, 49
Rosenfeld, Alvin, 176
Rosenthal, Gabriele, 182–3, 185
Rossel, Maurice, 134
Rothenberg, Jerome, 58, 62–81, 81n.1–2, 81n.5–6
Rotzoll, Maike, 93–4, 101n.5
Rumkowski, Chaim, 3, 25
Russell, Catherine, 158
Russell, Lord (of Liverpool), 15

Sade, Marquis de, 62
Sadism, 26, 66–7
Saidel, Rochelle G., 8, 174
Salomon, Charlotte, 93
Sauna, 187–8
Satzinger, Helga, 92

Schalling, Franz, 133
Schindler's List (film), 97
Schlöndorff, Volker, 153, 155–6, 160, 172n.10, 172n.12
Schoppmann, Claudia, 177–8, 180, 191n.1
Schubert, Heinz, 130, 132–46, 147n.5, 147n.8, 148n.12–13
Schütze, Fritz, 182–3
Schweidler, Max, 35, 55
Schwenger, Peter, 50–2
Scrolls of Auschwitz, 4, 11, 14, 22, 24, 27n.2, 27n.8, 33–4, 42–3, 50, 56, 58, 68, 78, 80, 81n.4, 85, 89, 97
sculpture, 46, 196, 203
Sebald, W.G., 151–2, 154, 171n.4
secondary witness, 19, 87
seeing, ways of, 42, 47–8
Serbia, 12
sex, 24, 47, 66–7, 175–81, 183–4, 190, 197–8, 201, 208
sexuality, 7–8, 174–8, 183, 186, 208
Shoah (Film), 1, 3–4, 7–8, 67, 89, 91, 130–7, 140–1, 144–6, 147n.2, 158, 226
silence, 3, 50, 59, 92, 100, 117, 153, 156, 170, 188, 191, 197, 218
Simferopol, 138–9, 141
Sketchbook, 6
Slovakia, 12, 196
Snyder, Timothy, 12, 131
Sobibór, 131, 134
Sonderkommando, 2, 4–9, 14–16, 22–4, 27n.2, 27n.10, 33–6, 39–40, 42–7, 53, 55, 58, 60–1, 68, 72–3, 75, 78, 80, 81, 85, 97, 114, 126n.10, 135, 141, 143, 147n.7, 148n.22, 158
songs, 6, 47
Soviet Union, 12, 130–1, 146
Spiess, Alfred, 149
Spira, Françoise, 153
spoon, 104, 113, 116, 124n.1, 188, 194, 196–8
SS, 6, 12, 25, 44, 94, 114, 116–17, 126n.9, 131, 138, 140, 144, 145, 147n.8, 148n.19, 176, 178–80, 187–8, 191n.2
Starachowice, 18

Stein, Edith, 37–9, 52–5
Steiner, Jean-François, 65–8, 81n.4
Stier, Walter, 133, 140, 147n.12
Stone, Dan, 6–7, 39, 41, 58, 86, 149n.27
Suchoff, David, 23
Suchomel, Franz, 133–4, 137, 139–42, 146, 147n.6, 147n.12
survivor, 1, 3, 8, 14, 17–22, 60, 65–6, 78, 81, 81n.4, 85–91, 94–7, 100, 101n.1, 115, 131–2, 137, 145–6, 147n.8, 174–8, 181–6, 190–1, 191n.3, 191n.6, 196, 211, 224
Sutzkever, Avrom, 4
Synecdoche, 12, 89, 123, 146

testimony, 1, 3–9, 11, 14, 16–22, 26, 33–6, 39, 42–3, 46, 49–54, 56n.5, 58, 62, 65, 73, 80, 85–9, 92, 96–8, 127, 137, 141, 146, 167, 182, 184–5, 201, 224–5
Theresienstadt, 100, 134
Third Reich, 13, 16, 137, 222–3, 225
trace(s), 5, 33–5, 41, 45–7, 53–5, 91–3, 99, 115–117, 120, 123, 135, 145, 153, 154, 159, 165, 167, 169–71, 194, 198, 200, 207, 218
transaction, 114–16, 119–20, 148n.12, 180
transcrypted, 219
transgenerational, 8, 197, 217
Trauerspiel, 159, 163–4, 170–1, 172n.10
trauma, 1–3, 8, 19–22, 39, 82n.10, 86–8, 91, 94, 97–8, 145, 180, 183–5, 194, 196–200, 203, 204–7, 210–211, 214–19, 220n.1–2
trauma (transport station of), 8, 194, 198, 200, 205, 215, 217–19
Treblinka, 4, 6, 63–7, 70, 81n.4, 82n.7, 134, 137, 141, 146
triangle, black, 177–8, 180, 188

Ukraine, 12, 131, 143–4, 146, 147n.4, 147n.8
Ungar, Steven, 153–4, 159, 170
United States, 147n.2, 191
USSR, 12
utensils, 113, 115–16, 124n.1, 126n.8

value, 4, 35, 73, 97, 114–17, 120–2, 124n.4, 125n.5, 126n.10, 127n.12, 146, 148n.22, 220n.2
Vélodrome d'Hiver, 200
Venezia, Shlomo, 46–7
Vice, Sue, 7–8
Vidal-Naquet, Pierre, 66
video testimony, 8, 182
Viñas, Salvador Muñoz, 35
Vincendeau, Ginette, 158, 172n.8
violence, sexualised, 67, 176–9
voies de traverse, 203, 205, 217, 219
Volksgemeinschaft, 14

Waal, Edmund de, 92–3, 99
Wachsmann, Nikolaus, 12
Warsaw, 4–5, 36, 65, 76–7, 189, 222
Waxman, Zoë, 4, 8, 17, 20, 174–5, 177–8
Wehrmacht, 130, 140–1

Weisman, Gary, 182
Werner, Wilhelm, 94
White, Hayden, 8–9, 20–1, 59, 86, 125n.5
White, Margaret Bourke, 1–2
Wiener, Reinhard, 39–45, 49, 52–3
Wiesel, Elie, 176
Wilkomirski, Binjamin, 95–6
Williams, Dominic, 7, 85, 89, 97
Wolfe, Robert, 17
Wyschogrod, Edith, 44

Yad Vashem, 39, 147n.2
Yiddish, 5, 14, 23, 27n.2, 27n.11, 62–4, 68, 72, 76–7, 81n.1, 81n.6, 211
Young, James, 66, 90, 97

Żywulska, Krystyna, 180–1

Printed by Printforce, United Kingdom